MW00413744

More than......

Breakfasts

...with

Blender Batter Baking

& Allergy Alternatives

3rd Edition

*for Health & Hospitality**

SUE GREGG

SueGreggCookbooks

PUBLICATIONS BY SUE GREGG

Sue Gregg Cookbooks

Main Dishes, 3rd edition
Soups & Muffins, 2nd edition
Meals in Minutes, 3rd edition
Lunches & Snacks, 3rd edition
Breakfasts, 3rd edition
Desserts, 2nd edition
Master Index & Menu Planner

Yeast Breads, 2nd edition
Holiday Menus
The Creative Recipe Organizer
Four Food Storage Plans

Eating Better with Sue, Video
The Busy Woman's Guide to Healthy Eating,
 with Emilie Barnes, (Harvest House, 1987, 1994, 2002)

Как Вам Это Нравится? *Recipes for Russian & American Appetites with Valentina Platova & Alex Krutov*

Curriculum

Baking with Whole Grains

Published and distributed by
Sue Gregg Cookbooks
8830 Glencoe Drive
Riverside, California 92503-2135
909-687-5491 www.suegregg.com

Breakfasts, 3rd Edition © 2002 by Rich & Sue Gregg
ISBN 1-878272-06-3

First Edition printed 1989, 1990, 1991, 1992
Second Edition printed 1993, 1995, 1997, 1998, 1999, 2000

Disclaimer

This cookbook is designed to provide information relating to the subject matter covered. It is sold with the understanding that the publisher and author are not engaged in rendering medical, nutritional, dietary, or other professional services. If expert assistance is required, the reader should seek the services of a competent medical professional.

This cookbook does not cover or reprint all of the information on the subject available to the author, publisher, or the reader. Research in the field of nutrition often seems conflicting, and when hyped by media and advertising, contradictory and confusing. You are urged to read all the available material, to inform yourself as much as possible about nutrition and food preparation, and then with the advice of competent professionals to tailor the information to your personal needs.

Health is not achieved through one shot schemes, potions, or pills. It is not acquired through diet alone. Anyone who decides to pursue it must expect to invest time, effort, and discipline. We are reminded, however, that even those who inherit or achieve even the best health do not live forever. *It is appointed to man once to die...* Therefore, the reader is urged not just to prepare for the immediate, but also to discover the Creator's eternal plan.

With every edition and printing of this cookbook every effort is made to make the information as accurate, complete, and up-to-date as possible. However, experience tells us that mistakes are inevitable in content, data calculations, and typography. This cookbook should be used only as a general guide and not as the ultimate source of information on food preparation and nutrition.

The purpose of this cookbook is to model and motivate, to educate and entertain. The author and the publisher, shall have neither liability nor responsibility to any person or entity with respect to any loss or damage caused, alleged to be caused, directly or indirectly by the information contained in this book.

If you do not wish to be bound by the above, you may return this book to the publisher for a full refund.

What others are saying...

I go all the way now with "Eating Better." My energy level has increased greatly! Another benefit has been a 20 lb. weight loss!
Betty Lamb, Jenison, Michigan

Your recipes have really encouraged my cooking. My husband is pleased. Happy husband means a happy wife!
Christa, San Bernardino, California

You have done an excellent job presenting healthful eating with taste appeal, ease of preparation, familiar dishes, color, and beauty with thanksgiving to our God and Creator.
Kathleen Hoffman, Somerset, Wisconsin

I love your approach. You use "real people" food but it's done in a healthy way. *Lori Leeke, Plano, Texas*

Your cookbooks have changed my life. Our weekly food budget has decreased from $125 to $70. I can't thank you enough.
Sheila Preston, Ontario, Canada

Your cookbooks are all I ever use. The recipes are hassle-free to make. No special ingredients to buy. They are healthy and taste great! My family loves them. Thank you for writing such wonderful books! *Chris Gordon, Everett, Washington*

We've had lots of allergy problems and have been on rotation diets, vegetarian diets, combination diets, no dairy diets...Cooking became a trial to be put off as long as possible. Your books are sensible...We have only begun, but so far it is all I'd hoped for and more. *Sherry Schindler, Bartlesville, Oklahoma*

*I've been using the **SueGregg Cookbooks** for 1½ years. After 10 years of marriage, what a blessing to hear "This is good! This is really good!" Recipe after recipe! Praise God!*
Kathie Moran, Sacramento, California

I love the cookbooks and menu planner! I've been converting recipes and using various health cookbooks for years, but these are far superior! Thanks! Sara, Pasadena, Texas

Thank God for bringing you into our lives. When my family asks, "Whose recipe?" and I answer, "Sue Gregg's."
Johnne Neiner, Pittsfield, Massachusetts

Contents

What's Behind This Book?

I am ever on a quest for the "perfect recipe." The "perfect recipe" meets four basic concerns: 1) appetite appeal, 2) nutritional value, 3) ease of preparation, and 4) cost control. In this book waffles, muffins, coffee cakes, and crepes made with whole grains in the blender are my "perfect" whole grain recipes, followed by great whole grain loaves of yeast bread (worth the extra preparation time). You will certainly want to discover Whole Grain Blender Magic! You will also be intrigued to learn in this third edition of a new (or perhaps very old) method for significantly improving access to the nutritional value of whole grains (see pp. 50-51). As you will discover, while all breakfast foods are addressed in this book, the focus is especially on whole grains.

You will notice that there is a lot of nutrient data included in this book. It reflects hours of computation time. In my first cookbook I did all this with calculator, paper, and pencil. Eventually *Nutrition Wizard*, a computer data program, available through *The Center for Science in the Public Interest*, speeded things up. What a boon! Yet I still had to program over 200 ingredients into it to make it useful. To calculate costs of ingredients I visited local supermarkets, health food stores, and researched catalogs.

Nutrition Wizard served until I purchased a faster computer. Then it failed to operate. Since CSPI did not update *Nutrition Wizard* to meet new computer demands, I finally decided to design my own nutrient data computer program with *Microsoft Excel* (with the help of our son, Dan, the computer literate family member!).

I spent hundreds of hours researching more up-to-date nutrient information (where available), updating the cost of ingredients to 1996 levels, and transferring all of it into a new program. Nevertheless, nutrient tables did not agree and none of them were complete. And costs are both necessarily localized and become quickly dated. This is certainly "weariness the body!" Yet a technological society demands such information. I also have appreciated the conclusions it has afforded me to make, as for example, in our *Nutritional Goals Chart* (pp.16-17). In summary, while the data is useful for its purpose, don't make too much of a purpose out of it. It can be a particularly helpful guide for those persons who must restrict fat, cholesterol, sugar, or sodium. It also makes useful comparisons between recipes possible. Otherwise, take it with a grain of salt as approximately reliable, though not exact.

Data calculation, being an inexact and incomplete science, I recommend that you focus on the nutritional quality of ingredients instead of on the numbers. Keep in mind, also, that the nutrient data numbers say nothing about a recipe's micronutrient value (vitamins, minerals, enzymes, phytochemicals, etc.) Therefore, learn which foods to use liberally and which to use in moderation, and don't overeat any of them. If you do that, the calories, grams, milligrams, and percentages will take care of themselves.

More than Breakfasts developed as some novels do. The author doesn't really know what her characters will do until she's finished the story! I've listened to women for 24 years. They continue to pose questions about nutrition and food preparation at my seminars and through correspondence. Awareness of the need for change has expanded along with interest. Yet for many there is still much mystery about what is available and what should be included in a healthy diet. For example, whole grains are like a foreign language, and fats, oils and dairy products are like a rat's maze. My aim is to dispel some of that mystery. That is why this book grew to 300 pages.

I have also continued what I began in **Lunches & Snacks**--to encourage teaching your children. I urge you to include them in what you are learning about foods. Capture natural curiosity. Answer the why as well as the how. Let them feel the pride of replacing you in the kitchen. That's why you will find sections, for example, on *The Science of Making Hot Cereals, The Art & Science of Making Yogurt, Fruit Trivia, The Anatomy of an Egg,* and the historical section on whole grains and dietary fiber.

You will find extensive cross-referencing with page numbers throughout this book. These are to help you quickly locate any additional information you may need.

A divider page with the contents listed on the back introduces each section of this book. Cut-out tabs are provided in the back of the book for these pages. You will note that six of the sections focus on a menu format rather than on a recipe category. Consequently, while most like recipes are grouped together, some are not. Various breads, for example, such as biscuits, loaf breads, muffins, coffee cakes, sweet rolls, etc., are separated into different menu sections where they best fit the particular menu pattern. Use of the Index should spare you any difficulty locating a recipe.

My prayer is that God will use this book for your enrichment, enjoyment, and blessing.

Sue Gregg

Cook's Prayer

The LORD our God, Maker of Heaven and Earth's Land,
He made the wheat, the germ, the bran--
   nutrient and fiber-rich for the strength of man,

And cheeses 'n chicken, fish, beef, 'n dairy--
A little goes a long way to refresh the weary.

Vegetables countless--nutrient-packed treasure;
Succulent fruits for dessert--what delightful pleasure!
Nuts 'n seeds for essential fats in good measure.

Beans 'n peas for more protein and fiber, please!
With plenteous water in which to cook them
   poured out by the LORD of the Seas.
What great gifts, these!

His store of food in all colors,
   all shapes, and all sizes
   are ever full of nutritious and tasty surprises!

Honey dripping from the comb,
   of this sweet offering could be written a tome.
Spices and herbs to jazz up flavor.
Even salt and egg yolks we count not out of His favor!

Now, O LORD our God,
Help us to put your bounty together
In balance and wholeness that we might eat better,
   for bodies stronger,
   and minds sharper;
   for spirits assisted,
   and service enlisted,
To sow the seed; to reap the harvest,
From the nearest land to the farthest.

The Breakfast

She is like the merchant ships, bringing her food from afar.
Proverbs 31:14

THE BREAKFAST

Planning the Breakfast Menu

When I was a high school student my home economics teacher taught a unit on breakfasts. I remember well a particular small group discussion. "Now," she said, " breakfast is very important. You'll be more alert, have more energy, and do much better in school if you eat a good breakfast. Is there anyone here who doesn't eat breakfast?" Sheepishly I half raised my hand. "Okay, Sue," she said, "And what kind of grades do YOU get?" Ever so humbly I whispered, "Straight A's?" "You would!" she replied.

I was one of those in 50% of all households that seldom eat breakfast. And this continued right through college, where I was still an honor student, until I married a no-nonsense farm fellow. An ironclad rule of our new home was a full breakfast eaten together daily. Did I reform? Absolutely. And I quickly learned to enjoy breakfast. But I still do best on a light one. So I am here to tell you that while some suggest to "eat breakfast like a king, lunch like a prince, and dinner like a pauper," breakfast pauper-style serves this sedentary female best. Others who are more active, especially men and children, will eat more. In any case, don't neglect yourself by going entirely without something nourishing for breakfast, nor let your children do it. Here are some good reasons:

A Few Claims for Breakfast!

~Breakfast will *take off unwanted pounds*, because it helps you regulate better what you eat the rest of the day, and because breakfast calories seem to be better metabolized than evening calories.

~People who eat breakfast *live longer*. Researchers who discovered this theorized that going without breakfast is a sign of self-neglect and that people who neglect themselves die younger.

~Breakfast stimulates *more productive work* because it improves your mental performance, your ability to concentrate, and increases your physical energy.

~Eating breakfast makes *problem solving easier* because blood sugar is raised to an adequately sustained level.

Sue's Breakfast Menu Planning Chart

FRUITS/JUICES	CEREALS	BREADS	EGGS/MAIN DISHES	SHAKES	PANCAKES, ETC.
Juices	**Cold**	toast	Soft-Cooked, 138	Apple, 186	**French Toast**
Orange Juice	Date Apple Granola, 119	Spelt Bread, 122	Hard-Cooked, 138	Apple Bran, 185	French Toast, 210
Apple Juice	Simple Granola, 116	KamutBread, 123	Poached, 139	Banana, 187	Low Cholesterol, 211
Grape Juice	Yummy Granola, 118	Sourdough, 286	Scrambled, 143	Basic Breakfast, 185	Maple Butter, 211
Frozen Blends, 13	meusli	English muffins, 124	Cheesy Egg Muffin, 141	Blueberry, 190	Tofu, 212
Apple-Grape, 260	Sprouted, 102	Sourdough, 284	Cheesy Spinach	Carob, 188	
Carrot-Apple, 260	Swiss, 115	biscuits, 125-26	Crepes, 252	Carob-Banana, 188	**Pancakes**
Carrot-Apple-Celery, 260	favorite boxed, 90-91	Sourdough, 285	Chick Curry Crepes, 251	Carrot, 188	Blender, 204
Cantaloupe, 261		muffins, blender	Chicken Pizza, 231	Coffee, 189	Cottage, 208
Watermelon, 261	**Hot**	Banana, 196	Enchiladas, 143	Date, 187	Finnish, 209
Citrus Combo, 261	favorite boxed, 91	Bran, 192	Gourmet Scramble, 141	Egg Nog, 189	Oat, 208
Kiwi-Apple, 261	oatmeal, 108-11	Molasses, 193	Fried, Sun-Up, 144	Molasses, 189	Orange, 208
	Roman Meal, 107	Good Morning, 194	Egg Frames, 144	Oat Bran, 191	Sourdough, 283
Fruits	Polenta, 107	Orange Date, 198	Omelet, 146	Orange, 186	
orange/apple wedges	barley, 114	Sunshine, 195	Frittata, 150	Papaya, 191	**Waffles**
grapefruit	buckwheat, 113	Wheat Germ, 197	Tofu Scramble, 151	Peanut Butter, 191	Blender, 204
applesauce	(kasha)	tortillas	Virginia's Egg	Pecan Fruit, 190	International, 207
in-season fruits	millet, 103, 112	coffee cakes, 233-240	Scramble, 228	Pineapple, 187	
Apple Breakfast Treat, 173	brown rice, 104	Almond, 233		Strawberry, 186	**Toppings** 210-217
Apple Nuggets, 175	rye, 105	Apple, 234	**Accompaniments**	Sunshine, 188	Almond Sauce, 215
Berry Delicious, 174	oat bran, 109-10	Apricot Pecan, 235	Breakfast Beans, 156		Apple, 216-217
Citrus Ambrosia, 173	spelt, 114	Blueberry, 236	Breakfast Sausage, 230		Berry Topping, 217
Cottage Fruit Crepes, 173	Kamut, 106	Cowboy, 237	**Fried Sweet**		Fr. Toast Topper, 210
Fruit Compote, 176	teff, 111	Orange, 238	Potatoes, 153		Fresh Fruit, 212, 216
Fruit Pizza, 231	quinoa, 102, 106	Peach Bran, 241	Kasha 'n Potatoes, 152		Nutty Banana, 218
Melon Ball Bowl, 172	bulgur, 102	Pineapple, 239	Potato Tostadas, 154		Pineapple, 218
Mixed Fruit Bowl, 172		Zucchini, 240	**Sweet Potato**		Pine-Applesauce, 218
Papaya-Pineapple, 174		crepes, 249-251	Sausage Bake, 155	**Other**	Whipped Cream, 214
Prune Compote, 176		scones, 232		Sue's Super Cottage	Yogurt, 35-37
Quick Apple Yogurt, 175		sweet rolls, 242-248		"Dessert," 268	Syrups, 213-214

Whether we eat a large, moderate, or small breakfast, it is still the easiest meal to plan and prepare, since most of us are willing to settle for less variety than at other meals. Many, however, who long for variety skip breakfast, either out of boredom or a lack of ideas that can be easily implemented. We need a simple plan with variety. I recommend the following:

WEEKLY BREAKFAST MENU

4 or 5 mornings: **Cereal Breakfast**

1 or 2 mornings: **Egg Breakfast**

1 morning: **Shake or Fruit Breakfast**

1 morning: **Waffle/Pancake or French toast**

Occasionally: **Special Occasion Breakfast**

The **Cereal Breakfast** usually includes hot and/or cold cereal or granola, fresh fruit piece or fruit juice, toast, or English muffin. On occasion a fresh hot baked bread such as muffins or coffee cake might replace the ordinary toast or English muffin.

An **Egg Breakfast** is about the same as the cereal breakfast, substituting the eggs for the cereal. Or the eggs might be added to the cereal breakfast, especially if the cereal is cold.

A **Shake Breakfast** usually suits individuals, especially those who work and are on the go, more than as a family meal. You might even want a *Meal-In-a-Glass* for breakfast on a more or less daily basis.

A **Fruit Breakfast** is especially appealing in warmer weather. For heartier appetites, muffins served with a shake or fruit will add something to sink the teeth into for a filling, satisfying meal.

A **Waffle/Pancake or French toast** includes toppings with fresh fruit or juice. With blender recipes waffles and pancakes are one of the quickest breakfasts to prepare.

Reserve sweet rolls, coffee cakes, more involved egg dishes, and sausage for a **Special Occasion Breakfast.**

Post *Sue's Breakfast Menu Planning Chart*, p. 8, or a similar planning chart of your own in your kitchen.

Breakfast Time Savers

Do these things the night before, or in advance.

Make Juice ————————

Start Hot Cereal;
Set Out Cold Cereals ————

Set Table ————————

Fill Coffee Maker ————
or Teapot

Start or Complete Baking ———

Set Out Special Appliances ———

THINK! What else can be done ahead?

Shopping

Arrowroot Powder Arrowroot powder is a nutritious, easily digested starch thickener processed from the tubers of the tropical plant, *Maranta arundinacea* or related species, grown mostly on St. Vincent Island in the West Indies. It works well in place of cornstarch using the same amount, although it is best to cook it at a little lower temperature. It does not hold up as well in reheating as cornstarch. Purchase in the spice section of supermarket, or in larger economy packages at a health food store.

Baking Powder I use *low sodium baking powder* without corn or aluminum, available at health food stores or *Rumford* which contains no aluminum. *See also*, pp. 279-80 for other alternatives.

Bagels *See* **Breads, Whole Grain**

Bran (oat, wheat) Available in both supermarkets and health food stores. More economical at health food stores. *See also* pp. 67, 272.

Breads, Whole Grain Loaf breads, English muffins, bagels, muffins, and tortillas are all available. Check health food stores. Read ingredients labels carefully to obtain 100% whole grain products without refined sugars, or hydrogenated or partially hydrogenated fats or oils (difficult to find in supermarkets).

Butter Unsalted butter for cooking and baking is one way to reduce sodium. It should be stored in the freezer. Since salt acts as a preservative, unsalted butter turns rancid much more quickly than salted butter. Unfortunately rare, raw butter is rich in lipase, the fat-splitting enzyme. The enzyme is destroyed by pasteurization. Non-hydrogenated margarines are beginning to emerge (see p. 264), such as *Earth Balance*, available at Trader Joe Markets and some health food stores. These usually contain canola oil (see comments p. 263).

Buttermilk Buttermilk gives a lighter texture to whole grain baked goods. It is an excellent medium to soak grains in for improved nutritional benefits (see pp. 50-51). It is low in fat, is an easily digested cultured milk and offers a pleasing flavor. Buttermilk is available with 2% butterfat, 1% butterfat and ½% butterfat. I use the lowest fat buttermilk available at the supermarket. Fresh buttermilk will give the best results in baking, but powdered buttermilk can be used and is also available. *Darigold* or *Now* brand is available at some health food stores. *Saco Cultured Buttermilk Blend* is sometimes available in supermarkets. Inquire of the management if you can't find any of these sources. Use 3 tablespoons buttermilk powder per 1 cup water. *See also* pp. 28-29 for other dairy or non-dairy alternatives to buttermilk. Our recipe nutrient information is based on using 1% fat buttermilk since it is more commonly available than ½% fat buttermilk.

Carob Powder Buy roasted carob powder for the best flavor. It is more economical purchased from a health food store, but is also available in supermarkets. Carob is a low fat legume, high in calcium and trace minerals.

Cereals *See* pp. 90-91.

Coconut, Unsweetened Readily available in health food stores. All coconut I have seen in supermarkets is sweetened.

Cornmeal Stoneground is available at health food stores. *See also* p. 65.

Cream Cheese, Light Available at most supermarkets. Light cream cheese is 40% lower in fat than cream cheese. *Light Philidelphia* brand is available. It is also known as *Neufchâtel* cheese.

Eggs I recommend fertile eggs from free range fed or cage free hens. They are generally fresher, tastier, and probably higher in nutrients, and without potentially harmful chemicals. Purchase at health food store or Trader Joe Markets. *See also* pp. 135-36.

Egg Substitutes *See* **Egg Alternatives**, p. 269.

English Muffins, Whole Wheat *See* **Breads, Whole Grain**.

Flaxseed Oil Available at health food stores. *See also* pp. 266-68.

Flax Seeds Available at health food stores. *See also* pp. 266-68.

Flour, Whole Grain Many whole grains and flours are available in health food stores. Refrigeration and fast turn over is essential for freshness. Keep flours in refrigerator or freezer. *See also* pp. 60-81.

Fructose, Crystalline Fructose is fruit sugar, usually extracted from corn. It is refined, but releases less insulin into the blood stream. Only half as much as white sugar is needed for recipes in most cases. I use it very sparingly, preferring honey most often. It is very expensive and available at health food stores. A 5 lb. bag is the most economical buy and will go a long way. Keep it tightly stored, allowing no moisture to get inside, in which case it will get hard as a rock.

Fruit Concentrates Thick liquid fruit concentrates are available at health food stores such as apricot and apple. Delicious mixed into yogurt and shakes. These come in jars and keep a long time. I keep them refrigerated after opening.

Fruit, Canned Purchase unsweetened canned fruits. Unsweetened applesauce, pineapple, pears, peaches, apricots, grapefruit sections and fruit coctail are all available in supermarkets. Read labels to be sure you get the unsweetened!

Fruit, Dried Buy unsulfured fruits. Sulfur places stress on the kidneys and also affects pH balance (see p. 276) which decreases their nutritional value. Unsulfured dried fruits are available in health food stores or Trader Joe Markets.

Fruit Juices Real unsweetened fruit juices are right next to fruit drinks and sweetened juices in supermarkets. Read every label. Juices in bottles are the best of the canned juices. Of the unsweetened frozen juices, although orange juice still remains the favorite, there is an increasing available variety. For example, *Chiquita Caribbean Splash* and *Raspberry Passion, Dole Mountain Cherry, Pineapple-Orange, Mandarin Tangerine, Orange-Pineapple-Banana, Welch's Grape,* and *Lady Lee Grapefruit.*

Grains Most grains and flours are readily available in health food stores, or through food co-ops or mail order sources. *See also* pp.60-81.

Ground Turkey Ground turkey is available in many supermarkets and health food stores. It is generally from 85% to 99% fat free by weight, depending on the proportion of white and dark meat and how much turkey skin has been added. The amount of fat makes a difference in the juiciness and tenderness. Choose as low fat as available and acceptable to you. For *Breakfast Sausage* (p. 234) I prefer to use plain ground turkey, adding my own seasonings, instead of commercially available turkey sausage which contains preservatives. *See also* **Main Dishes**, p. 21.

Honey Most honey in supermarkets has been processed with nutrient destroying heat. The best quality is unfiltered, unheated honey. Purchase in 60 lb. buckets for the best price. Local bee keepers are a good source. If you cannot find or pay for this quality honey, purchase uncooked, unfiltered honey from the supermarket. See also **Desserts**, pp. 24-25.

Jams Several honey sweetened and unsweetened jams and spreads are available. Unsweetened spreads should be refrigerated since they contain no sugar which acts as a preservative. Many supermarkets carry unsweetened jams and fruit spreads. Health food stores carry both unsweetened and honey sweetened spreads. *See also* recipes in **Lunches & Snacks**, pp. 138-39.

Kefir Cheese A cultured sour cream with acidophilus, kefir cheese is a tasty alternative for cream cheese. Available at health food stores.

Lecithin Liquid or granules available in health food stores. *See also* pp. 270-71.

Maple Syrup Use pure maple syrup available in both supermarkets and health food stores. It is an expensive item, but contains nutrients not found in pancake syrups made with refined sweeteners. It is available in grades A, B, and C. Grade C is strongest in flavor and the richest in nutrients. To insure that the syrup is free of formaldehyde residue which contaminates the sap, purchase Vermont or Canadian syrup. There may be high levels of lead in some maple syrup, acquired from processing equipment and/or lead seams in metal cans. Canadian supplies are safest, followed by syrup in glass or plastic containers. I recommend moderation in use. For alternative home prepared maple syrup and toppings, *see* pp. 217-22.

Milk *See* pp. 21-26.

Milk, dry powder Buy non-instant type at health food store. *See also* pp. 25-26.

Molasses Molasses is the by-product of refining sugar cane to produce white sugar. The nutrients removed from the sugar end up in the molasses. Light molasses has the least of the nutrients, dark molasses contains more, and blackstrap molasses contains the most. Blackstrap molasses is available in health food stores. It is strong flavored and rich in calcium, copper, iron, and phosphorus, and is a good source of B-vitamins. Purchase molasses that is unsulfured. *Plantation* is one available brand.

Nuts & Seeds Good prices and good quality of shelled nuts and seeds are easier to find in health food stores, except for walnuts. Look for dry roasted nuts (roasted without oil) or unroasted nuts. Buy all nuts and seeds unsalted. Store in refrigerator or freezer. They are high in oil content and therefore can go rancid easily. To roast or grind your own *see* p. 120.

Nut Butters Peanut butter is not the only one! Several good brands of almond, cashew, and tahini (sesame) are available in health food stores or Trader Joe Markets. These are expensive, but highly nutritious alternatives to butter as spreads and provide some variety to peanut butter. Keep refrigerated. Buy peanut butter without sugar or hydrogenated vegetable oil. *Laura Scudder's* is one of several acceptable supermarket brands.

Oils I purchase all oils at the health food store except extra virgin olive oil which is available in supermarkets and Trader Joe Markets. I prefer to buy expeller pressed oils. *Spectrum Naturals* and *Arrowhead Mills* are excellent brands. Excellent organic oils are available from SunOrganic Farm (p. 79). *See also* pp. 262-67; **Main Dishes,** pp. 26-27.

Peanut Butter *See* **Nut Butters**.

Salt I use a sea salt that is labeled "unrefined" or "sun-evaporated only." *RealSalt* (formerly called *Orsa* salt) is an excellent brand available in some health food stores or may be ordered in bulk by mail from Redmond Minerals, PO Box 219, Redmond, UT 84652 (1-800-367-7258), www.realsalt.com Sea salt does not contain dextrose or aluminum.

Seeds *See* **Nuts & Seeds**

Sour Cream Low fat and fat-free sour creams are available, such as *Knudsen Nice 'n Light* (lowfat) and *Knudsen Free Light Sour Cream Substitute* (fat-free). Both may be found in supermarkets. Look for other brands also. I enjoy blending equal portions of low fat sour cream and nonfat yogurt.

Spike Seasoning A tasty seasoning for eggs, *Spike* contains 39 herbs and spices and is about half sodium. It should not be used for the purpose of cutting down on sodium. Health food stores and some supermarkets.

Stevia An herb product for low sugar cooking and baking. Highly concentrated, ½ tsp. = ½ cup sugar. A helpful booklet is *Stevia Nature's Sweetener* by Rita Elkins, M.H., Woodland Publishing, Inc., PO Box 160, Pleasant Grove, UT 84062, and cookbook: *Stevia Sweet Recipes* by Jeffrey Goettemoeller, Vital Health Publishing, PO Box 544, Bloomingdale, IL 60108.

Sucanat Available in health food stores, *Sucanat* is organically grown. Originally designated as evaporated cane juice containing all the nutrients of the whole sugar cane, it is now listed on the ingredients label: organic sugar and molasses. Organic sugar with molasses looks and tastes exactly like the original, but it is hard to varify if the nutrient level is exactly the same (see **Desserts**, p. 26). The molasses, however, is organic blackstrap molasses which is a plus. *Sucanat* has a fuller, less sweet flavor than white sugar. To substitute for honey, use at least twice the amount: ½ cup *Sucanat* to ¼ cup honey. To substitute for white sugar, use the same amount.

Sue's "Kitchen Magic" Seasoning A wonderful seasoning made from soy, corn, alfalfa, and wheat. As a hydrolyzed vegetable protein it contains naturally occuring MSG. One teaspoon contains 710 milligrams of sodium. When used in recipes, the addition of salt can usually be cut in half. See order blank for purchase at back of this book. *Bragg Liquid Aminos*, available at health food stores, is virtually the same flavor less concentrated, made from soybeans but not hydrolized (thus no MSG). It may be substituted in recipes using 3 to 4 times the volume (to taste) as *Sue's Seasoning*. See our www.suegregg.com for more information.

Sunflower Seeds *See* **Nuts & Seeds**.

Sweeteners Most sweeteners can be used interchangeably, as desired, in our baked recipes. Natural, less refined sweeteners include barley malt syrup, date sugar, honey, maple syrup, molasses, rice syrup, sorghum, *Sucanat*, crystalline fructose, and *FruitSource* All Natural Sweetener (made from grapes and rice). *See also* **Fructose, Honey, Maple Syrup, Molasses, Stevia, Sucanat**, and ***Desserts***, pp. 23-30.

Tofu Tofu is the most digestible form of soybeans and is available in most supermarkets in the refrigeration section. It comes either soft, regular, or firm. It is very inexpensive. Tofu made from organically grown soybeans can be purchased in health food stores for a slightly higher price. Tofu that will keep several months, such as *Mori Nu* brand, is also available.

Wheat Germ Use vaccum packed wheat germ which is guaranteed fresh until the seal is broken, such as *Kretchemer* brand at supermarkets or *Mother's* or *Arrowhead Mills* brands at health food stores, Keep in freezer after opening. It is available in supermarkets. *See also* p. 273.

Whole Wheat or Whole Wheat Pastry Flour See Grains, p. 13.

Yogurt I use nonfat or lowfat yogurt often in recipes. Some brands are more pleasing than others. Yogurt should contain active or live bacteria, preferrably including *L. acidophilus* and *B bifidum*. Type of cultures or bacteria should be stated on the carton. *See also* pp. 26-28.

Nutritional Goals

The typical American diet includes 37-42% of daily calories in fat, 7-14 grams dietary fiber, 450-500 mg. cholesterol, and 4,000-6,000 mg. sodium (the estimates on sodium are declining).

Contrast these figures to the daily goals of 30% or less fat calories, 30-40 grams dietary fiber, at least 55% complex carbohyrates, 250-300 mg. cholesterol, and 1100 to 3300 milligrams sodium.

The data below is compiled from 7 representative breakfast menus (pp. 89, 129, 159, 181, 201, 221). The lower totals reflect the smaller menu amounts for women, the larger totals, the larger menu amounts for men. The 7 menus represent weekly: 4 cereal breakfasts, 1 egg breakfast, 1 waffle\pancake breakfast, and 1 fruit or shake breakfast,

GET PLENTY OF THESE (List not intended to be complete)	DAILY GOAL Amount	AVERAGE OF 7 BREAKFASTS	
		Amount	% of Daily Goal
COMPLEX CARBOHYDRATE	55% to 65% of Calories	69 - 70% of Calories	_____
DIETARY FIBER	25 to 40 grams	8 -15 gm.	23-68%
VITAMIN A	RDAs[1] 5,000 I.U.	1048-1405 I.U.	21-28%
VITAMIN C	60 milligrams	70 - 87 mg.	117-145%
VITAMIN B-1 (Thiamine)	1.5 milligrams	.63-1.14 mg.	42-76%
VITAMIN B-2 (Riboflavin)	1.7 milligrams	.59 - 1.02 mg.	35-60%
VITAMIN B-3 (Niacin)	20 milligrams	4 - 7.3 mg.	20-36%
CALCIUM	1,000 milligrams	357 - 634 mg.	36-63%
POTASSIUM	3,750 milligrams	951 - 1564 mg.	25-42%
IRON	15 milligrams	3.9 - 7 mg.	26-47%

Nutritional Goals

plus on a rare occasion, 1 special occasion breakfast (calculated for this chart as eaten once in 3 months). When these breakfast menu averages are taken together with menu averages from **Main Dishes** (pp. 11-12), **Meals in Minutes** (pp. 72-73), **Soups & Muffins** (pp.6-7), and **Lunches & Snacks** (pp. 146-47), the total meets each of the daily goals, and in several instances exceeds them.

We seek goals that are realistic for family eating, neither strict nor therapeutic. Yet when the latter are desirable, our realistic family approach can be more easily modified to meet individual needs than the typical American diet.

LIMIT THESE	DAILY GOAL	AVERAGE OF 7 BREAKFASTS
CALOIRES	27-30% Day's Total	477 - 830
PROTEIN	10% to 15% of Calories	16% of Calories
FAT (TOTAL)	30% of Calories	14% to 16% of Calories
(Saturated fat)	(10% of Calories)	(4% of Calories)
(Monounsaturated fat)	(10% of Calories)	(6-8% of Calories)
(Polyunsaturated fat)	(10% of Calories)	(4% of Calories)
CHOLESTEROL	250-300 mg.[2]	75-81 milligrams
SODIUM	1100-3300 mg.[2] (or 2400 mg)	593-1082 milligrams
SUGAR	Reduce consumption by half[3]	3.6 - 7 tsp.
AVE. COST		$1.05 - $1.65

[1]RDAs are for the typical adult (a statistical person). [2]Less for children.

[3]In 1981 the average per capita sugar consumption per year was 125.6 lbs. A minimal reduction to 63 lbs. per year amounts to a little over ⅓ cup (16 teaspoons) of sugar per day.

How to Read a Recipe

The example below explains how the nutrient data and details relate to the recipes. Do not regard data as exact (see pp. 2-3)

Nutrient data based on first listed ingredient, *(eg. nonfat cottage cheese)*

or first amount listed *(eg. 1 tbsp. flaxseed oil)*

Exchanges rounded off to nearest ¼ exchange[1]

RECIPE SAMPLE

This recipe illustrates information you will want to understand; not a recipe to prepare and serve!

AMOUNT: 1 Serving

1. Blend together:
   ¾ cup nonfat or lowfat cottage cheese

   1 - 2 tablespoons flaxseed oil *(p. 12)*

   ¼ teaspoon vanilla, optional

Per serving (vanilla included)
  Exchanges: 1 Milk, 2.75 fat;
225 Calories, 20 g protein (21%),
12 g fat (5%), 68 g carbohydrate (74%),
15.5 g dietary fiber, 4 mg cholesterol,
100 mg sodium, $.95

Page where more information may be found

Data states whether or not item is included

Nutrient Data: fat, protein, carbohydrate, fiber grams (g) rounded to nearest ½ or whole; mg=milligrams

Cost rounded off upward to nearest $.05; based on '96 prices[1]

[1]For full explanation and chart using the exchange system see **Main Dishes**, pp. 14-15. For basis of food cost, see **Main Dishes**, p. 38.

NUTRIENT DATA SOURCES

Nutrient data for this book has been compiled from *Sue's Nutridata* © 1993 computer program based on the following sources:

Package Nutrition Labels where available

Carper, Jean. *Jean Carper's Total Nutrition Guide: Complete and Up-to-date Based on USDA New Scientific Analysis of Vital Nutrients of More Than 2500 Foods.* New York: Bantam Books, 1989.

Jacobson, Michael: Center for Science in the Public Interest. *Nutrition Wizard.* Washington D.C., 1986. Computer data base program.

Nutrition Search, Inc. *Nutrition Almanac.* New York: McGraw-Hill Book Co.,1979.

Pennington, Jean A.T. and Church. Helen Nichols. *Food Values of Portions Commonly Used, 14th Edition.* New York: Harper & Row, Publishers,1985.

Milk Alternatives

He will eat curds and honey when he knows enough to reject the wrong and choose the right. Isaiah 7:15

MILK ALTERNATIVES

Milk, A Muddle in America

Some nutritionists say milk is for calves, not for people. Controversy over the value and safety of milk drinking, and of dairy products in general, abounds. What are we to make of it all so that we can decide what is best for ourselves and our families? What will we put on our breakfast cereal and how will we get our calcium quota if we abandon our breakfast glass of milk?

Let's start from a Biblical perspective. The apostle Paul spoke these startling words to Timothy: *The Spirit clearly says that in later times some will abandon the faith and follow deceiving spirits and things taught by demons. . . .They forbid people to marry and order them to abstain from certain foods, which God created to be received with thanksgiving by those who believe and who know the truth. . . .For everything God created is good, and nothing is to be rejected if it is received with thanksgiving, because it is consecrated by the word of God and prayer. 1 Timothy 4:1, 3-5.* Is milk among the good things God created for food?

According to the *Illustrated Davis Dictionary of the Bible*, milk was "An important article of diet, especially in the East. The milk of cows (*2 Sam. 17:29; Isa. 7:22*), sheep (*Deut. 32:14*), goats (*Prov. 27:27*) and camels (*Gen. 32:15*) was and is still used. . . . Milk was used in its natural state and as curds and as cheese (*Deut. 32:14, Judg. 5:25, 2 Sam. 17:29*). It was kept in skins and served in dishes (*Judg. 4:19, 5:25*)." It is also instructive to observe Abraham's version of hospitality: *He brought some curds and milk and the calf that had been prepared, and set these before [the three angels]. Genesis 18:8.*

It appears that Biblical evidence and historical eating patterns stand in opposition to what some nutritionists teach about milk. I conclude, therefore, that to declare milk off nutritional limits for human consumption is a controversial proposition, at best.

However, there are some qualifications. *1 Corinthians 6:12* might apply here: "*Everything is permissible for me*" *--but not everything is beneficial.* Additional questions to answer include:

Has anything been done in the processing of milk that might make it unhealthy or unsafe as a nourishing food?

Are we consuming too much of a good thing (gluttony)?

Is there a personal allergic reaction or intolerance to a particular milk product to be considered?

21

In response to these questions I have included several alternatives, one of which, I trust, will meet your own qualifications for tasty and nourishing breakfasts:

DAIRY CHOICES
Commonly Available:
Cow's Milk
Goat's Milk

Processing Methods
Pasteurized
Homogenized
Ultra-Pasteurized
Raw (unpasteurized)

Available Levels of Fat
Whole Milk
Lowfat Milk
Nonfat (Skim) Milk

Lactose Reduced
Dairy
Non-Dairy

Cultured
Yogurt
Buttermilk
Kefir
Acidophilus Milk

NON DAIRY CHOICES
Soy Milk
Soy Yogurt
Nut Milks
Rice Milk
Juices

Dairy Choices[1]

He nourished him. . .with curds and milk
from herd and flock. . . Deut. 32:13, 14

Cow's Milk and Goat's Milk

Both cow's and goat's milk are available. Both are rich sources of protein, calcium, phosphorus, potassium, vitamins A, D, E, K, and B-vitamins, especially riboflavin.

The composition of goat's milk is closer to human milk and generally a better alternative than cow's milk. The disadvantages are, of course, availablility and cost, and for many, taste, as well.

Many people have a problem with milk because of *lactose (milk sugar) intolerance*, or the inability to properly digest the lactose in milk. On an average 70%, of the world's population, excluding infants and young children, are lactose intolerant to one degree or another. This is due to the diminishing supply of lactase, the lactose digesting enzyme in the human body. Among American Caucasians of northern European and British descent, however, lactose intolerance averages only 8%. Lactose intolerance among the Danes and Swiss is higher, while among Caucasians worldwide intolerancre average 40%. In contrast,

[1]*See also* **The 15 Minute Menu Planner**, pp. 123-134.

70% of American blacks and 90% of Asians are lactose intolerant. Lactose intolerance may be generally related to the historical use of milk in one's ancestral line.

Some research has been done suggesting that milk may assist in lowering blood cholesterol, especially cultured milk. The amount consumed in the studies was 2 to 4 quarts a day. High quality milk products may be even more beneficial than we now understand.

Pasteurized Milk

Practically all milk in the United States is pasteurized. *Pasteurization* is the accepted method of controlling harmful bacteria in milk by heating it to 160° for 15 seconds, then cooling it. Pasteurization is also destructive to some of milk's nutrients causing:

38% loss of vitamin B-complex
12% loss of vitamin B-12
destruction of vitamins A and C
10% reduction in availability of calcium
4% reduction in protein digestibility
destruction of the digestive enzyme, phosphatase
destruction of the lipids (lecithin, an emulsifier of cholesterol)

Homogenized Milk

Most pasteurized milk is also homogenized. *Homogenization* of milk is the process that breaks down the fat molecules in the milk so that the fat will stay evenly suspended throughout the liquid instead of rising to the top as it would otherwise naturally do. This also prolongs the shelf life of the milk. Kurt A. Oster, M.D., and Donald J. Ross, Ph.D, authors of *The XO Factor* have conducted extensive research on the milk enzyme, *xanthine oxidase*. According to their theory, the smaller fat particles allow xanthine oxidase to enter the blood stream and damage the arterial walls, thus contributing to heart disease. I believe this is a plausible theory worthy of further investigation. In the meantime, I don't recommend the use of homogenized milk because, if the xanthine oxidase theory is correct, it has very serious implications in regard to heart disease. This narrows our dairy choices for milk since most whole and lowfat milks are homogenized. There is no problem with nonfat (skim) milk since there is virtually no fat present.

Ultra-Pasteurized Milk

Some homogenized milk products are *ultra-pasteurized*. In this processes milk is heated to the flash point of 282°F for 3 seconds. This is more destructive to milk's nutritional value than pasteurization. Its one advantage is in destroying any xanthine oxidase present in the milk.

Lactaid, half 'n half cream, and whipping cream are ultra-pasteurized milk products.

Raw Milk

Raw milk is unpasteurized, unhomogenized milk. It is far superior in nutritive value and the assimilation of its nutrients is much greater. If raw milk is certified it must meet very strict processing and testing regulations, thus greatly reducing the risk of harmful bacteria in the milk. *Stueve's Natural* raw certified milk, formerly produced in Southern California is unfortunately no longer available. Much controversy surrounded the safety of even certified milk. Eventually a warning label was required by law on *Stueve's Natural* certified milk containers cautioning use for newborns, the elderly, pregnant women, persons taking corticosteroids, antibiotics or antacids, and persons having chronic illnesses or other conditions that weaken the immune system.

Stueve's Natural raw certified milk was the first choice for our family for many years. The nutritional superiority of raw milk is worthy of consideration and investigation even though *Stueve's Natural* is no longer available. Read more about it in **The 15 Minute Meal Planner** (p. 125). Some raw milk is sold in other states. Check into local certification requirements for brands available to you. For a brochure comparing nutritional values of raw certified milk and pasteurized milk, *Which Do You Choose?*, send a self-addressed stamped envelope to **SueGreggCookbooks**, 8830 Glencoe Drive, Riverside, CA 92503.

You get uncertified raw milk directly from the cow on a farm. It does not come under government regulations for certification and cannot be commercially sold. Most farm families, however, have thrived for generations on their own raw milk.

If you want to avoid homogenized milk and have access to raw or raw certified milk, but are concerned about its safety, you can pasteurize it yourself without homogenizing it (recipe p. 30).

Lactose Reduced Milk

Many persons are lactose intolerant (see p. 22). One 8 oz. glass of regular milk contains 12 grams of lactose (milk sugar). *Lactaid*, a lactose reduced milk with lactase enzyme added, contains only 3.6 grams lactose. Ultra-pasteurized lowfat and nonfat *Lactaid* are available.

Another solution for lactose intolerance is the use of *Lactaid Lactase Enzyme*, in tablets or liquid, available from a drug store, health food store, or mail order from Lactaid, Inc., P.O. Box 111, Pleasantville, N.J. 08232. Other, less expensive alternatives are cultured milks (pp. 26-29).

There are many non-dairy lactose reduced milks and non-dairy creamers. I don't recommend any of them. They are primarily a combination of water, corn syrup solids and partially hydrogenated vegetable oil, ingredients that subtract from, rather than add to health (see p. 264). They are no substitute for the nutritional value of real milk.

Whole Milk

Whole milk is under severe criticism for its fat content. About half the calories of whole milk come from fat. Don't be fooled by the 3.5% or 4% fat label on whole milk products. This is the amount of fat by weight, but not by calories. There is a big difference! I do not recommend whole homogenized milk for anyone. For children, whole unhomogenized pasteurized milk (rarely available), or whole raw certified milk are better choices. Most adults prefer lowfat or nonfat milk. Although lower fat milk is acceptable, it is the fat in the milk that assists the body to assimilate the fat-soluble vitamins, vitamins A and D. Milk fat is also easier to digest than fat in meats.

Lowfat Milk

Lowfat milk is 1% to 2% fat by weight (up to 25% of the calories). Most people prefer some fat in milk for palatability. Virtually all lowfat milk is homogenized.

Nonfat (Skim) Milk

Nonfat milk is less than 0.5% fat or virtually fat free. If homogenized milk is the only milk available to you, I would recommend you use nonfat milk. The drawback is the taste and the fact that vitamins A and D in the milk will not be as well assimilated. You can fortify it with the addition of dry milk powder to improve the richness and the nutritional value (see *Enriched Nonfat Milk*, p. 30). I have also included the recipe our son, Dan, came up with when *Steuve's Natural* raw certified milk was temporarily pulled from the shelves (see *Dan's Milk*, p.31). *Dan's Milk* provides another alternative to providing milk fat content while avoiding homogenized milk.

Nonfat dry milk powder is excellent for reconstituting as a beverage, fortifying liquid skim or nonfat milk, for making yogurt, and for using in baked goods. You can use either instant nonfat dry milk powder or non-instant. The latter is less processed, works more successfully in yogurt, and is suitable for all baking. It is higher than instant milk powder in protein, energy value, B-vitamins, and particularly in calcium, phospohorus, and potassium. It also stores better over a long period of time without going stale.

Non-instant milk powder is generally available only in health food stores. Nonfat dry milk stores very well in a cool dry place up to 1½ years, and longer under refrigeration. Nonfat dry milk makes an especially economical yogurt at about $1.20 per quart as compared to $2:00 or more per quart for most commercial yogurt (recipe p. 36).

I recommend *evaporated skim milk* only for an occasional recipe. The extra processing required to produce it further diminishes the original nutrient value. In contrast to nonfat dry milk, it loses nutrients during storage as well, and often contains additives such as calcium chloride, disodium phosphate, and sodium citrate. Unopened cans are best stored in the refrigerator. Pour unused portion of an opened can into a jar and cover tightly before storing in refrigerator.

CULTURED MILK

The culturing of milk is a very ancient tradition. Yogurt, for example, has been a mainstay in the Balkans, Turkey, Greece, Egypt, India, China, and Arab countries for centuries, but has only become prominent in America since the 1960's.

Cultured milk products are my favorites, not merely because I enjoy the taste, but because of the wonderful nutritional advantages cultured milks have over sweet milk. Many who are lactose intolerant can tolerate milk in some cultured form. In all cultured milks, much of the lactose or milk sugar has been converted to lactic acid by some type of bacteria. The type of bacteria varies depending on the particular product. Some have greater nutritional benefits than others.

The disadvantage of cultured milks is the sour taste, but it is a taste well worth developing. There are so many things you can do, especially with yogurt. The sour taste of yogurt is a marvelous compliment to many other foods.

Yogurt

Of all the cultured dairy products, yogurt is the most versatile, the most widely available, and the most acceptable for taste, especially as a dairy alternative to milk for most lactose intolerant digestive systems. Yogurt contains the same nutritional benefits of the milk from which it is made and more.

Yogurt assists the intestines in destroying harmful bacteria by producing an acid environment. If yogurt causes gas it is because the friendly bacteria are fighting the odiferous harmful bacteria to destroy them. This condition will be temporary unless one is so intensely lactose intolerant that even yogurt causes adverse reactions.

The standard bacteria used to make yogurt are *Lactobacillus bulgaricus* and *Streptococcus thermophilus.* Yogurt should contain *"live"* or *"active" cultures.* Some yogurts are pasteurized after culturing which kills the bacteria. The only way to be certain the bacteria is active in the yogurt is to try some of it for making homemade yogurt. Quality yogurt should also be free of stabilizers, preservatives, and refined sugars. There is a wide variety of inferior yogurt choices, so read the labels carefully.

Yogurt eaten regularly, if it contains active cultures of both *Lactobacillus acidophilus* and *B. bifidum,* may encourage friendly bacteria production in the digestive tract. This will especially aid in restoring the normal flora destroyed by antibiotics. Yogurt that is 7 days old (more tart) is more effective for this. It is *L acidophilus* that the body needs and that is produced in the intestines; but according to *Probiotics,* © 1990, by Leon Chaitow and Natasha Trenev, during the yogurt making process this bacteria is repressed by the *L. bulgaricus* bacteria, unless *B. bifidum* is also present (in which case the latter is repressed instead). Even this combination is not yet well tested enough to guarantee that an active *L. acidophilus* will not be repressed. Three excellent brands containing both *L. acidophilus* and *B. bifidum* bacteria are *Nancy's, Brown Cow Farm,* and *Trader Joe's* (a Southern California brand). The latter two are whole milk yogurts, pasteurized without homogenizaion, and are delicious. *Nancy's* is available in nonfat and lowfat and has a delicious honey yogurt.

The lactic acid of yogurt and other cultured milks renders them *predigested* which means the body can assimilate the protein more easily than from sweet milk. In one hour, the protein of yogurt is 91% digested in comparison to only 32% of sweet milk protein. The lactic acid also enhances iron and calcium absorption (the more tart the yogurt, the greater the absorption of calcium), and encourages the intestinal production of vitamins B-2, B-3, biotin, folic acid, and vitamin K.

Eating yogurt can relieve both constipation and indigestion. One cup per day can be beneficial in cases of diarrhea and dysentery. When traveling abroad eating 1-2 cups of yogurt with *L. acidophilus* and *B. bifidum* or taking acidophilus in capsules or liquid form can fortify against dysentery. Yogurt has been found helpful in cases of peptic ulcers, colitis, and gastroenteritis, and is excellent in general for sensitive digestive systems.

Buttermilk

Buttermilk used to be the mineral-rich fluid remaining after the churning of butter. No longer. It is usually nonfat milk that is cultured with bacteria such as *Leuconostoc citrovorum* and *Streptococcus lactis* or *Streptococcus cremoris* and has butter granules and/or cream added to it. Unfortunately stale pasteurized milk is often reclaimed for use in producing buttermilk. Some dairies, such as Alta-Dena Dairy, use fresh pasteurized milk.

Buttermilk ranges from ½% fat to 2% fat (by weight). Two percent fat buttermilk is most commonly available. I use buttermilk in baking because of its consistency and flavor. Since it is a cultured milk it is easy for the body to digest. In all baking any other type of milk can be used in place of buttermilk. If yogurt is used, thin it a little with water to be about the same consistency as buttermilk. When substituting sweet milk or water in place of buttermilk, baking soda is not needed in the recipe. You can make your own buttermilk from fresh pasteurized or from a safe local source of raw milk (recipe p. 32).

Kefir

Kefir, with similar consistency to buttermilk, is made by fermenting milk with a blend of cultures, including *Lactobacillus caucasicus*. Of cultured milks it has the finest curd and is therefore the easiest to digest. According to the authors of *Probiotics* kefir far surpasses other cultured milks in its benefits. It is unfortunate that it is not more widely available and that American taste buds are not adapted to it. *Alta Dena Dairy* produces both plain and in delicious fruit flavored kefir. Commercial kefir is usually produced from whole milk. *Nancy's* is another brand produced by Springfield Creamery Inc. in Eugene, Oregon.

If you use a lot of plain kefir, making your own will be much less expensive (p. 40). Homemade kefir is especially nutritious because the milk need not be heated before adding the starter. A quart of commercial plain kefir will keep well for a couple of weeks to use as a starter. Look for it in a health food store. You can also purchase a powdered kefir culture.

Acidophilus Milk

Lactose in acidophilus milk is greatly reduced by culturing it with *lactobacillus acidophilus*. *Sweet Acidophilus Milk* is processed by adding the bacteria to the milk when it is cold so that it tastes like ordinary milk. The bacteria is inactivated until it reaches the warm environment of the stomach. If sweet acidophilus milk is used in baking or heated in a hot drink, the bacteria will be destroyed before it is consumed. Both acidophilus and sweet acidophilus milks are, unfortunately, homogenized. For this reason I don't recommend them.

28

Non Dairy Choices

Soy Milk & Soy Yogurt

Of the non dairy alternatives, soy milk is most widely available and the least costly for persons who are altogether allergic to milk products or committed to a vegan vegetarian diet. The protein of soy compliments grain protein to provide complete protein.

Soy milk is simplest to make with a soy milk powder. There are several brands in health food stores. I consider *Better Than Milk Soy Beverage* the best tasting. It is available in liquid and powder. The powdered form is less costly. Soy yogurt is very simple to make from soy milk and quite palatable (recipe, p. 37). It has the same lactic acid benefits as dairy yogurt. Soy milk or yogurt work equally well in place of milk or yogurt for all breakfast dishes and recipes.

Unfortunately, soybeans and unfermented soy products have come under severe criticism. Much information has been made available on the Internet and many are asking serious questions about the nutritional wisdom of relying on soy products in place of dairy foods. Of the available information, I especially recommend *The Ploy of Soy, A Debate on Modern Soy Products* by Sally W. Fallon, MA and Mary G. Enig, Phd, published by the Price-Pottenger Nutrition Foundation, Inc. A copy can be ordered at (619) 574-7763 or through *www.price-pottenger.org.* This thorough review costs about $6.00.

Nut Milks

Nut milks can be substituted for milk for drinking, for shakes, and in baking. Nut milks are not at all difficult to prepare. They are high in fat burning essential fatty acids and fat burning amino acids, thus one should not consider nut milk as "fattening." For drinking and using on cereals, I consider nut milk much tastier than soy milk.The biggest drawback is the high cost of nuts. *See* recipes, p. 34. An excellent reference is *Not Milk...Nut Milks!* by Candia Lea Cole, Woodbridge Press, Santa Barbara, CA 93160, 1992.

Rice Milk

Rice Dream Non Dairy Beverage, containing brown rice, safflower oil, and salt, is in liquid form and available in health food stores. It is quite thin, but works in most recipes. Rice milk is a boon for persons allergic both to dairy and soy products. The protein value will be lower (*see* p. 58).

Juices

In baking, apple or pineapple juice will usually work in place of any type of milk. You may need to adjust the amount to achieve the same batter consistency. Expect some difference in the texture.

Home Pasteurized Milk

In the event that you want to avoid homogenized milk, but are concerned about the safety of raw milk, here is an alternative. Note the nutritional losses from pasteurization, p. 23.

Heat at 145° for 30 minutes
Cool rapidly to 40° - 50°

1. Assemble Equipment:
      Quart Glass Canning Jars
      Deep Kettle
      Wire Rack
      Candy Thermometer
      Indoor-outdoor Thermometer
      Raw Milk

2. Fill quart jars with milk to within 2" of the top and place over rack in deep kettle.

3. Fill kettle with water to top of milk level in the jars.

4. Place candy thermometer in one of the jars.

5. Heat until candy thermometer registers 145° and hold at that temperature for 30 minutes.

6. Cool rapidly to 40°-50° by placing jars in chilled water. Use an indoor-outdoor thermometer to test milk temperature.

7. Refrigerate immediately.

> **Jar Tip:** It is important to use canning jars to stand the change in temperature from hot to cold. Other jars such as mayonnaise jars may crack.

Enriched Nonfat Milk

To improve the nutritional value and flavor of skim or nonfat milk.

Blend together in blender:
      1 quart skim or nonfat milk
      ½ cup non-instant nonfat dry milk powder *(p. 14)*

Per 1 Cup (8 oz.)
      Exchanges: 1.5 Milk; 145 Calories, 14 g protein (40%), 1 g fat (5%), 20 g carbohydrate (56%; 20 g sugars), 8 mg cholesterol, 210 mg sodium, $.40

Reconstituted Nonfat Milk

This recipe is for use with non-instant, nonfat dry milk powder (p. 14).

1. Choose one of these mixing methods:
    ~ Add milk powder to cold or room temperature water
      in blender and blend.

    ~ Pour warm water into mixing bowl; gradually add milk
      powder while mixing vigorously with a wire whisk.

Use proportions of:
    1 cup dry milk + 4 cups water = 1 quart milk
    ½ cup dry milk + 2 cups water = 1 pint
    ¼ cup dry milk + 1 cup water = 1 cup milk
    2 Tbsp. dry milk + ½ cup water = ½ cup milk

2. Optional--Whisk or blend in for added palatability:
    ¼ cup honey or crystalline fructose per quart

3. Refrigerate for at least two hours or overnight for best flavor.

Per 1 Cup (sweetener not included)
*   Exchanges: 1.25 Milk; 109 Calories, 11 g protein (40%), less 0.5 g fat (2%),*
16 g carbohydrate (58%; 16 g sugars), 6 mg cholesterol, 161 mg sodium, $.30

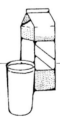

Dan's Milk

*Our son, Dan, who finds nonfat milk unpalatable and has growing
young children besides, uses this combination to avoid homogenized
milk where no safe raw milk is available.*

Mix together:
    1 gallon nonfat or skim milk
    ½ pint (1 cup ultra-pasteurized *Half 'n Half* (see p. 24)
    ½ pint (1 cup) ultra-pasteurized whipping cream (see p.24)

Per 1 Cup (8 oz.)
*   Exchanges: 1 Milk, 1.5 Fat; 142 Calories, 8 g protein (23%), 6.5 g fat (42%),*
12 g carbohydrate (35%; 12 g sugars), 28 mg cholesterol, 121 mg sodium, $.30

Buttermilk

You can make your own buttermilk with fresh, raw milk, Reconstituted Nonfat Milk (p. 31) or fluid skim milk.

1. Bring milk and buttermilk to room temperature; combine in quart jar, stirring well:
   3½ cups nonfat (skim) milk
   ½ cup buttermilk *(p.11)*
   ⅛ teaspoon salt

2. Cover and let stand at room temperature until clabbered (thickened and soured), about 9-10 hours.

Per 1 Cup (8 oz) with 2% fat buttermilk
Exchanges: 1 Milk; 94 Calories, 9 g protein (38%), 1 g fat (10%),
12 g carbohydrate (52%; 12 g sugars), 6 mg cholesterol, 136 mg sodium, $.25

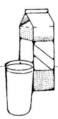

Kefir

Ingredients for kefir can be taken right from the refrigerator without bringing them to room temperature. I culture my kefir in the oven with gas pilot light overnight. This recipe cannot be used for succeeding batches of kefir. Start with commercially prepared kefir each time.

1. Combine in a quart jar:
   3½ cups whole milk *(safe source of raw milk, if available, p. 24)*
   ½ cup plain kefir *(p. 28)*

2. Cover and incubate (p. 41) at 95° - 110° overnight.

VARIATION
In place of commercial kefir, use **Kefir Culture**, a dry powder available at health food stores. Follow package directions for use. Succeeding batches of kefir can be made from previous batch, starting with fresh dry culture once a month.

Per 1 Cup (8 oz.)
Exchanges: 1.5 Milk, 0.25 Fat; 160 Calories, 8 g protein (21%), 9 g fat (51%),
12 g carbohydrate (29%), 35 mg cholesterol, 120 mg sodium, $.20

Soy Milk

The quickest way to make soy milk is to purchase a soy powder such as Better Than Milk Soy Beverage (p. 29), and follow the package directions. But you can also make your own from fresh soybeans in about 20 minutes. Very economical. See caution on soy, p. 29.

AMOUNT: About 1 Quart

1. Cover beans with water and soak for 24 hours:
   1 cup soybeans (fresh, less than one year old)
   2 - 3 cups water

2. Drain soybeans. For a milder flavored milk, rub off the soybean hulls under water and discard.

3. Pour **2 cups boiling hot water** into blender and add half the drained soybeans. Liquify. Line a saucepan with cheesecloth and strain the liquified soybeans through it.

4. Repeat step #3 with other half of soybeans and **2 more cups boiling hot water**. Rinse out blender with an extra ¼ **cup water** and pour through cheesecloth.

5. Bring edges and sides of cheesecloth together, twist, and squeeze to extract all the milk.

6. Bring just to a boil over moderately hight heat, stirring constantly with a wire whisk (foam will suddenly rise to the top); reduce heat and **simmer 7 minutes**; remove immediately from the heat.

7. Cool. To increase shelf life, cool quickly by setting saucepan in ice water for 10 or 15 minutes, stirring occasionally.

8. Remove solids from the cheesecloth, rinse it out, and strain milk through it again.

9. Blend in, if desired and chill thoroughly in refrigerator:
   1 tablespoon honey
   1 tablespoon safflower oil
   dash salt

> **Special Tip:** The solids left in the cheesecloth are called okara. It is rich in nutrients and can be saved for use in cooking. Spread it out on a baking pan and bake 5-10 minutes at 350° to dry out and lighten it. Add to vegetable soups, scrambled eggs, or use ¾ cup, lightly packed, in place of ¾ cup flour in pancakes, waffles, or muffins

Per 1 Cup (8 oz.) with all ingredients
   Exchanges: 0.75 Meat, 0.5 Bread, 1.25 Fat, 0.5 Fruit; 165 Calories, 10 g protein (23%), 8.5 g fat (44%), 14 g carbohydrate (33%; 7 g sugars), 1.5 dietary fiber, 0 mg cholesterol, 34 mg sodium, $.20

Almond Milk

See about nut milk on p. 29. Almond milk is easy to assimilate, is high in protein, monounsaturated fat (p. 262), rich in minerals, and a highly alkaline drink beneficial in maintaining pH balance (p. 276). Nutrient data is not given here because straining the milk removes about ⅔ cup nut pulp which makes approximately accurate data indeterminate.

AMOUNT: 3 Cups

1. Combine and let stand overnight or minimum of 30 minutes:
    1 cup whole almonds, unroasted, unsalted
    2 cups boiling hot water

2. (Optional) Rub off the skins.

3. Place nuts with soaking liquid in blender and add:
    2 cups water
    ⅛ teaspoon salt
    1 teaspoon lecithin granules *(provides creaminess; p. 13)*
    1-2 tablespoons honey
    ½ teaspoon vanilla

4. Blend thoroughly until smooth for 2 or 3 minutes.

5. Strain through fine mesh large square cheesecloth: place cheese cloth inside a large mixing bowl with cloth edges draped generously outside the edges of the bowl; pour in the milk; lift 4 corners and sides of cheese cloth and twist cloth above the milk; press milk thorougly out of the cloth with your hands until only a very dry moist pulp remains.

6. Store in refrigerator.

Per 1 Cup (8 oz.) with all ingredients: $.55

VARIATIONS
In place of ¼ - ½ cup almonds use any of the following:
    ¼ - ½ cup cashews, unroasted, unsalted *(p. 14)*
    ¼ - ½ cup sesame seeds *(p. 14)*
    ¼ - ½ cup unsweetened coconut *(p. 12)*

Cashew Milk

Use **1 cup cashew nuts** (unroasted, unsalted) in place of almonds in *Almond Milk* recipe above; increase salt to **¼ teaspoon salt**.

Per 1 Cup (8 oz.) with all ingredients: $.55

Sue's Yogurt

After experimenting with many recipes this is the one I like best. See pp 38-42, for explanations of each of the steps involved in making yogurt.

AMOUNT: 1 Quart

1. Pour hot water into clean jar or jars and let stand to warm while making yogurt.

2. Heat to 120°-180° in a saucepan or double boiler:
   1¾ cups water
   2 cups lowfat milk *(p. 25)*

> **Special Tip:** Test temperature with a candy-deep fry thermometer or heat until a scum begins to form on top of milk (this is about 180°).

3. Cool to 110° - 115° (takes about 45-50 minutes).

4. Pour about half of it into the blender and blend with:
   ¾ cup non-instant nonfat dry milk powder *(p. 14)*
   ¼ cup plain yogurt *(nonfat preferred with acidophilus and bifidum bacteria, p.27)* **or dry Bulgarian Yogurt Culture** *(p. 35)*

5. Whisk back into remaining milk and pour into clean warm jar or jars; cap firmly.

6. Let stand (incubate, p. 41) at 105° - 118° until firm, usually 3-4 hours. Check every ½ hour after 3½ hours.

7. Refrigerate immediately.

8. Save **¼ cup yogurt** to make the next batch. Yogurt no older than 5 days will give the best results.

Per ½ Cup
   Exchanges: 0.75 Milk; 75 Calories, 6.5 g protein (36%), 1 g fat (15%), 9 g carbohydrate (50%; 9 g sugars), 7 mg cholesterol, 96 mg sodium, $.20

> **Budget Tip:** Home prepared yogurt is definitely less expensive than commercial yogurts. Compare the costs of the 3 recipes at $1.20 - $1.60 per quart with the cost of $2.00 per quart, or more, for different commercial brands. Be sure to compare prices with yogurt containing active cultures.

Judy's Yogurt

Enjoy the richness of whole milk yogurt with this recipe! I recommend using it only if you use quality goat milk or raw certified whole milk.

AMOUNT: 1 Quart

Follow **Sue's Yogurt** recipe using the following:

> **1 Quart** *(safe source raw milk or goat milk preferred, p. 24)*
> **3 tablespoons non-instant nonfat dry milk** *(p. 14)*
> **3 tablespoons lowfat plain yogurt** *(p. 27)*
> > *(nonfat preferred containing acidophilus and bifidum bacteria)*

Per ½ Cup
> *Exchanges: 1 Milk; 92 Calories, 5 g protein (23%), 4.5 g fat (44%),*
> *8 g carbohydrate (33%; 9 g sugars), 18 mg cholesterol, 78 mg sodium, $.20*

Yogurt

One advantage of making nonfat yogurt with nonfat dry milk powder is that the water can be heated just to the temperature for adding the yogurt starter without waiting for it to cool.

AMOUNT: 1 Quart

1. Pour hot water into clean jar or jars and let stand to warm while making yogurt.

2. Place in blender and blend:
   > **3½ cups warm water** (between 105° - 115°)
   > **¾ cup + 2 tablespoons non-instant nonfat dry milk** *(p. 14)*
   > **¼ cup nonfat plain yogurt** *(with acidophilus bacteria and bifidum, p. 27)*

3. Pour into clean warm jar or jars; cap firmly.

4. Let stand (incubate, p. 41) at 105° - 118° until firm, usually 3-4 hours. Check every ½ hour after 3½ hours.

5. Refrigerate immediately.

6. Save **¼ cup yogurt** to make the next batch. Yogurt no older than 5 days will give the best results.

Per ½ Cup
> *Exchanges: 0.5 Milk; 51 Calories, 5 g protein (41%), less 0.5 g fat (2%),*
> *7 g carbohydrate (57%; 7 g sugars), 3 mg cholesterol, 74 mg sodium, $.15*

Soy Yogurt

Alternative to dairy yogurt. It can be cultured at room temperature.
See caution on soy, p. 29.

AMOUNT: 1 Quart

1. Pour **3 cups water** into a 1 quart measure or bowl and heat in microwave oven on full power for 1 minute, 35 seconds to approximately 112° (or heat in pan on top of range).

2. Blend together in blender:
    1 cup soy milk powder *(p. 29)*
    2 tablespoons honey
    ½ to 1 teaspoon vanilla, optional

3. Adjust temperature to 112°, heating or cooling, as needed.

4. Blend in:
    1 tablespoon dry *Bulgarian Yogurt Culture* *(p. 41)*
    or soy yogurt

5. Pour into clean jar or jars, cap, and let stand at room temperature 14 - 18 hours just until set.[1]

> **Special Tip:** Yogurt is set when it pulls away from the sides of the jar. Don't worry about the small amount of liquid that may be floating on top.

6. Refrigerate immediately.

7. Save at least **1 tablespoon yogurt** to make the next batch.

[1]May also be cultured at about 105° for 4-8 hours.
See p. 41 for various methods.

Per ½ Cup
   Exchanges: 0.25 Fat, 0.5 Fruit; 28 Calories, 1 g fat (19%),
6 g carbohydrate (76%; 5 g sugars), 0 mg cholesterol, 16 mg sodium, $.15

The Art & Science of Yogurt Making

THE SCIENCE
1. Milk contains a sugar called *lactose.*

2. Certain types of bacteria (see *Yogurt*, p. 27) will *ferment* the milk at a warm temperature by converting most of the lactose into *lactic acid.* "To maintain the bacteria at the most favorable temperature for development" is called *incubation.*

3. This *fermentation* results in a tart sour taste and a custard-like consistency. The more tart the yogurt, the more lactic acid has been formed, and the more the health benefits are increased (p. 27).

In fermentation, part of the milk turns to *curd.* If the yogurt is stirred before it sets up, you will see the curd (milk solids) separate from the *whey* (the liquid portion). The curd is separated from the whey in making *Yogurt Cheese* (**Lunches & Snacks**, p. 56).

THE ART (Getting the science to work)
Cleanliness of utensils and containers, and temperature control are the most important in yogurt making. The successful activity of the live bacteria depends upon these. Although you can merely follow the yogurt recipes, here is a summary of equipment and ingredients, and steps for making any yogurt recipe. Explanations of these steps follow.

Equipment and Ingredients (p. 39)
saucepan or double boiler
candy thermometer (optional)
wire whisk
strainer (optional, helpful when adding nonfat dry milk)
clean jars and lids (glass canning jars are perfect, unless
    you have a commercial yogurt maker)
measuring cup or tablespoon
equipment for selected incubation method (p. 41)
milk and/or non-instant nonfat dry milk powder
fresh plain yogurt or package dry yogurt culture for starter

Summary Steps for Making Yogurt (p. 39-42))
1. Prepare clean equipment, especially the jars and lids.
2. Heat the milk to 120°-180°.
3. Cool the milk to 106°-115° (100° minimum, maximum 120°).
4. Blend in room temperature plain yogurt, 2-4 tablespoons per
    quart milk, or a dry yogurt culture starter.
5. Pour into warm prepared jars and cap.
6. Incubate at 106°-115° (100° minimum, 120° maximum).

7. Check for doneness every ½ hour after 3 hours.
8. Write the date on jars. Refrigerate immediately when set; let refrigerate 12 hours before serving.
9. Make the next batch of yogurt when the yogurt to be used from the last batch for starter is not over 5 days old.

EQUIPMENT & INGREDIENTS (see Summary, p. 38)

~Any kind of milk can be used. The taste, texture, and nutrient value of the yogurt will be similar to the type of milk used.

~The addition of non-instant nonfat dry milk powder will make a firmer, higher protein yogurt. 3 tablespoons minimum to a quart of milk is a good guideline. Instant nonfat dry milk does not work very well.

~Yogurt can be made entirely from non-instant dry milk powder (see the recipe, p. 36). If so, it does not need to be pasteurized, so the milk can be heated just to the right temperature to add the starter (100-110°). This omits the need to cool it.

~A freeze-dried package of dry yogurt culture is most reliable for successful yogurt, but not a necessity (see step #4, p. 40).

~To use commercial fresh yogurt, get the kind with the appropriate bacteria (see *Yogurt*, p. 27) This is important for the health benefits; it must contain *live cultures.*

STEPS FOR MAKING YOGURT (see Summary, p. 38)

1. Preparing clean equiqment

The saucepan and utensils should be very clean and dry. Wash the jars and lids in very hot water with detergent and rinse well. Fill jars with boiling hot water until ready to pour in the yogurt.

2. Heating the Milk

To 120° The milk should be heated to at least 120° to kill properties that interfere with the bacteria that must ferment the milk. This lower temperature will do the least damage to the whey and casein protein of the milk. You'll need a candy-deep fry thermometer to register when the milk reaches this temperature.

To 180° Heating the milk to 180° is also described as *scalding*. Milk is scalded when a scum begins to form on top. It is a way you c a n easily judge the temperature without relying on a thermometer, and it will produce a sweeter, firmer yogurt. But this higher tempera-ture will also *denature* (reduce the natural value of) some of the pro-teins and caesin of the milk.

Boiling   In the Middle East the milk is boiled and reduced in volume by one thired giving a thicker and firmer, richer yogurt, and a very acid, tart flavor. It will also damage the milk proteins more severely and may also destroy some of the nutrient value.

To Heat the Milk   A double boiler or a pan over another pan with hot water will make it easier to prevent *scorching* (slightly burning the milk so as to affect the taste). It will also prevent accidently letting the milk boil over which can happen suddenly when heated over direct heat. If you heat the milk over direct heat, use a moderately low temperature.

3. Cooling the Milk

The milk must be cooled to the same temperature necessary for incubation (106°-115° or 100° minimum, maximum of 120°) before the yogurt starter is added. Use the candy thermometer to register the temperature.

Without a thermometer, the milk should feel lukewarm on the wrist, or you should be able to hold your finger in the milk comfortably to the count of 10.

4. Blending in the Yogurt (A process called *inoculation*)

Having the yogurt starter at room temperature will help keep the milk temperature appropriately warm.

For a milder yogurt add a smaller amount:
2 tablespoons yogurt per quart

For a more tart yogurt add a larger amount:
4 tablespoons yogurt per quart

Using commerical plain yogurt works very well. Buy plain yogurt with *live bacteria* (see *Yogurt*, p.27). This is a must for the health benefits.

A packaged freeze-dried yogurt starter can also be used, such as *Bulgaian Yogurt Culture*. Purchase from a health food store and follow the package directions for preparing the yogurt. If you don't use it right away, keep it in the refrigerator.

5. Pour into Jars & Cap

Empty the water out of the jars. Cap loosely so that when you open them to test the yogurt for doneness, you don't jostle the jars too much causing the curds to separate from the whey.

6. Incubation (Keeping the milk at the most favorable temperature so the bacteria will turn it into acceptably textured and tasty yogurt). Keeping the appropriate range of temperature (106°-115° or 100° minimum-120° maximum) is a tricky proposition. Yogurt cultured at 115-120° will produce more lactic acid and thus a more tart yogurt with greater health benefits. A milder yogurt with less lactic acid will be produced at 100-105°. It requires some experimenting to find out what will work most consistently with the equipment you have on hand. Here are several ways it can be done:

Commercial Yogurt Maker These cost from $12 to $60. A yogurt maker is the easiest method, but the volume capacity of most of them is only 1-1½ quarts. If you want to make larger batches the commercial maker won't suit you. If you like having individual smaller containers of yogurt, it will be perfect.

Oven If you have a gas oven with a pilot, the oven temperature might be just right for yogurt making. If this works for you, it can actually be easier than using a commercial maker, especially if you like making yogurt in quart jars. Be sure to tack a note to the oven door or temperature dial to remind you that yogurt is incubating inside. Otherwise you may turn the oven on later to do some baking (I've done this!) and ruin your yogurt. If you have an electric oven, preheat it to 100° and turn it off. You'll need an oven thermometer to test the temperature. Set the yogurt in a pan of warm water inside the oven.

Thermos Bottle Use a wide mouth thermos for ease of getting the yogurt out, with a glass insulator to retain more of the heat. Wrap a towel around the entire thermos.

Pan of Warm Water Set the yogurt jars in a pan of 106-115° water with water level half way up the jars. Cover entirely with towels. If possible set the pan on top of a heating pad turned to medium to maintain the water temperature or on top of a warmer. Replenish the water with warmer water as needed (checking the temperature occasionally). Do not let it overheat from heating pad or warmer.

Picnic Cooler Chest Do the same as if using a pan of warm water, covering tightly with the lid instead of towels. To rewarm the water as needed, scoop out some of the cooled water and pour in hot water. Use a thermometer suitable to test temperature if you need to, or follow the rule of the finger test (see #3. p. 40).

Outdoors on a Hot Day On a 90°-110° day take advantage of the direct sun. If the jars are clear glass, cover each one with a sock to prevent nutrient loss. Light will destroy some of the vitamin B-2.

7. Check for Doneness

Incubation takes 3-12 hours depending on incubation temperature. To test for doneness, lift the lid without moving the jar and take a tiny taste from the top with a spoon (without stirring it).

The best texture and taste is maintained if yogurt is refrigerated immediately when done, so after 3 hours check it every ½ hour. Once you see that your method of incubation regularly requires about the same amount of time, you probably won't need to do this.

8. Refrigerate

Date the jars. Refrigerate immediately and refrigerate for 12 hours before using. This will maintain best texture and taste.

9. Preparing the Next Yogurt Batch

For your succeeding batches of yogurt you do not need to begin with a fresh container of commerical yogurt or dry starter if you save some yogurt from the last batch. Make new yogurt with it while it is still at its best for producing a successful new batch--within 5 days of first making it. The longer the yogurt is kept in the refrigerator after 5 days the more tart it will become. The more you allow this to happen before making a new batch, the more often you will need to start over with yogurt from a fresh box. Homemade yogurt keeps well up to a week, while commerical yogurt keeps well about 2 weeks.

TROUBLE SHOOTING YOUR YOGURT

If it doesn't set up right, it may mean that:
~the milk was too hot when the yogurt starter was added.
~the temperature was too hot during incubation.
~the milk was too old (especially nonfat dry milk powder).
~the yogurt starter was too old (inactive), especially if dry starter.
~the milk was not heated high enough to pasteurize it.
~the yogurt was agitated too much in testing during incubation.
~equipment used to prepare the yogurt was not clean enough.
~there were antibiotics in the milk, such as penicillin residue, which killed the live bacteria.

If it turns out too tart, it may mean that:
~the yogurt starter was too tart.
~the incubation temperature was too high.

If it turns out too mild, it may mean that:
~the incubation temperature was too low.

42

Grain Wonders

All this comes from the LORD, Almighty,
wonderful in counsel and magnificent in
wisdom. Isaiah 28:29

GRAIN WONDERS

²³Listen and hear my voice;
   pay attention and hear what I say.
²⁴When a farmer plows for planting,
   does he plow continually?
Does he keep on breaking up
   and harrowing the soil?
²⁵When he has leveled the surface,
   does he not sow caraway
   and scatter cummin?
Does he not plant wheat in its place,
   barley in its plot,
   and spelt in its field?
²⁶His God instructs him
   and teaches him the right way.

²⁷Caraway is not threshed with a sledge,
   nor is a cartwheel rolled over cummin;
caraway is beaten out with a rod,
   and cummin with a stick.
²⁸Grain must be ground to make bread;
   so one does not go on
   threshing it forever.
Though he drives the wheels of his
   threshing cart over it,
   his horses do not grind it.
²⁹All this also comes from the
      LORD Almighty,
   wonderful in counsel
   and magnificent in wisdom.

Isaiah 28:23-29

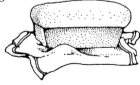

Whatever Happened to Whole Grain?[1]

We may not understand the way that ancient harvesting methods worked as mentioned in the Bible, yet it is clear from *Isaiah 28:23-29* that God had an ordered plan for producing and harvesting the food we eat and that plan was *magnificent in wisdom.* Surely God's plan was intended to produce health-giving grain for mankind's use!

For centuries the bread of peasants in Europe was a coarse, dark, and heavy loaf made of perhaps a little wheat and a quantity of rye or barley, or of barley and oats. For example, from the time of Charlemagne a bread even as hard as *Trencher Bread* was common in the European household. *Trencher* came from a French word referring to a wooden plate. This coarse square-cut flat bread was so hard it served as the plate shared between two people on which they placed their food!

> Lay a clean trencher before you, and when your pottage is brought, take your spoon and eat quietly; and do not leave your spoon in the dish, I pray you. Lay salt honestly on your trencher, for that is courtesy. Do not put the meat off your trencher into the dish, but get a voider and empty it into that. Do not play with the spoon, or your trencher, or your knife; but lead your life in cleanliness and honest manners. Heap not they trencher high with many morsels. . .
>
> *Advice to a Child,* 1500

It is little wonder that civilizations have attempted to produce breads more appealing in texture and color. Little progress was made in these attempts until the 19th century. Fine flour was expensive and thus limited to use by the wealthy before then. All this changed, however, when Governor Washburn of Minnesota tasted his first white French roll at an exhibition in Paris in 1876.

Washburn returned to America and introduced the steel roller mill, an economical method of making white flour available. This flour stored well, traveled across the pioneer miles well, and baked into nice high light loaves of pleasant textured bread. What defined status for the wealthy now became accessible to all. Homemakers were thrilled and no one was the wiser for its nutritional bankruptcy.

[1]*The Great Grain Robbery*, a 20 minute video cassette, is available from **SueGreggCookbooks**. $5.00 rental fee (30 days). Include separate refundable check for $30 marked "Video Depost."

When the Depression hit in the 1930's people relied more on inexpensive foods, including white bread. This resulted in a rampant spread of the Vitamin B-1 deficiency disease, beri beri. There just was not enough sustaining nutrients in white bread. Enrichment was thus introduced, adding three synthetic B-vitamins and iron to white flour. But the full nutritional value of over 30 nutrients was not restored, nor was fiber loss even considered (see chart, p. 53).

Enriched white flour products of all kinds have not only become entrenched in our society, but have rapidly spread throughout the world. The desire for convenience, ready availability, and familiarity of taste and preparation far outweigh awareness and concern for nutritional value--even for those who believe in God's magnificent wisdom.

It is a tragedy that we have been kept in such ignorance about whole grain wonders. I want you to appreciate the nutritional riches of whole grains. With tasty recipes you can be liberated from dependence on nutrient and fiber-depleted wheat flour!

A Little Fiber History

It is the glory of God to conceal a matter; to search out a matter is the glory of kings. Proverbs 25:2

God's truth is timeless and eternal, but our discovery of it is ever growing. We certainly have been slow in our discoveries of nutritional truth! A history lesson in fiber to illustrate:

Before 1880's

~There was little or no understanding of the presence of fiber in foods or its value to health.

~Little success throughout history had been achieved in producing lighter flours for breads, at least for the general populace, though attempts had been made.

~The only choice of grains was unrefined whole grain or flour.

1880's

~The steel roller mill was introduced; large-scale production of refined white flour began, making it available to large populations.

~The value of food fiber to health was still unknown.

1890's

~The United States Department of Agriculture (USDA) began to compile nutrient data information on a variety of foods, and to record it on a long chain of tables.

1950

~The first complete *Composition of Foods Tables*, called *USDA Handbook No. 8* was published.

1950 - 1970's

~*USDA Handbook No. 8* and all other nutrient data publications listed fiber data based on measurement of "crude" fiber. *Crude fiber* is the measurement of two forms of fiber in foods: cellulose and lignin.

~Crude fiber, containing no nutrients and indigestible, was thought to have no value to human health.

1970's - 80's

~More forms of fiber were discovered. The fiber value of foods was found to be much higher than the crude fiber values. The value of fiber to health was now being revealed in research studies. Fiber received a new name-- *dietary fiber.*

~Dietary fibers were classified into two types. Cellulose, hemicelluloses, and lignins were classified as *insoluble fiber.* Pectins, gums, and mucilages were classified as *soluble fiber.* Most plant foods have a combination of both types. These two types, it was discovered, perform different tasks in the body (see chart, p. 52).

~Dietary fiber was discovered to be many times higher than crude fiber, on the average 4 to 5 times higher in a given food, but may go as high as 38 times higher in some foods (according to *Center for Science in the Public Interest*).

~Publications still listed only crude fiber measurements in foods. A few news and magazine articles began to print limited food lists giving dietary fiber data. A number of boxed cereals also still listed only crude fiber measurements.

~Crude fiber measurements no longer had meaningful value for the consumer in terms of health.

~The USDA continued to publish limited publications with dietary fiber counts, as measurements became available through testing and research.

1990's

~The long awaited revised *USDA Handbook No. 8* giving dietary fiber measurements is not yet available (at this writing).

~Dietary fiber measurements are still not available for many foods.

~Standardization of dietary fiber measurements have not yet been fully established, so there are many inconsistencies between publications. The USDA data is the most accurate where available.

~Standard nutrient data publications are just beginning to be revised with dietary fiber listings. They are incomplete.

~Many dietary fiber measurements must still be made by good "guestimates," especially for the whole grains.

~The package standardized nutrition label is probably the most consistently available source of dietary fiber measurements.

The dietary fiber data given in the recipes and charts of this book may not be totally consistent with other sources you find. I have endeavored to use the most current and most reliable resources available whenever possible (see p. 18).

Benefits that researchers at first attributed to fiber may be the result of other nutrients in fiber foods. Yet nutrients--for example, vitamins and minerals--work more efficiently together than alone. This is called *synergism*. Perhaps dietary fiber also works synergistically with the wide range of nutrients. This would not be a surprising discovery coming from the hand of our Creator, the heavenly Father, magnificent in all his works!

Why not eat whole, unrefined high fiber foods: whole grains, beans, fruits, vegetables, nuts and seeds, just like our forefathers did before the advent of the steel roller mill and the discovery and measurements of dietary fiber? God has provided them all along for us.

Choose whole foods, based not on the latest research, which is still incomplete, but because by faith we know the Creator of these foods.

Then God said, "I give you every seed-bearing plant on the face of the
whole earth and every tree that has fruit with seed in it. They will be
yours for food. . . .I give every green plant for food." And it was so.
God saw all that he had made, and it was very good.
Genesis 1:29, 30, 31

Dietary Fiber-Hidden Treasure

Dietary fiber[1] in foods may be defined as what makes up the plant cell walls and properties associated with them. It has traditionally been termed *roughage* or *bulk*, although this doesn't describe soluble fibers very well. It is primarily non-digestible, but not all. You cannot tell if a food is high in fiber by eating it. Some coarse or crunchy foods (celery, for example) are low in fiber. Fiber is found only in plant foods. Breakfast is an ideal meal for getting grain and/or fruit fibers.

The average dietary fiber intake for the American diet is about 11-15 grams per person daily. this contrasts to 40--60 grams daily in countries (Africa, for example) where people are not suffering diseases and health conditions now attributed to the absence of sufficient high fiber foods. There are varying recommendations for Americans, but I believe that 35-40 grams daily for adults is a suitable goal. This goal can easily be achieved by using recipes and menus from **SueGreggCookbooks.** Amounts for children, of course, should be less than this, and will automatically be less on the same diet as long as they do not overeat.

A caution: It is wise to add high fiber foods gradually to prevent digestive discomfort. Some people will not have initial trouble with this, but many do. One popular method people use to increase fiber intake is to add an excessive amount of wheat bran to an otherwise poor diet. This isn't what we recommend. Instead, make your transition *One Recipe at a Time.*

A *Fiber Analysis*, the chart on p. 52, identifies the types and forms of fiber and what they do. This information is based on what research has thus far revealed about fiber. Who knows what fabulous new piece of news will be added to the fiber puzzle tomorrow. *Proverbs 25:2* is still relevant in the 21st century.

Maximizing Whole Grain Nutritional Benefits

A major concern about fiber relates to *phytates* or, phytic acid content. It is well documented that the phytates in high fiber foods bind a certain portion of protein, fat, vitamins and minerals (as calcium, phosphorus, iron and zinc), preventing them from being absorbed by the body. This is especially true of the calcium content of whole grain which is four times that of white flour. Yet the phytates inhibit calcium's absorption which promotes an imbalance in the calcium-phosphorus ratio. The nutrient-binding effects of phytates can be

[1]See also, *Making Friends with Fiber*, **The 15 Minute Menu Planner**, pp.91-100.

50

be minimized or eliminated by soaking the whole grain. Soaking, sprouting or fermenting the grain or flour (see "How to" below) activates the grain enzymes to "predigest" the nutrient components of the grain to make them more available to the body. This is a similar action as takes place when making sourdough (see p. 281) which the Hebrews in the Old Testament practiced extensively (given that they had no access to commercial yeast as we do today). We should not assume, however, that phytates are "all bad." They also have a health role to play. Jean Carper in *The Food Pharmacy Guide to Good Eating* reports promising research that phytates are involved in maintaining blood sugar levels, lowering cholesterol, and as *antioxidants*, which work against free radicals in the body. Free radicals are cancer promoting (see also p. 262). This sounds like more synergism at work!

How to Soak Whole Grains

The suggested time for enzymic action to break up the phytates is seven hours (or overnight). This added step in preparing whole grains actually encourages convenience because you have your recipe half made in advance, leaving the quick final steps only for the last minute. The procedure is simple and only slightly different depending on what you are making.

- *Yeast Breads* (e.g. p. 122). Mix dough for yeast bread by the *sponge* method, which combines the water, part of the flour and yeast mixture in advance (or night before). Allow two risings in the bowl after kneading the dough before shaping and final rising in the pans.

- *Blender Recipes* (as waffles/pancakes, muffins, coffee cakes, crepes). Do the initial blending, omitting the egg. Let stand at room temperature. Just before baking, fold in egg and reblend on highest speed 1 minute, then briefly blend in the leavenings. This procedure. for example, is incorporated in the following recipes: *Blender Banana Muffins, Blender Waffles/Pancakes, Almond Coffee Coffee Cake* and *Blender Crepes* (pp. 196, 204, 233, 249).

- *Standard Quick Bread Recipes* (i.e. those made by hand with flour as muffins, scones, biscuits, cookies, cakes, loaf breads; see *Breakfast Biscuits*, p. 125, for example). Blend dry ingredients without leavenings into liquid ingredients without egg. Cover and let stand at room temperature. Blend in egg, then leavenings just before baking. Briefly blend in both evenly without overmixing.

- *Hot Cereal.* Use one of the slow methods of cooking such as those given on pp. 99-101, or simply soak the grain or cereal flakes in the water overnight before cooking. *Sprouted Cereal*, p. 102, is another option.

A Fiber Analysis

INSOLUBLE FIBERS	SOLUBLE FIBERS
3 types cellulose hemicelluloses lignins	**3 types** Pectins (in fruits) Mucilages Gums

Food Sources
bran of whole grains:
  wheat bran, corn bran
  rice bran[1]
legumes
	Food Sources
	oats (bran)
	dried fruits
	apples, pears (flesh)
	membranes of oranges
	most vegetables
	seeds
	barley[1]
	spelt

Characteristics do not dissolve; absorb water, forming bulk pass through body undigested speed passage of food through digestive system	**Characteristics** dissolve in water to form a kind of gel; lack bulking ability slow passage of food through digestive system almost completely digested

Assist digestive regularity
contributing to prevention
and regulation of:
    appendicitis
    colon cancer
    constipation
    Crohn's disease
    diverticular disease
    hemorrhoids
    hiatal hernia
    obesity
    spastic colon
    ulcerative colitis
    varicose veins
 	
Cellulose forms mucus in the
intestine, destroying parasite that
causes irritable bowel syndrome.
	Help regulate appropriate
	blood sugar and cholesterol
	levels contributing to preven-tion
	and regulation of:
	    coronary heart disease
	    diabetes
	    gallstones
	    high blood pressure
	    hypoglycemia
	
	[1]Recent studies show that rice
	and barley bran lower choles-
	terol, perhaps not because of
	the fiber, but because of
	antioxidant properties in the
	oil of the grain (see p. 262).

A Kernel of Truth

What has happened in milling wheat flour to make white flour, by removing the bran and germ, is a good example of how we have been robbed of important nutrients that God created for our benefit.

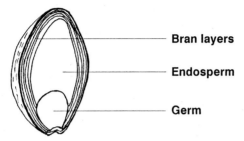

Bran layers

Endosperm

Germ

A Kernel of Wheat (a cross section)

Whole Wheat Flour Nutrients	Nutrient Loss in White
thiamine (B-1)[1]	77%
riboflavin (B-2)[1]	67%
niacin (B-3)[1]	81%
pyridoxine (B-6)	72%
choline	30%
folic acid[1]	67%
pantothenic acid	50%
vitamin E	86%
chromium	40%
manganese	86%
selenium	16%
zinc	98%
iron[1]	75%
cobalt	89%
calcium	60%
sodium	78%
potassium	77%
magnesium	85%
phosphorus	91%
molybdenum	48%
copper	68%
fiber	89%

[1]vitamins B-1, B-2, B-3, folic acid and iron are added to white flour in synthetic form by a process called enrichment. The chart reflects losses without enrichment.

God's Grain Wonders

*The streams of God are filled with water to provide
the people with grain, for so you have ordained it.*
Psalm 65:9

Origin & History of Grains

Since the beginning of civilization, grain has been the most important staple food throughout the world. About 70% of the world's cultivated soil today is dedicated to grain growing. Identified as true grains are those of the cereal grasses or *Graminae* family. These include barley, rice, corn, kamut, millet, oats, rye, sorghum, spelt, teff, triticale, and wheat. There are also several other staple seeds that are not members of the cereal grasses. However, they are used like grains and share with the grains in nutritional value. Therefore, we will treat these as grains. These include amaranth, buckwheat, quinoa, and wild rice. All of these, except triticale, have been in existence for thousands of years.

Most information sources on grains remind us that dependence upon grain was the single most important activity that moved man from the nomadic to a settled lifestyle of cultivating crops. This is interesting in light of the fact that Cain cultivated crops (*Genesis 4:3*). Man's first cultivation of grains was perhaps rather earlier in history than most would believe!

Historically, most world religions have had a goddess of the grain. For example, Ceres, from which our word cereals is derived, was the goddess of agriculture in Roman mythology. In light of the religious significance attached to grain, the purpose for which God gave the Israelites manna (a grain-based food) while they wandered in the desert for 40 years is of special significance: *He humbled you, causing you to hunger and then feeding you with manna, which neither you nor your fathers had known, to teach you that man does not live on bread alone but on every word that comes from the mouth of the LORD (Deuteronomy 8:3).*

Many peoples eat a grain-based diet. The grain, as the basic food supplying nutrients and energy, is supplemented with legumes, nuts, seeds, fruits, vegetables, and small amounts of dairy, meat, and fish. The result is a low fat, high fiber diet. In contrast, today's American diet is not a grain-based diet, but a meat-dairy based diet supplemented with mostly refined grains, and a serious lack of fruits, vegetables, nuts, seeds, and legumes. This has resulted in a high fat, low fiber diet deficient in many vital nutrients. It is not surprising that most Americans cannot tell the difference between whole grain wheat, oats, or brown rice, cannot even identify buckwheat or rye, and only recognize millet as birdseed. Actually much of our grain is fed to the animals, and we eat the animals.

Nutritional Value

Grains are the most nutritionally complete food for sustaining life. They are high carbohydrate foods, low in fats, and contain good amounts of incomplete protein[1] (*see* chart, p. 58). They contain a broad range of vitamins and minerals, including B-vitamins, vitamins E and K, calcium, iron, magnesium, and phosphorus, plus small amounts of essential fatty acids and valuable dietary fibers.

These nutritional goldmines also are very filling and satisfying because of their high energy value (calories). The myth that "bread is fattening" is finally being broken. Recent research has exposed some interesting facts. For example, only 3% of fat calories are burned during digestion, while 25% of complex carbohydrate calories are burned. In addition, the indigestible fiber of complex carbohydrates that provides the satiety quality of whole grains provides no calories. This effect in the digestion of complex carbohydrates as compared to fat digestion has been called the *thermic effect*. "Bread is fattening" no doubt applies to refined flour foods, but not to whole grains.

While whole grains are primarily carbohydrates we must reorganize our thinking. Foods with complex structures should not be put into one nutrient category. This again emphasizes the value of *synergism*--the effect on the body nutrients have when working together. For example, the value of B-vitamins is enhanced in the presence of vitamin E. The multitude of interactions between food nutrients is intricate and complex. The result is that the whole is greater than the sum of its parts. This is important to understand in evaluating our refined cold cereals that have been fortified with synthetic vitamins. When the cereal grain is stripped of its original complex relationship of nutrients and then "enriched" with an incomplete list of nutrients, how can we expect them to do the same thing as the original? In addition, researchers are discovering more and more resident nutrients in grains in addition to vitamins and minerals. Obviously, refined cereals have not been fortified with these because they haven't been known.

Some nutritionists advocate rotation of the grains in the diet so that allergic reactions will not be acquired from overeating one grain repeatedly. Historically many peoples have relied on one local grain without adverse reactions. The problem of allergy does not lie with the grains, but perhaps more likely with repeated use of them in refined forms. In addition, our bodies usually adapt best to the grains of our ancestors.

[1]*See* **Lunches & Snacks,** p. 90, **The 15 Minute Meal Planner**, pp. 101-103.

For example, Asians thrive best on rice, many Africans on millet, and Mexicans on corn. It is wise, therefore, to consider our ancestral roots in our choice of grains, and perhaps not overuse grains that we may not be so readily adapted to. For most Americans of European ancestry, in particular, this suggests use of a variety of grains to avoid overdependence on any one grain.

Baking & Cooking Characteristics

How whole grain flours act in baking depends mostly on the gluten content. High gluten grains, for example, are best for yeast bread recipes. The gluten, a protein part of the grain, develops elasticity as it is kneaded. This in turn traps the gas formed by the yeast as it grows and gives the bread its rise and lightness of texture. Gluten-free and low-gluten grains, therefore, do not produce light textured yeast breads. A portion or combination of any of them, however, may be added to any of the high-gluten wheat flours with success. Up to ¼ the amount of wheat flour can be replaced with other grain flours to produce a pleasing result. Thus, if a recipe calls for 6 cups of wheat flour, 1½ cups of other flours may replace 1½ cups of the wheat flour. It is best to knead the dough just with the wheat flour before adding the other flours. This can only be done by machine, however, as the dough would otherwise be too sticky to knead by hand.

The grains may be classified as having no gluten, low gluten, or high gluten content:

Gluten-free grains	Low-gluten grains	High-gluten grains
brown rice		hard red wheat
corn	barley, oats	hard white wheat
millet	rye	kamut
amaranth	buckwheat	spelt
quinoa	triticale	
sorghum	teff	
	soft wheat *(pastry)*	

Gluten flour is a commerical product made from white flour that is often added in a small portion to whole grain yeast breads, particularly those with a portion of gluten-free or low-gluten flours added. It is added to increase lightness. The summary of steps in gluten flour making include:

1) mixing water with white flour to produce a soft dough
2) kneading the dough until it is elastic and rubbery
3) washing the dough to rinse away the starch, leaving a rubbery mass
4) drying the rubbery mass and grinding it into gluten flour

Gluten flour is very expensive, costing ten times that of the whole wheat. I don't use it in my recipes, even when combining wheat with other grains. It is a refined portion of the flour. In my testing it did not significantly improve the final result.

In baking quick breads without yeast such as muffins, pancakes, waffles, biscuits, crepes, coffee cakes, cakes, and cookies, low-gluten grains and whole wheat pastry flour generally work well. In quick bread baking where baking soda, baking powder, or whipped egg whites are used for leavening, you do not want the gluten elasticity to be developed because it will toughen the texture of the baked goods. The high-gluten exceptions are kamut and spelt (see pp. 61-64). These latter two seem to work beautifully in just about everything.

Baking quick breads opens a wide door to using all the grains successfully. Each grain supplies its own unique flavor and texture. Some of the grain flours are more pleasing than others in flavor, hold together better, or are lighter in texture than others, particularly for muffins, biscuits and quick loaf breads. For flatter breads, however, such as crepes, pancakes, or waffles, just about any grain, alone or in combination is a delightful success. Some whole grain flours require slightly higher or lower temperatures to bake, or a bit longer. Quinoa waffles, for example, take longer to bake than kamut-oat waffles. *Blender Oat Pancakes* require a little more time on the griddle at a little lower temperature, yet oat muffin recipes require a higher oven temperature for a shorter time.

All the grains will cook up successfully as breakfast cereals, or as a grain dish for the main meal (with the exception of amaranth). Cereals may be creamed, cracked, flaked, left whole, or sprouted (see pp. 92-93).

The many grain options that can successfully be used in breakfast cereals and baked goods are a real boon for persons with grain allergies or gluten intolerance.

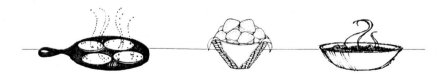

Grains have Protein!

Dairy products compliment grain proteins to provide complete, highly usable protein: for example milk and eggs with whole grain in muffins, waffles, French toast and other baked goods, milk served with breakfast cereals, and eggs served with whole grain toast, rolls, or biscuits. Legumes (dry beans) also compliment grain protein, such as Chili with Cornbread or including a portion of bean flour in yeast breads.

Protein Value of Grains by Weight

Kamut	17.3%
triticale	17%
oats	14 - 16.7%
quinoa[1]	16.2%
amaranth[1]	15.7%
spelt	13.1 - 14.28%
wild rice	14%
wheat, hard spring (durum)	12 - 14%
wheat, hard spring/winter (bread)	12 - 14%
teff	12%
rye[1]	12%
barley[1]	10 -12%
sorghum	11%
buckwheat[1]	10 -11%
millet[1]	6-11%
wheat, soft (pastry)	9.1%
corn	9%
brown rice[1]	7.5 - 9%

[1]These grains contain higher amounts of *lysine*, the amino acid that is normally low in grains. The protein value of grains high in lysine is a more complete (usable) protein on its own, but all grain proteins are well utilized when served in tahe suggested food combinations listed above. If one were on a subsistence diet of grain only, the lysine content would become more significant (see examples of high-lysine corn, and millet, pp. 66, 72).

Grains are Low Fat!

All grains are low fat, high energy foods. Grains that are both higher in fat and protein than other grains are considered especially high energy foods.

Fat Value of Grains
(% of Calories)

oats	15.0%
amaranth	14.0%
quinoa	13.5%
triticale	12.0%
corn	10.5%
millet	8.2%
spelt	6.9%
barley	5.5%
kamut	6.6%
teff	4.5%
wheat	6.9%
buckwheat	6.4%
rye	5.9%
brown rice	4.7%
wild rice	1.8%

The fat in grains contain valuable *essential fatty acids* in a whole food package. Don't choose a lower fat grain over a higher fat grain just to cut down on fat!

Great Grains

. . . the valleys are mantled with grain;
they shout for joy and sing.
Pslam 65:13

Wheat - King of Grains

Wheat is thought to be the oldest of the grains, originating in the Fertile Crescent between the Tigres and Euphrates Rivers. The Bible often mentions wheat; it was an important food in Israel and Egypt. The Egyptians made a fine art of baking with wheat and when they discovered yeast, Egypt became the bread basket for the Roman Empire. Baking became such an important vocation that bakers were exempt from military service and the Roman government provided each baker's family with a house.

Columbus brought wheat to the West Indies, Cortes brought it to Mexico, and English colonization brought it to North America, Australia, and Africa. Although Virginia and Massachusetts colonists brought it to our eastern shores quite early, it did not grow well there. Not until pioneer expansion to the West did wheat become an important crop.

Wheat has been universally prized for its high gluten content, essential to light textured yeast breads (see p. 56). Today, 50% of the world's population relies on wheat as a staple grain. In the United States per capita consumption is 126 pounds per year. Scientists have developed different wheat varieties that will grow in almost any country in the world under a wide range of geographic and climatic conditions. More acres of land are now dedicated to growing wheat throughout the world than any other food. At least 30,000 varieties of wheat have been developed. Over 200 of these are grown in the United States. With the exception of kamut and spelt, all are hybridized to increase yields, to obtain uniformity, to improve qualities of resistance to disease, to improve baking qualities, and to accept chemical treatment.

The *genus* of the wheat family is *Triticum*. *Triticum durum* wheat, for example, is used almost exclusively by the commerical food industry for pastas. It is a very hard wheat, not suitable for bread baking. Semolina is a refined form of durum wheat used in pastas. *Triticum aestivum* identifies common bread wheat. Spelt is *Triticum spelta* and kamut, *triticum polonicum*. For our baking purposes we will concern ourselves with six kinds of wheat: hard winter red wheat, hard spring wheat, hard white wheat, whole wheat pastry flour, kamut, and spelt.

Hard Red Winter & Spring Wheats

Whole wheat flour comes from varieties of hard wheat grown mostly in the winter. Hard winter red wheat, developed in Canada, is one of the finest for yeast bread baking. With the highest gluten content, whole wheat flour makes the best yeast breads. It is sometimes labeled as bread flour, but most often simply as whole wheat flour. It can be used in all recipes, but will not give as light a texture as whole wheat pastry flour in quick breads, muffins, and desserts that do not use yeast. Hard red spring wheat is also fine for baking and may be preferred by some.

Whole wheat flour purchased from the supermarket cannot match the freshly milled whole grain in texture and flavor. In addition it has been bromated or phosphated to produce lighter baked goods. Graham flour is coarsely ground whole wheat flour, but usually the wheat germ has been removed from it to prevent rancidity. It is best to buy freshly stoneground whole wheat from a health food store (inquire when it was ground) or better yet, buy the whole grain wheat, called wheat berries (see p. 78), and grind your own fresh flour (see p.84).

Wheat germ and wheat bran are valuable parts of the whole wheat that have been extracted from white flour and sold separately. These may be added to recipes to further supplement the nutritional value (see pp.272-273).

Hard White Wheat

We concur heartily with Dean Folkvord in Wheat Montana's brochure, "Our Golden 86 is a new variety of hard white spring wheat. it has protein levels and yields comparable to hard reds, yet produces a bread light in color and texture that has all the nutrition of traditional whole wheat. It also has a light, sweet taste that's unique to this variety." The bran of hard white wheat is lighter in color. You may prefer it to hard red wheat in yeast breads, but it is not currently widely available. Contact Walton Feed at 135 North 10th, PO Box 307, Mont Pelier, ID 83254 (1-800-847-0465), or Wheat Montana, PO Box 647, Three Forks, MT 59752 (1-800-535-2798).

Whole Wheat Pastry Flour

Whole wheat pastry flour comes primarily from varieties of soft wheat grown in the spring. It is both lower in protein (see chart, p. 58) and gluten content than whole wheat bread flour. The lower gluten content makes lighter textured quick breads and desserts of all types. Whole wheat pastry flour is not generally available in supermarkets, but readily available in health food stores, along with whole wheat pastry grain (berries).

61

Kamut (kah-MOOT)

Kamut could be the food find of the 20th century! In 1989, David Goldbeck, co-author with Nikki Goldbeck of *The Supermarket Handbook*, named kamut one of the ten best foods in his *True Food Newsletter*. It is a rediscovered, transplanted to America, 6,000 year old ancient wheat. The wheat of the Bible may have been more like Kamut than our present common varieties of wheat. Public awareness of kamut is spreading rapidly. Its availability in cereals and pastas has extended beyond healthfood stores even to some supermarkets. kamut is fabulous! Here's why:

~It is wheat, so it acts like wheat in all recipes, including yeast bread recipes. It has the necessary gluten content to give light and tender results.

~It is 20-40% higher in protein than whole wheat (see chart, p. 58), slightly higher in 8 of 9 minerals, considerably higher in magnesium and zinc, and up to 65% higher in amino acids.

~The texture is lighter than whole wheat or whole wheat pastry flour. kamut-oat waffles (p. 205) are the lightest we've ever tasted, and it makes wonderfully textured *Kamut Bread* (p. 123).

~Many people sensitive to wheat are able to eat kamut without allergic reaction. At least two controlled studies have demonstrated that 70% of those with negative responses to wheat can enjoy kamut products. If you have similar allergies, consult your physician.

~It is easily digestible, yet since it is higher protein and higher in fat than wheat, it is considered a higher energy food.

~The same amount of kamut can be used in any recipe without altering the quantity of any of the other ingredients, or changing the baking temperature. New recipes are not really needed for kamut.

~It has its own unique taste, not at all like whole wheat. The baked goods are lighter in color, a psychological plus for persons attached to eating white breads.

~It makes the lightest pastas we have tasted. I have finally found a really enjoyable whole grain macaroni that meets my nutritional standard. Kamut pastas are available in some health foods stores.

Kamut is currently marketed under the registered trademark, Kamut®, of the Kamut Association of North America, indicating the pure, uncrossed, non-hybridized organically grown ancient grain. Kamut is an Egyptian word for wheat.

How was kamut discovered? The story does not come out of the research laboratory. Instead, it emerges with a mystery of its own.

While in Portugal In 1949, a U.S. Airman from Montana, was given 36 kernels of grain, believed to have come from Egypt. He sent the grains to his father, a wheat farmer in Fort Denton, Montana, who planted them. Thirty two of the 36 kernels germinated. In just six years 1,500 bushels of the grain were accumulated. Shown at a country fair the grain aroused little curiosity. Consequently it was sold for cattle feed.

In 1977, Bob Quinn, son of another Montana farmer, Mack Quinn, remembered seeing the grain at that county fair as a youth. He managed to collect a pint of the grain and gave it to his father who planted it in his garden. Meanwhile, Bob, with a Ph.D. in plant biochemistry, began research on the grain.

The Quinns took a sample of the grain to the Natural Products Expo West '86 in Anaheim, California. Here, a commercial interest started. The Quinns, in Big Sandy, Montana, began serious production planting 20 acres in 1987 and 60 acres in 1988. They gave the grain its registered trademark name, Kamut®. There is a limited supply of kamut, but with the promise it holds for many persons allergic to common wheats, we can anticipate that much more of it will be grown in years to come. The 1992 harvest, produced on over 4,000 acres in Montana and Canada, yielded over 5 million pounds.

Genetically kamut belongs to the wheat family. The slightly yellowish grains are longer and larger than wheat kernels. Kamut contains gluten and can be substituted in recipes calling for wheat. It has a pleasing flavor all its own.

Kamut grain or flour, packaged by may be purchased at health food stores. Kamut pastas are more limited in availability, but are also found in health food stores. Kamut may be purchased by mail order as well as from SunOrganic Farm (see p. 79). As awareness and use of kamut grow, I expect to see an increase in the availability of kamut grain and flour, and in the variety of pastas. In 1990, the KAMUT Association of North America (KANA) was formed with Bob Andersen as Executive Vice President. Literature and product source information may be obtained from KANA, 295 Distribution St., San Marcos, CA 92069 (619) 752-5234.

Spelt

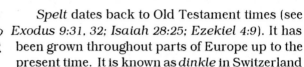

Spelt dates back to Old Testament times (see *Exodus 9:31, 32; Isaiah 28:25; Ezekiel 4:9*). It has been grown throughout parts of Europe up to the present time. It is known as *dinkle* in Switzerland and *farro* in Italy. When European customers began requesting spelt in America, *Purity Foods, Inc.* investigated the use of spelt for human use (most produced had been for animal feed). The company began marketing spelt products in 1989.

In structure, spelt is closer to our bread wheats than kamut, yet it shares a similar nutrition content. Likewise, many persons allergic to common wheats are finding that they can tolerate spelt, although controlled studies have not yet confirmed this.

Containing both soluble and insoluble fibers (see chart, p.52), spelt is easily digested and has been considered beneficial for indigestion, gas, and nausea. It is rich in essential fatty acids and higher in fiber than wheat. With a higher fat and protein content than common wheat, spelt is a higher energy food. The nutrients are found in the inner kernel of the grain in contrast to wheat, where they are found in the bran and the germ.

Delicious with a nutty flavor, spelt makes a wonderfully soft textured yeast bread. *Spelt Bread* (p. 122) has replaced my *Delicious Whole Wheat Bread* as our favorite. In fact, spelt has replaced hard winter red wheat for yeast bread baking in our household since it contains the essential gluten content for light textured breads. I also use it frequently in place of whole wheat pastry flour in quick bread baking with pleasing results.

Spelt requires less liquid (or more flour), than whole wheat flour in recipes. I use about 1¼ cups spelt flour in place of 1 cup whole wheat flour or decrease the liquid from 1 cup to ⅔ - ¾ cup. In several of our recipes we have included spelt as a choice, but as with kamut, it can be used successfully in most recipes.

Pastas made with spelt are also available. However, since spelt is lower in starch and gluten than durum wheats, with a higher fiber content, spelt pastas are not as smooth and firm as Kamut and durum wheat pastas. Nevertheless, it holds up well when cooked. I prefer spelt's rich nutty flavor over the flavor of whole wheat pastas.

For more information on spelt and spelt products check local health food stores or write to Purity Foods, Inc., 2871 W. Jolly Rd., Okemos, MI 48864 (517) 351-9231. *Vita Spelt* brand pastas, whole grain, flakes, and flour are available.

Corn

Corn is America's great contribution to the family of grains. It was probably first grown thousands of years ago in South America and was a staple for the Incas, Aztecs, Mayans, and nomadic Indian tribes. American Indians taught the first European settlers how to plant it, grind it, and use it in palatable ways.

The word *corne* is actually an old English generic term for whatever grain is the staple of a particular locality. For example, the Scots would refer to oats as corn, and the English to wheat as corn. In some translations of the Bible the word corn is used for grain (see *Psalm 78:24, King James Version*) The pilgrims called the local staple of America, Indian corne, although it is actually *maize (Zea Mays)*.

When the first settlers from Europe came to America's shores they discovered that the three most important local foods were corn, fish, and game.

One of the first things that every settler in a new land has to learn is that he must find food in that land; that he cannot trust long to any supplies of food which he has brought with him, or to any fresh supplies which he has ordered to be sent after him. He must turn at once to hunting, fishing, planting, to furnish him with food grown and found in the very place where he is. . . .[It was the] abundance, adaptibility, and nourishing qualities [of corn] that not only saved the colonists' lives, but altered their many methods of living, especially their manner of cooking and their tastes in food. (p. 126, **Home Life in Colonial Days**, Alice Morse Earle in the year 1898).

Today, the Midwest states supply 50% of the world's supply of corn, although it is grown in all 50 states. In the U.S. more wheat is grown and used than corn, however. With the increasing use of white flour from wheat, yearly per capita consumption of field corn (the kind used for cornmeal) in the U.S. has dropped from 117 pounds in 1877 to a about 7 pounds. Cattle and pigs consume more field corn in America than do people. Yet corn is the third most produced grain worldwide after wheat and rice. In two generations after Columbus took corn to Europe, it spread over Europe, Africa, China, India, and Tibet. Corn is commonly available in several forms:

Dent corn (field corn) used for cornmeal
Popcorn
Sweet corn we eat on the cob, canned, and frozen
Masa parched corn with lime used in Mexican tortillas
Blue corn *(Hopi Corn)*, sweeter and milder than yellow corn, used in pancakes, tortillas, and corn chips

There are red, yellow, white, and blue varieties of corn. Flint corn is the beautiful multicolored corn with red in it. It, too, may be home ground for cornmeal. The most commonly available cornmeal is yellow corn that has been *degerminated* (the corn germ is removed). *Stonground* cornmeal that has not been degermed, or whole kernel corn for home grinding are available from health food stores, food co-ops, or mail order sources (see p. 79).

Corn may be considered the least nutritious of the grains. Of course, this does not mean it is not nutritious. It is especially high in magnesium and yellow corn is the only grain that contains vitamin A (about 600 I.U. per 1 cup stoneground). Blue corn contains more manganese and more complete protein than yellow corn. *Arrrowhead Mills* brand of blue cornmeal is available in health food stores.

Corn is especially low in lysine, the amino acid that most cereal grains are low in. In societies where corn is the primary food with little other protein sources, millions of children suffer from *kwashiorkor*, protein malnutrition. A high-lysine corn, 70% higher in lysine, has been developed in an attempt to meet this need. It is a hybridized corn and more expensive than stoneground cornmeal or whole kernel corn. It is not essential to most Americans' diets which include plenty of high protein foods. Jean Carper in *The Food Pharmacy* reports that corn contains chemicals that contribute to lower the risk of contracting certain cancers, heart disease, and dental cavities.

Popcorn remains the All American favorite way to consume dry corn in its whole form. Popcorn has a very hard hull. When the kernel is heated, the water inside turns to steam. Since there aren't any openings in the hull for it to escape, the kernel explodes. Popcorn that does not pop well has lost some of its moisture. To restore it, you can sprinkle water over the top of the popcorn in the jar, seal it and allow it to stand for several days before popping it. Our recipes using corn include *Cornbread*, corn in waffles (pp. 205, 207), *Polenta* (p. 107), crusts for *Tamale Pie* and *Chicken Pot Pie, Corn Tortillas, Corn Chips, Pineapple Cornmeal Muffins* and *Blueberry Corn Muffins.*

Oats

Before becoming an important crop, oats were weeds among the barley, probably in western and central Europe. Today the U.S. is the largest producer of oats (*Avena sativa*). Russia, Canada, and Scotland are also major producers. Oats have been traditional to the Scots and are our most widely used grain for hot breakfast cereals and granolas. The following describes how rolled oat flakes are produced:

1. Husked grains are partially cooked by passing them through a steam chamber.
2. The partially cooked grains are flattened by heated rollers.
3. The flattened grains are dried.

Rolled oat flakes retain virtually all the nutritional value of the original grain. When flattened by rolling, there is no loss of the germ or bran and the manufacturing process does not destroy the vitamins. If you look at *Old Fashioned Quaker Oats* you can see the rib of the whole grain down the center of each rolled flake. *Quick Quaker Oats*, on the other hand, are flakes from oats that have been steel cut first, and then rolled.

Besides rolled oats, steel cut oats and Scotch oatmeal are available. In the latter, the oat groats have been stone-cut rather than steel cut. There seems to be a difference of opinion about whether whole, rolled, steel-cut, or stone-cut oats retain more nutrient value. Yet most agree that whatever differences exist, they are minimal. All forms of oats provide valuable whole grain nutrition.

Oats provide high energy, containing one of the highest amounts of grain protein and fat (see pp.58-59). They are rich in iron, phosphorus, and inositol, with a good amount of minerals. Oats are the grain highest in thiamine (vitamin B-1) and are a fair source of riboflavin (vitamin B-2) and vitamin E. Oats also contain silicon, valuable to healthy hair, skin, eyes, and nails.

While oatmeal was almost getting buried by 1980's oat bran-mania, researchers discovered that whole or rolled oats were just as effective in contributing to lower blood cholesterol. This is encouraging! Oats are much more tasty than oat bran and easier to use in a wide variety of recipes. Oats naturally do contain oat bran, the soluble fiber found so effective for cholesterol lowering (see chart, p. 52). A daily cup of uncooked old fashioned or quick oats has about the same cholesterol-lowering effect as ½ cup oat bran. Research suggests that this amount will lower total blood cholesterol about 3%. For persons with very high cholesterol levels (over 300), however, oats do not seem to be effective. Though oats have become best known for cholesterol-lowering soluble fiber, they also act as a mild laxative.

Dr. Samuel Johnson, an Englishman:
Oatmeal! Food for horses in England and men in Scotland.
James Boswell, a Scot:
Aye, and where will you find such horses, or such men?
1772

Oats may be eaten either raw or cooked. Uncooked oats may be soaked before eating as in *Swiss Breakfast*, p. 115, or eaten raw in meusli, granola-type cereal with uncooked oats. Oats added to baked goods slows spoilage. When using oats in pancakes, bake them a little longer at a lower temperature. Oven baked quick breads with oats usually call for a higher temperature at 400°-425°.

Whole oat grain is referrred to as *oat groats*. They are not as readily available as other grains, especially at health food stores. Groats may be used interchangeably with rolled oats for oat flour in recipes although the yield of 1 cup groats is different than 1 cup rolled oats (see chart, p. 85). Rolled oats do not feed through a stone grinder as easily as groats unless mixed with other whole grains. They may be ground dry in a blender at high speed for about 1 minute, in the liquid of a blender recipe or in a coffee bean mill.

A bowl of hot oatmeal served daily for breakfast is one of the easiest ways you can provide whole grain nutrition on a strict food budget (see chart, p. 77).

Brown Rice

Rice (*Oryza sativa*) is the second most used staple grain in the world. Unfortunately It is primarily eaten as white rice. In Asia, rice provides about half of the people's total calories. *Dhanga*, the sanskrit word for rice means "supporter or nourisher of man."

Alexander the Great discovered this semi-aquatic marsh grass of southeast Asia and India and brought it to Greece from India. The Moors introduced it to Spain and the Spaniards took it to Italy, the West Indies, and Souh America. In 1694 an unexpected storm at sea blew a ship from Madagascar to the shores of North America. As a token of gratitude for the help for repairs he received, the ship's captain gave the colonial governor in Charleston, South Carolina a small amount of rice.

Today the United States produces annually about 10 billion pounds of rice in warm, moist climates not suitable for corn and wheat. It is grown along the Gulf Coast of Texas and Louisiana, in central Arkansas near the Mississippi River, and around the Sacramento Valley in California. Although only 2% of the world's rice crop is grown in the United States, it supplies 20% of the rice export market.

Americans eat about the same amount of rice as cornmeal, about 7 pounds yearly in contrast to about 450 pounds per capita in Southeast Asia, or 100 pounds in Brazil. The average is higher, of course, among the Mexican and Asian American population. People who eat more natural foods average 25-200 pounds a year.

Of the 7,000-8,000 varieties of rice, the common varieties available in our markets include long grain, medium grain, short grain, and basmati rice, and a less familiar sweet rice. Long grain brown rice has a fluffier, drier texture, closer to that of white rice. Most Americans prefer this texture. Short grain brown rice cooks up chewier and stickier. Medium brown rice is inbetween. Basmati rice is a long grain brown rice with an elegant flavor of its own, especially suited to the gourmet meal. Sweet rice is a very glutinous sticky rice that the Japanese especially like to use for a popular dish called *mochi.*

Brown rice is not used extensively in baking, but persons who are gluten intolerant do rely on it. Rice flour is slightly grainy in texture and can add crispness to crackers and cookies, can lighten yeast bread when added to wheat, and makes a good thickener in place of white flour. Brown rice works well in waffles and pancakes (p. 205), and in cookies with barley flour (**Desserts**, pp. 20-21). *Cream of Brown Rice Cereal* (p. 104) with its light color is a tasty alternative to *Cream of Wheat,* a refined wheat cereal. It is also the most economical cereal along with *Polenta* and oatmeal (see chart, p. 77).

Some claim that white rice is still a good food. But it cannot compare nutritionally to brown rice which, as a rich source of vitamin B-complex, iron, and calcium, contains 5 times the thiamine (B-1) and vitamin E, 3 times the dietary fiber, niacin (B-3), B-6, and magnesium, twice the iron and pantothenic acid, and 50% more zinc than white rice. Although rice is at the bottom of our protein chart (p. 58), it is high in the amino acid lysine making it one of the most valuable cereal grain protein sources.

Jean Carper in *The Food Pharmacy* reports that brown rice can lower blood pressure, fight diarrhea, prevent kidney stones, clear up psoriasis, and contains chemicals that assist in preventing cancer. Of course, research has now included rice bran on the list of soluble fibers that can effectively lower blood cholesterol (see chart, p. 52).

Since America's rice crop is heavily sprayed, second only to cotton, it may be well to consider using organically grown rice, available through health food stores, food co-ops, and mail order sources (see p. 79).

Barley

 For the Hebrews, Greeks, and Romans barley was the most important grain, especially for bread, until it was replaced by wheat and rye during the Middle Ages. Historically the Roman gladiators were known to build their strength on barley. It is mentioned in the Bible as having been a prominent crop. The Egyptian crop of barley was destroyed by the plague of hail (*Exodus 9:32*), Ruth first gleaned in Boaz's field during the barley harvest (*Ruth 2:23*), and it was barley loaves that Jesus multipled one evening on a hillside for over 5,000 people (*John 6*).

Today, barley is the 4th most used grain worldwide. It is still popular in Scotland in stews and soups. *Scotch Broth* is characterized by the addition of barley. Scandinavians and Turks have grown strong on it along with the Scots. The Dutch, Spanish, and English brought barley to America. There are over 2,000 varieties. Barley is identified by the genus, *Hordeum*.

Pearl barley is the most commonly available in America. The hull and two hard outer layers of the grain are removed in pearl barley putting it nutritionally in the same class with white flour and white rice. This is just about the only form of barley you can find in supermarkets. For soups and casseroles, pearl barley is the most palatable form.

Until recently whole hulled barley was hard to find. Now it is available through health food stores and mail order (see p. 79). Only the inedible hull and one hard outer layer has been removed leaving most of the nutritional value intact. Hulled barley cooks up well for a breakfast cereal (pp. 95, 114) and makes an excellent whole grain flour that may be used totally in place of wheat for light quick bread recipes, or to lighten baked goods by replacing 2 tablespoons of each cup of wheat flour with 2 tablespoons of barley flour. Barley flour can be used successfully in place of wheat in coffee cakes and waffles/pancakes (pp. 205, 233-240), and in place of wheat in cakes and cookies (**Desserts,** pp. 20-21).

Barley is one of the grains high in lysine, increasing its protein value. It contains moderate amounts of phosphorus and calcium, and small amounts of B-vitamins. It also contains water-soluble fiber (see chart, p. 52), and can relieve constipation as well. It is a non-gas-forming grain that is easy to digest. It assists in lowering cholesterol and contains antioxidants. As with whole grains in general, it may assist in preventing cancer.

70

Rye

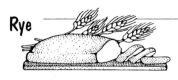

Commercial loaves of rye bread are popular in America. They are usually combinations of white flour and light or dark rye flour. Light rye flour is comparable to white flour in nutritional value. Dark rye flour includes more of the whole grain. An all rye yeast bread loaf makes a very heavy, dense loaf. Rye works best in combination with whole wheat flour. Rye has a distinct flavor that many do not like, or think they don't like because they confuse its flavor with the flavor of the caraway seed often added to rye breads. A palatable form of rye for cereal is rye flakes, used to make *Cream of Rye* (p.105). We also use whole grain rye in our own *Roman Meal* mix (p. 107). While little used in quick breads, we do offer it as a pleasing choice for *Blender Molasses Muffins* (p. 193).

Rye probably came from eastern Europe or Asia. To the Greeks rye (*Secale cereale*) was a weed. The Romans cultivated it. It was a staple grain throughout Europe in the Middle Ages. The typical loaf of bread in England was made of rye and barley. Rye bread has continued to be popular among the Russians and Scandinavians. Dutch immigrants brought rye to America early in the 19th century, and the pioneers took it to the West. As the use of wheat increased, the use of rye decreased in most parts of the world. Nevertheless, it has continued as an important crop in cold climates grown on infertile soils inhospitable to other grains, especially in northern Europe. Russia is the largest producer of rye, followed by Canada, Poland, and Germany. North and South Dakota are the leading states in rye production in America.

Millet

Think of the little yellow birdseed and you will have identified millet. Yet millet feeds far more than the birds. Fully one third of the world utilizes millet as grain feeds for animals and for human consumption.

Millet was a staple in China before rice. During Biblical times it was common in the Middle East. It is grown extensively in southern Europe and in Asia. In the United States farmers grow mostly foxtail millet (*Setaria italica*). Most millet in the United States goes for animal feed, to raise seed, or to enrich the soil. But it is a primary staple food for millions in parts of Africa, Asia, and India. In India the Hunzas use millet extensively. The diet secrets of the Hunzas have been studied for years because of their outstanding health and longevity.

71

Millet is actually any of a wide variety of small-seeded hay or cereal grasses. For example, barnyard millet grown mainly for hay is *Echinochloa frumentacea*, and broomcorn millet, grown primarily for seed in both Europe and the United States, is *Panicum milaceum*.

Millet is a gluten-free grain and almost no one is allergic to it. With an excellent balance of amino acids, millet is one of the best quality grain protein sources. It has more iron and vitamins than any other cereal and is very easy to digest. The following World War II story concerning millet was recounted from *China's Millions*, a missionary publication:

When the Japanese occupied Changtze, where Miss Lungren and Miss Bachmann were stationed, the ladies were cut off from all supplies and lived for four months on a diet of millet porridge three times a day....Miss Bachmann's health - she had been suffering from digestive trouble - greatly improved. It is interesting to hear that an American Mission doctor in Peking has discovered the virtues of millet porridge for digestive trouble and now gives it a regular place on her own menu, and feeds her friends on it too. (p.142, *The Flying Scotsman*, a biography of Eric Liddell by Sally Magnusson).

Millet as a hot cereal is very different to American tastes. I am not particularly fond of it but I do like my own cereal recipes for it. A little butter stirred into the cereal can greatly improve the taste. In baking, millet works best in combination with other grains. Tortillas and chapatis can be made with half whole wheat and half millet flour. Millet used alone or in combination with other grains makes excellent waffles and pancakes (pp.207, 212). In yeast breads up to 1/5 the amount of wheat flour can be replaced with millet flour successfully. Millet is quite dry in muffins and quick loaf breads if used alone. In flatter breads, such as crepes, pancakes, and waffles, millet as the only flour will work well.

Triticale (tri-ti-KAY-lee)

Triticale, first raised in Sweden in the 1930's, is man's "accomplishment" of blending two different grains, wheat and rye. Tritcale gets its name from *Triticum* (wheat) + *Secale* (rye), combining the higher gluten and protein content of wheat with high lysine content of rye. The result is a grain higher in protein and nutritive value than wheat (see chart, p. 58).

Triticale produces a heavier yeast bread than wheat, though much lighter than rye. The gluten is softer, necessitating gentle kneading and only one rising of the dough. Yeast bread turns out well using triticale alone, or with 1 part triticale to 2 parts whole wheat flour. Triticale bread can be lightened by adding vitamin C crystals to the liquids (⅛ teaspoon per 2 loaves bread), and/or 2 tablespoons liquid lecithin (see p.13).

For persons with a mild sensitivity to wheat, triticale is often acceptable. Use it like wheat. It will be a little heavier and more dense with its own special flavor.

Buckwheat

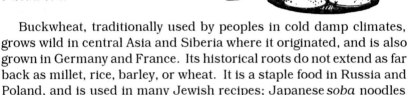

Buckwheat, traditionally used by peoples in cold damp climates, grows wild in central Asia and Siberia where it originated, and is also grown in Germany and France. Its historical roots do not extend as far back as millet, rice, barley, or wheat. It is a staple food in Russia and Poland, and is used in many Jewish recipes; Japanese *soba* noodles are made from buckwheat.

A member of the sorrel family (*Polgonaceae*), buckwheat is not a grain, but a fruit related to rhubarb. It is a triangular seed containing no bran or germ. In America we use it primarily in pancakes and waffles. Buckwheat also makes good crepes.

Buckwheat contains almost all the B-vitamins and is high in calcium, vitamin E, and lysine. Unique to buckwheat is *rutic acid* which contributes to health of the arteries, veins, and circulatory systems. Few people are allergic to buckwheat, one of the most nutritious of grains. Three forms of buckwheat are commonly available:
    sprouting buckwheat
    raw buckwheat groats (i.e. grain)
    kasha

The least expensive, sprouting buckwheat is the unhulled buckwheat groat, almost black or charcoal gray. It is our first choice of buckwheat as a single grain or in combination with other grains in pancakes and waffles (p. 205). It will also grow into sprouts, and if planted, into buckwheat lettuce. Moderately expensive, raw buckwheat is the hulled, untoasted grain, ashen in color. Kasha, which is most expensive, is nutty brown toasted buckwheat and generally most popular for hot cereal. In addition to the grains, light buckwheat flour from raw buckwheat groats and dark buckwheat flour may be purchased commercially.

All three forms of buckwheat may be used for flour in waffles, crepes, and pancakes. You can make your own kasha by toasting raw buckwheat groats. Heat a tablespoon of oil in a heavy pan until hot; add the buckwheat groats and stir until nutty brown. Both kasha and raw buckwheat make a tasty hot breakfast cereal (see p. 113).

Sorghum (SAWR-gum)

Sorghum (i.e. *Sorhum vulgare*) is the major cereal grain of Africa, and used in India, Japan, and China. Slave traders first brought sorghum to the West Indies from Africa. It is grown in the United States primarily in the Great Plains region. Sorghum thrives in hot, dry climates. Varieties are used as grain, cattle feed, sweet syrup, and broom fiber.

Sorghum is little used as a flour in the United States. We are most likely to find it as a sweet syrup. In Africa the women spend up to 2 hours each day to pound sorghum into flour for porridge, pancakes, and flatbreads.

Sorghum may be cooked and eaten like rice using 1 part sorgum to 4 parts of water. It is a grain I have not attempted to use and I expect it is the least used cereal grain in this country. It is often called *milo*.

Quinoa (KEEN-wah)

A member of the goosefoot family (*Chenopodium quinoa*), quinoa is grown in the altiplano of the Andes in Bolivia, Ecuador, and Peru, and some in Chile and Argentina. A pilot crop grows in Boulder, Colorado.

Quinoa has historically been the staple food of the Andes, traditionally eaten like rice, toasted and ground to make tortillas, and fermented to make *chicha*, a drink. As the "mother grain" of the Incas, quinoa was of such central importance to that civilization, that by destroying its cultivation, the Spaniards subdued the Inca Empire in one year.

Quinoa cooks up quickly in 15-25 minutes into a light, fluffy "cute curly" yellow grain. It has the gourmet look and a very delicate flavor. The flour makes light crepes and waffles in our blender recipes. It is gluten-free, providing another grain choice for the gluten intolerant. With high protein and high lysine content, quinoa is one of the most nutritious grains. It is very expensive.

74

A substance on the surface of quinoa seed called *saponins* imparts a bitter taste and must be rinsed away. I rinse the seed in a strainer 1-2 minutes the evening before using it, soak it in a bowl of water overnight, drain it, and rinse again about 1 minute. This procedure is included in our recipes for quinoa crepes, waffles, and creamed cereal.

Amaranth

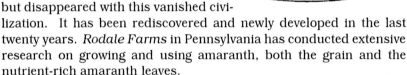

A staple of the Aztecs, amaranth all but disappeared with this vanished civilization. It has been rediscovered and newly developed in the last twenty years. *Rodale Farms* in Pennsylvania has conducted extensive research on growing and using amaranth, both the grain and the nutrient-rich amaranth leaves.

Not a grain, amaranth is a tiny seed belonging to the family, *Amaranthus*. There are 60 different species. It is highly nutritious with high lysine content and high protein. It is higher than most grains in calcium and phosphorus.

Amaranth does not work acceptably on its own in recipes. It has a very sweet pungent flavor and is very glutinous in texture. It is best used in combination with grains, using up to 15% amaranth (2-2½ tablespoons of 1 cup flour). This amount adds a sweetly pleasant flavor and moistness to texture. It also may be used in combination as flour with arrowroot powder--about 75% amaranth flour and 25% arrowroot powder (for example, see *Amaranth Muffins*, **Soups & Muffins**, p. 87).

Amaranth flour is very expensive and generally only available in small amounts. The tiny seed may easily be made into flour in a coffee bean mill or in a blender, either dry, or with the liquid ingredients used in the recipe. I have not included recipes with amaranth in **Breakfasts.** Use the guidelines here to do your own experimenting. Commercially, amaranth is found combined with other grains in cold cereals, cookies, and crackers. For example, *Health Valley Amaranth Graham Crackers* (not at all like graham crackers) are a delightful reminder of animal crackers in crunch and taste.

Teff

For thousands of years teff (*Eragrostis tef*) has been the staple grain in the highlands of Ethiopia. Ethiopians typically make it into a large fermented flatbread called *injera*.

The name of teff means "lost" because the seed is so tiny that you probably couldn't find it if you dropped it. 150 teff grains weigh about as much as one wheat kernel. Teff has been brought to America in recent years with a pilot crop grown in Idaho.

Teff has a high nutritional rating. The nutritious bran and germ are a large proportion of the tiny grain. Mineral content is high with very high calcium and iron. It is, however, low in lysine. It is very expensive, sold in very small amounts and not widely available.

With low gluten content, teff is best used in quick breads. It may be white, red, or brown. *Arrowhead Mills* brand of Teff, available at health food stores, is very dark and cooks up into a very grainy-like cereal (p. 111). For a small cookbook of teff recipes prepared by Rebecca Wood, including waffles, muffins, hot cereal, and banana bread, write to Maskal Forages, Inc., 1318 Willow, Caldwell, Idaho 83605 (208) 454-3330.

Wild Rice

Not a true rice or a true grain, wild rice is an aquatic grass (*Zizania aquatica*) native to northeastern North America. It is a lovely gourmet dish cooked whole for main meals, either in place of brown rice or in combination with brown rice. It is expensive and worthy of the special occasion. It is not used in baking, as far as I know. For an unusual treat it would go well with a special scrambled egg dish or omelet for a holiday brunch. I often mix ¼ cup wild rice with brown rice in cooked rice or a pilaf.

Wild rice has enough protein, carbohydrate, and nutrients to sustain a long and healthy life supplemented with little other food.

> *Yet he gave a command to the skies above*
> *and opened the doors of the heavens;*
> *he rained down manna for the people to eat,*
> *he gave them the grain of heaven.*
> *Men ate the bread of angels;*
> *he sent them all the food they could eat.*
> *Psalm 78:23-25*

All Grains are Low Cost!

Why spend money on what is not bread,
and your labor on what does not satisfy?
Listen, Listen to me, and eat what is good.
Isaiah 55:2

Cost Comparisons of Grains

Low Cost	Moderate Cost	High Cost
whole wheat (bread flour)	barley, hulled	kasha
brown rice	brown rice	quinoa
(non-organic)	(organic)	amaranth
oats, rolled	millet	teff
rye	oat groats, hulled	wild rice
cornmeal	kamut	
pastry wheat	spelt	
	buckwheat, raw	

Some grains do cost more than others, yet as a food group, grains are a low budget food item. The higher the proportion of grains to dairy and meats in the diet, the less costly meals will be, even when more expensive grains are included.

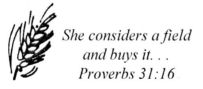

She considers a field
and buys it...
Proverbs 31:16

Whole Grain Shopping List

Where do you find these whole grains anyway? For most women this is real uncharted territory! Logically, you will find most grains and whole grain flours in health food stores. You might find both grains and flours in open bins from which you weigh out the number of pounds, or you may find grains and flours packaged in 12 oz., 1 lb., 24 oz., 2 lb., or 5 lb. packages. Some stores buy in bulk and do their own packaging. Others order prepackaged flours and grains from companies such as *Arrowhead Mills* and *Nature's Cuisine*, or they carry them both ways.

There are also mail order sources and food co-ops. The savings realized from these sources will vary considerably depending upon the quantity purchased and the cost of shipping and handling. Some mail order sources are listed in **The 15 Minute Meal Planner**, pp. 304-305. You will also find an extensive list printed in **The Yeast Connection Cookbook** by William G. Crook, M.D. & Marjorie Hurt Jones, R.N., pp. 354-59. This book is readily available at most health food stores. Try to locate a source close to you. Get their catalog and ordering terms. Check out the prices and range of offerings to compare with local health food store prices. Check the Internet.

The most reliable and serviceable company in my area that sells quality whole grains and flours, along with other great food items, is SunOrganic Farm in Valley Center, CA (near San Diego). SunOrganic Farm specializes in organically grown foods. Grains and flours are available in 1 lb., 3 lb., and 25 lb. sizes. I buy some grains in the 3 lb. and some in the 25 lb. (larger sizes cost less per pound). Of course, the more you purchase in one order, the less the shipping and handling costs per pound.

I appreciate that SunOrganic Farm ships UPS. This means I get my order within 3 days, and in most areas you should get an order within a week. Since SunOrganic Farm (address, p. 79) will take phone orders with *Visa* or *Mastercard*, I make my order by phone. The phone call costs me less in time and gasoline than going to the health food store. To show you how I save on costs, I have prepared a sample order for you. This is what I would recommend you order initially to get started in using **Breakfasts** recipes. Once you have made such an order, and experienced using these grains, you will know how to adjust future orders to suit you.

Suggested Starter Grain Order

3 lb. whole yellow corn	$2.20
3 lb. whole wheat pastry berries	$2.20
3 lb. whole millet	$2.40
3 lb. barley, hulled	$2.75
3 lbs. buckwheat, raw	$2.75
3 lb. spelt, whole	$4.00
3 lb. kamut, whole	$2.75
3 lb. quinoa, whole	$5.55
3 lb. brown rice, long grain	$3.20
Total: 27 lbs.	$27.80

UPS Shipping, Zones 2 to 8	+ 7.37 to 18.29
Total: 27 lbs. + UPS Shipping	**$35.17 to 46.09**
Average cost per 1 lb.	**$1.30 to 1.71 per lb.**
Average cost at Health Food Store	$2.00 per lb.

This order will provide you with about 65 cups of grain that will make about 184 cups of flour -- enough for 40-50 recipes. For example, if you make 3-4 blender recipes every 2 weeks, each calling for about 1 ½ cups grain---i.e. 1 or 2 waffle or pancake recipes, and 1 or 2 muffin recipes---this shipment would last about 6 months, $1.00 or less per recipe for the grain. Most grains will keep very well for that length of time (see p. 81). If you own a grain mill, of course, you will want considerably more grain.

The prices in this order are taken directly from a 2000-2001 catalog. Since prices change, be sure you get the updated prices either by phone or by sending for the latest catalog. You will notice that even if you live in zone #8 (from SunOrganic Farm[1]) you will still probably pay less than at the local health food store for the same grains in the same amounts (or the flours, which are usually somewhat higher in price). Keep in mind that when mail order prices increase, so will health food store prices, so even if prices change, the price savings comparisons should remain similar.

I encourage the use of whole grains in preference to whole grain flours as much as possible. They are fresher, store longer, and will deliver the best flavor, texture, and nutrient value. There are many recipes in **Breakfasts** and **Soups & Muffins** that you can prepare using the whole grains in the blender even if you do not own a grain mill, and they can also be used whole or cracked in a blender for tasty hot cereals.

[1]SunOrganic Farm, P.O. Box 2429, Valley Center, CA 92082
1-888-269-9888, Fax 1-760-751-1141, www.sunorganic.com

Whole Grain Storage & Care

Now that you have a supply of whole grains, how should they be stored? The best place is the freezer if you have the space. That is the way commercial warehouses who don't use fumigants do it. This will guarantee complete inhibition of resident bugs. The refrigerator will do the same, although you aren't likely to have as much room there as in the freezer.

If you don't have freezer or refrigerator space, most grains will keep indefinitely at room temperature as long as no infestation occurs. Oats will keep 2 years and brown rice 9-12 months at room temperature. Keep all grains tightly covered in the darkest, coolest, driest place available. For the frequently used small amounts that you want to keep on your kitchen counter, If you have 3 lb. coffee cans with plastic lids, they are perfect for 5 lbs. of grain. Glass jars with snug fitting lids (with rubber or sealing rings in areas where humidity is high) will display your grains attractively.

Whole grains will not lose nutritional value in storage. Rancidity and infestation are the primary concerns. If you follow the storage time guidelines in the last paragraph, rancidity should not be a problem. But what to do about those creepy crawlies? I have done the following, as needed, and these steps have worked successfully:

#1 Use the grains up within a year, keeping them in dry, cool, dark place, tightly covered, or in freezer. Unless the weather turns very hot for a season, you probably will not have a problem. If freezer space is limited rotate the bags of grain through the freezer for 3 days.

#2 Put a bay leaf or two in each container.

#3 If you discover live critters, here is how to get rid of them:

a) *If the grain is buggy* Put the grain in the freezer 3 days to kill them. Stir small amounts of grain at a time in a colander over the sink; the dead bugs will should fall through the holes of the colander.

To double-check grain you had to remove crawlies from: When you are ready to use it, pour a cup of grain on a piece of paper towel. Vibrate the paper towel with your hands to flatten the grain easily into a single layer. If you don't see crawlies, you probably don't need to check any more of the grain needed for the particular recipe you are making.

b) *If the grain is wormy* Set a house fan on a chair on the back patio. Set a bucket in front of the fan, but on the patio floor. Turn the fan on about medium speed. Hold your container of grain above and close to the front of the fan and pour the grain slowly into the bucket. The fan will blow the critters away, and if you don't believe me, put some white sheets of paper on the patio beyond the bucket (tape some 8½ x

11 typing paper together). When you've poured your grain into the bucket, just see all those little critters crawling on the paper! We've only had to do this once in 18 years. We repeated this process 3 or 4 times until we could see no more crawlers on the white paper. Here's how it works: the grain is heavier than the crawlers and will not blow past the bucket (unless your fan is turned on too high).

   c) Store the cleaned grain in the freezer if you have the room, to insure no more infestation.

These critters' eggs come with the grain. You can't buy the grain without them. As long as they are dormant, you needn't concern yourself with them. They only become actively visible if conditions are right, such as very warm or humid weather. They are a sign that your grain is worth eating. If left unattended too long, you will notice some holes eaten in the grain, possibly some powdered grain, or small groups of grain held together with what looks a bit like webs or dust. The fan should blow this defective grain away with the critters.

If this sounds like a lot of work to you, do step #1 well and you probably won't have to do it, or assign a responsible child to do it (how he would love to do it!), or console yourself with the thought of those dear African mothers (p. 73) who spend 2 hours daily grinding sorghum by hand to make their flour.

Flour Storage

Whole grain flours will gradually begin to lose nutrients from the time they are milled. Some research even indicates that there is significant nutritional loss just 72 hours after milling. Most flour may be kept at room temperature about 1 month without danger of rancidity, and 2-3 months in the refrigerator or freezer. Wheat will keep refrigerated 5-6 months or frozen for 12 months. Triticale will keep in refrigerator up to 12 months. It is difficult to extract creepy crawlers that may get into improperly stored flour. Unless there are just 2 or 3 that can be easily removed, throw the flour out. For best results bring flour to room temperature before using it. Cold flour does not facilitate rising of the recipe as well as room temperature or warmer flour.

Whole Grain Blender Magic!

With my blender, I have always been able to grind rolled oats and tiny grains such as millet, quinoa, amaranth, and teff into flour, to coarsely grind cornmeal from whole corn (this takes a sturdy blender), and to unevenly crack most other whole grains for hot cereal. Then, a neighbor shared a whole wheat pancake recipe with me that called for adding the grain, *whole and raw*, to the liquid ingedients in the blender. The high speed blending action of the blender then completely "milled" the grain.

The result was incredible! Instead of making whole wheat pancakes, however, I converted my recipe for kamut-oat waffles to the blender procedure, using 1 egg to replace my usual 3 egg yolks + 3 beaten egg whites. These blender waffles were the lightest, most tender I had ever made. Why hadn't I thought of this years ago? Convinced this blender process was working, I started experimenting with more waffle/pancake recipes, muffins, coffee cakes, crepes, and cornbread. They all turned out successfully, using all kinds of grains (except instant or parboiled brown rice).

What's most exciting about this is that most households have blenders. You don't have to have a grain mill. This is the ultimate in convenience --requiring less than 10 minutes of your time to get the blender process going and completed. What could be easier?

Now there are limitations to this. There must be enough liquid in proportion to the grain to keep the blender churning for 3 minutes to grind the grain without putting excessive stress on the blender. Any batter recipe with a ratio of about 1 cup grain to 1-1¼ cups combined liquid ingredients usually works. The steps are simple:

1. Put all the liquid ingredients (except egg) with grain *whole and raw* (not flour) in the blender.
2. Blend on highest speed 3 minutes. As the batter blends, it will thicken because the grain is being ground into flour. Sometimes a bubble will form over the blades and stop the churning. Slowing or changing the blender speed will help to get the batter churning again. If necessary, add a bit more liquid. Do not worry if you still feel grit in the batter from not-quite-ground grain.
3. Cover blender, unplug it and let stand at room temperature overnight or about 7 hours. This significantly improves the nutritional benefits (see pp. 50-51) and softens the grain to facilitate further "grinding." It is also a great convenience measure, dividing your work into two short easy steps.
4. Add egg and reblend about 1 minute. This normally completes the grinding of the grain. Change blender speed as needed as in step #2 above.

5. Blend or thoroughly stir in leavening and spices (baking powder, soda, salt, cinnamon, etc) just before baking. It is a good idea to first stir the leavenings and salt through a small strainer with a spoon to remove any lumps (even though a powerful blender will do the job). I usually include the spices in this process for the sake of convenience, even though they don't need sifting.

6. Fold in any ingredients such as nuts that need to be, just before baking.

These steps are incorporated or recommended in *Breakfasts* blender batter recipes, and, with the exception of steps #3 and #4, in several muffin recipes in *Soups & Muffins* and in *Blender Cornbread in Meals in Minutes* (steps #3 and #4 can be easily added to these recipes).

Most blenders work well for batter recipes, but I recommend one that will crush ice cubes. I suggest cautious use of an old or dull-bladed blender. Turn it off if the motor begins to smell hot and give it a rest. Please, I won't take the blame if "Aunt Matilda's" blender burns out! If your blender isn't adequate, this method is worth a new blender for $30-$40. In this cost range, seek a blender with a more durable gear which is made of metal, upon which the blender bowl sits (such as the Osterizer). The 12 or 16 speed Osterizer Blender or any heavy-duty blender such as a Vita-Mix , a Bosch Kitchen Machine blender or DLX blender works well.

I can't begin to tell you how easy it is to use the blender method with whole grains for batter recipes. I love it and use it wherever possible even though I have a grain mill. Just remember, you are not going to be making any yeast loaf breads, biscuits, or cookie doughs in your blender! Quick loaf breads and even some muffin recipes will not have enough liquid for the blender method. So if you adapt recipes other than those in this book to the blender, do take care to follow the guidelines given here.

TO ADAPT BLENDER RECIPES
TO STANDARD MIXING WITH FLOUR

You may wish to convert our blender mixing steps to standard mixing with flour. Here's how to do it:

1. In a mixing bowl, blend the liquids except egg/s.
2. Whisk in the flour: convert the grain measure to flour measure: 1 cup grain = approximately 1½ cups flour (see chart, p. 85).
3. Cover bowl and let stand at room temperature overnight or about 7 hours.
4. Proceed with the recipe as with steps #4 to #6 above, but blend in remaining ingredients evenly but briefly taking care not to overmix the batter.

The Value of a Grain Mill

When I first heard that grain mills[1] for home milling existed, I had no idea what one looked like, let alone how it might work! My university home economics education on grains had not gone past the bag of white flour.

My first grain mill was a high-speed stone mill encased in a beautiful dark oakwood box. Can you imagine my surprise when this fabulous new machine did not turn my first cup of whole grain oats into rolled oats? How little I knew about grain milling! My new mill, however, did transform baking and nutrition at our house. I, Dad, and the kids made everything from whole wheat pizza to whole wheat cookies (everything was whole wheat in those days). Never again did a bag of bleached white flour enter my kitchen.

The high-speed stone mill did a good job. It was noisy and it did tend to dust the kitchen. My second mill was a high-tech micronizer. It was small and compact in white plastic casing--a beautiful kitchen appliance. It produced very fine flour very fast on impact. I really wished its ear-piercing jet scream could have been muffled[2] and that the micronizer teeth were not so vulnerable to the occasional little rock that inevitably appears even in super clean grains. Nevertheless, it was and is a worthy little grain mill.

My third mill was a heavy duty, quiet, non-kitchen-dusting, fine flour-grinding, easy-to-adjust, slow-speed stone mill that should outlast my grandchildren. Simple. Durable. Not only could I drop the grain in the hopper and walk away to do other chores, I could even talk on the phone with it running.

If I were to tell you what one appliance will add more to the nutrition and taste delights of your family than any other, I would say "a grain mill" without hesitation. A blender would follow closely, but you've already got one of those. There is just nothing to match those beautiful loaves of home baked yeast breads made with freshly ground whole grain. A grain mill allows you to make every kind of whole grain baked good. And the grain does not have to be wheat. With the wide variety of grains coupled with the growing need to cope with allergies, a grain mill offers the ultimate in variety and convenience. Not only that, but you can bake your own breads and goodies for a fraction of what it would cost to buy them (if you could buy them!). Besides, those home-baked goodies will increase your resistance to expensive restaurants.

[1]For more information see *Grain Mill Reviews* under *Resources* at www.suegregg.com.
[2]The answer is the Whisper Mill, the quiet impact mill. See Links to Products under *Grain Mill Reviews* at www.suegregg.com..

GRAIN TO FLOUR CONVERSION CHART

GRAIN	¼ cup Flour	⅓ cup Flour	½ cup Flour	1 cup Flour	2 cups Flour
wheat, corn, brown rice, millet, triticale, amaranth	3 tbsps. grain	3½ tbsps. grain	5 tbsps. grain	⅔ cup grain	1⅓ cups grain
kamut, oat groats, teff, buckwheat (kasha)	3 tbsps. grain	¼ cup grain	6 tbsps. grain	¾ cup grain	1½ cups grain
barley, spelt, rye, quinoa	2½ tbsps. grain	3½ tbsps. grain	5 tbsps. grain	½ cup + 2 tbsps. grain	1¼ cups grain
oats, rolled	⅓ cup rolled	½ cup rolled	⅔ cup rolled	1⅓ cups rolled	2⅔ cups rolled

For quick estimate: ⅔ **cup grain = 1 cup flour** (or 1 cup grain = 1½ cups flour) -- a good rule of thumb to follow

Grain measurement is approximately to get you started, so always measure the flour after grinding. Scoop flour lightly into measuring cup; level it off without packing the flour.

To mill tiny grains as amaranth, quinoa, millet, or teff, or rolled oats in a slow speed stone mill, mix them with larger grains before milling. To mill these grains or rolled oats alone, grind them in the blender or a coffee bean mill.

For quick reference, post this grain chart inside a kitchen cupboard near your grain mill or baking area.

Grain Wonders-Bibliography

Bailey, Adrian. *The Blessings of Bread.* New York: Paddington Press LTD, 1975.

Carper, Jean. *The Food Pharmacy.* New York: Bantam Books, 1988.

Earle, Alice Morse. *Home Life in Colonial Days.* Stockbridge, Massachussetts, 1974.

Jones, Michael Whiteman. "Modern Market Rediscovers Ancient Grains." *Natural Foods Merchandiser* (July 1991).

Leonard, Thom. "New Grains on the Block." *East West* (March 1991).

Peterson, Vick. *The Natural Foods Catalogue.* New York, New York: Arco Publishing Company, Inc., 1978.

Strehlow, Dr. Wighard. *The Wonder Food Spelt*, 1989.

Tyler, Lorraine D. *The Natural Nine - Cooking with Whole Grains.* Salt Lake City, Utah: Magic Mill, 1984.

Wood, Rebecca. "The Incredible 'New' Wheat." *East West* (November 1989).

Wood, Rebecca. *The Whole Foods Encyclopedia.* New York: Prentice Hall Press, 1988.

World Book Encyclopedia. Chicago: Field Enterprises Educational Corporation, 1969.

The Cereal Breakfast

Faithfulness springs forth from the earth, and righteousness looks down from heaven. The LORD will indeed give what is good, and our land will yield its harvest. Psalm 85:11-12

THE CEREAL BREAKFAST

SUBJECTS

RECIPES

CEREALS

The Cereal Breakfast

Fresh Fruit or Juice
Cereal (Hot, Cold, or Granola)
Cereal Toppings (Milk and/or Yogurt,
Honey or Maple Syrup,
Raisins, Nuts, or Seeds)
Hot Bread (English Muffin, Toast,
Bagels, Biscuits, or Tortillas)
Spread (Jam, Butter)

Nutrition Goals Menu[1]

½ Pink Grapefruit
¾-1½ cups Yummy Oatmeal (p. 118)
½-1 cup Nonfat Milk
¼-½ cup Nonfat Yogurt
1-2 tsps. honey
1-2 Slices Whole Grain Toast
1½-3 tsps. Jam

[1]Small: $.85	*8% Fat*	*433 Calories*
[1]Large: $1.40	*9% Fat*	*816 Calories*

[1]This menu is included in the "Average of 7 Breakfasts" Column on the *Nutrition Goals Chart*, pp. 16-17. Small servings represent menu for adult female; large servings represent menu for adult male.

Cereals, Commercially Yours!

The variety is an endless maze. In one supermarket cereal survey I counted 117 cold cereals and 27 variations of hot cereal! Nor did this list include any that are now available in health food stores. Here are a few guidelines for nutritionally better choices.

SUPERMARKET OFFERINGS

While I can suggest a handful of better supermarket choices, you need to know how to interpret the nutritional value for yourself, not by the generalizations in large print such as *100% Natural* or even by reading the nutrient data labels, but by reading the list of ingredients and the ratio of complex carbohydrates to total sucrose and other sugars. Select the following:

~Cereals made only with whole grains or flours

~Cereals without partially hydrogenated vegetable oil (see p. 264)

~Cereals with little or no refined sugars

Few cereals in the supermarkets meet all three of these standards. Even those made of whole grain usually contain either, or both, partially hydrogenated vegetable oil and refined sugars.

First read the ingredients list. If refined sugars (sugar, brown sugar, corn syrup) are listed, then locate the carbohydrate information usually on the side of the box near the lower end. It lists the number of grams of complex carbohydrate (or starch - the grain part), and the number of grams of sucrose and other sugars per serving. Note the examples for comparison in the following chart:

Cereal	Complex Carbohydrate	Sucrose & Other Sugars
Cheerios	19 grams	1 gram
Ralston Whole Grain Wheat Chex	18 grams	3 grams
Kellogg's Cracklin' Oat Bran	10 grams	7 grams
Kellogg's All Bran	7 grams	5 grams
Nabisco 100% Bran	5 grams	6 grams

Cold Cereals - Supermarkets:

Cheerios (low sugar)

Nutri Grain Nuggets (whole wheat, barley)

Nutri Grain Almond Raisin (brown rice, corn)

Ralston Whole Grain Wheat Chex (low sugar)

Malti Bran Chex (low sugar)

Shredded Wheat

Nutri Grain Wheat

Grape Nuts (low sugar)

Kashi

Hot cereals in supermarkets don't offer you much more than a mind boggling array of oatmeal variations from instant varieties to regular old fashioned oats. *Malt 'O Meal, Cream of Wheat,* and *Farina*

90

are not whole grain. I consider the following to be the best choices (you may need to look in a health food store for *Roman Meal*):

Hot Cereals - Supermarkets:

Oat Bran

Roman Meal (oats, wheat, rye,
    wheat bran, flax seed meal)*

Ralston (untoasted whole wheat)*

Quaker Oats

Wheatena (toasted crushe wheat,
    wheat bran, wheat germ)

*Availability is limited (see recipe, p. 107)

HEALTH FOOD STORE OFFERINGS

A wide variety of both hot and cold cereals are available. Often cold cereals contain barley malt or concentrated fruit juices for sweetening. Both are nutritionally acceptable. Most of the flaked cold cereals do not contain salt and, therefore, taste flat. I recommend the salted ones for palatability. However, some are good without salt, such as puffed cereals and *Oat Bran Crunch*. The cereals I consider better tasting, although I seldom buy them are:

Cold Cereals - Health Food Stores:

Kölln Oat Bran Crunch

Puffed Wheat (whole)

Puffed Milled (whole)

Puffed Rice (whole)

Puffed Corn (whole)

Barbara's Raisin Bran

Barbara's Breakfast O's

Arrowhead Mills Kamut Flakes

Arrowhead Mills Spelt Flakes

There are also meusli and granolas of all kinds. Meusli is typically a combination of untoasted flakes of whole grain, nuts, seeds, and dried fruits, sometimes sweetened with a natural sweetener. Usually unsweetened and without fat added, meusli is generally easier on the digestion than granolas. Read all the labels, Much of the granola available is high in fat. On the other hand, an increasing variety without fat is also available. *Health Valley Amaranth Crunch*, for example, is a tasty no-fat, fruit-sweetened granola. Commercial cold cereals and granolas are very expensive food items, both in supermarkets and health food stores.

Most hot cereals are considerably less expensive than cold cereals (see chart, pp. 95-97). About every whole grain--ground, cracked, or flaked--is available for hot cereal. Here are a few:

Hot Cereals - Health Food Stores:

Kasha or Cream of Buckwheat

Roman Meal

Quick 'n Creamy Brown Rice

Teff

Erewon Oat Bran with Toasted Wheat Germ

Triple Bran (oat bran, rice bran, corn bran)

Kashi (7 whole grains, sesame seeds)

Scottish Style Oats

Corn Grits

Cracked Wheat

Cream of Rye

Bits O' Barley

Oat Bran

The Science of Making Hot Cereals

Preparing whole grain cereals except oatmeal is a new experience for most Americans. When, at the age of 38, I put my first whole grain oats into my new grain mill expecting it to come out like rolled oat flakes, I realized what a strange world whole grains were, even for most adults! We need all the help we can get to feel at home with them. I hope you will enjoy this section. It is a good lesson for the children, as well.

Grains are classified as starchy carbohydrates, though they also contain valuable protein and fat (see charts, pp.58-59). Hot cereal is made by adding water to the grain, then cooking, soaking, or sprouting it. When water is added to the grain, the grain will expand and soften to become edible. Hot Cereals can be prepared to eat in several forms:

whole kernels This is the grain before it is broken open in any way.

cracked kernels The whole kernels have been broken into smaller pieces.

rolled or flakes The whole kernels have been flattened very thin. Rolled oats is an example.

flour The whole, cracked, rolled kernels, or flakes are milled into very fine particles with a flour mill or blender.

Added water penetrates the shell of the grain. If the shell is broken by cracking, rolling, or grinding it, the water reaches the soft starchy center faster. Faster moving molecules of water speed up the process by generating heat. The starchy inner kernel absorbs the water, swells, and becomes sticky and edible. Thus, two of the conditions that determine how fast grains will soften and expand (cook) are the *temperature of the water* and the *form of the grain.*

A third condition that affects cooking time is the *hardness of the grain.* Some grains are softer than others and thus cook more quickly. For example, buckwheat, quinoa, and teff cook in boiling water in a shorter time than wheat, rye, or millet. The effects of these three conditions are reflected in the cooking times required in the following examples when cooked by the *Direct Heat Method* (p. 99).

~Rolled grain or flakes will cook or expand in 10-15 minutes (*Oatmeal Surprise*, p. 108). Rolled grains cut into smaller pieces (e.g.*Quick Quaker Oats*) cook faster than whole rolled flakes (e.g. *Old Fashioned Quaker Oats*) or in less than 5 minutes.

~A finely milled grain or creamed cereal will expand and cook in 10-20 minutes (*Cream of Brown Rice*, p. 104).

~Cracked grains require 20-60 minutes depending on the coarseness of the crack (*Polenta*, p.107).

~Whole grains take 20-90 minutes to cook (see chart, p. 98).

Cooking hot cereals over direct heat in the shortest time possible (*Direct Heat Method*) is only one way to cook them. I recommend soaking cereal overnight to be cooked by the *Direct Heat Method* or cooking them by a slow methods for several reasons (see below). They can be cooked overnight. In overnight cooking, the water temperature can be reduced to slow the cooking process in several ways:

~In a thermos (p.101)   ~In the oven at 150° - 175° (p. 101)

~By steam (p. 100)   ~In a crock-pot on low (p. 99)

Two other methods that slow the process of softening and expanding cereal grains require no cooking at all:

~*Sprouting grains* requires a couple of days to expand. Only grain in whole form can be used. (*Sprouted Cereal*, p. 102).

~*Soaking* Oat flakes can be softened enough to eat by soaking for a few hours. Less heat used means it will take longer for the grains to expand. They will not expand as much as if cooked. These cereals are served cold (*Swiss Breakfast*, p. 115; *Apple Breakfast Treat*, p. 173).

Normally we don't think of slowing down the cooking of hot cereal. We would rather do it as fast as possible using a nutritionally inferior and less flavorful instant cereal. But less processed cereals cooked more slowly at lower temperatures are advantageous in every way:

~*Convenience* Overnight preparation saves time during the morning rush.

~*Nutritional Value* The slow cooking process breaks down *phytates* in the grain that otherwise prevent some of the mineral content from being absorbed (see pp. 50-51). Slow cooking also improves cereal protein digestion.

~*Taste* Slowly cooked cereals are more flavorful.

~*Cost* You are more likely to eat less costly hot cereals more often, thus relying less on expensive cold cereals and instant hot cereals.

Most of the methods of slow cooking will work well on most cereal grains, but not entirely. I have listed what works best for several grains (p. 95). Try different grains and methods. You will probably find one or two methods and three or four grains you want to eat most of the time.

A Spiritual Application

...since the creation of the world God's invisible qualities~
his eternal power and divine nature~have been clearly seen,
being understood from what has been made...   Romans 1:20

The Bible says that we can know God by the things he has made. Consider this fact: All foods are made edible by water. Yes, a raw carrot is edible without adding water to it. That is because it already contains sufficient water to be edible in the raw state. In fact, a carrot is 88% water. On the other hand, grains contain practically no water. They are a tight package filled with life-giving nutrients and fiber, inaccessible to us until we expose them to water. We must add water to make them open up, soften, and expand to become edible and release their nutrients and fiber to the use of our bodies.

Read *John 7:37-39* in the Bible. To what does Jesus compare the Holy Spirit? Think about how the Holy Spirit comes into our lives through faith in Jesus Christ and opens, softens, and expands our hearts and minds toward God. Unless the Holy Spirit comes into our lives through repentance of sin, and faith in Jesus Christ, our hearts will remain hard toward God. This was the case of Pharoah in Egypt when God brought the 10 plagues upon the Egyptians. What water does to a kernel of grain to make it edible is what the Holy Spirit does in our lives to make us responsive to God.

Jesus describes our relationship with himself by the very act of eating:

Here I am! I stand at the door and knock.
If anyone hears my voice and opens the door,
I will go in and eat with him, and he with me.
Revelation 3:20.

Look for truth about God in nature and how it works. You will find it everywhere, even in the kitchen and at the dining table! This provides many wonderful opportunities to teach your children spiritual truths.

Applying Cooking Methods to Different Grains

For proportions of water to grain, see chart, p. 98. To increase nutritional value, soak all grains and rolled flakes overnight (see pp. 50-51).

Barley   All methods work well.

Buckwheat or Kasha   All methods work. Raw buckwheat is milder in flavor than kasha and requires a little longer cooking.

Cornmeal   All methods will work if you follow the first 3 steps in the recipe for *Polenta* (p.107) and then boil 5 minutes over direct heat.

Kamut Cook cracked by direct heat. For whole, soak 2 hours before cooking. Crock-pot or steam 8-10 hours.

Millet All methods work if parboiled[1] for 5 minutes except the oven method. Steaming gives the most pleasing texture.

Oats   Cooked whole or cracked oats is fantastic! All methods work, but I prefer the texture of steamed oats. Oats cooked by the oven method might be parboiled[1] 5 minutes for increased softness.

Quinoa   All methods work. A great grain. Don't overlook it!

Rye   Rye is a very hard grain and a very chewy cooked cereal. The thermos and oven methods are not suitable. I recommend crock-pot cooking as the best, but not the only successful method. Presoak 2 hours. For most, rye flakes will be more pleasing (p.105).

Spelt All methods work except the oven method. A chewy, great grain! May be presoaked 2 hours, if desired.

Teff Oven method is not suitable. Steam or follow box directions.

Wheat Soak 2 hours before cooking, then crock-pot or steam 8-10 hours.

[1]parboil: to boil in advance

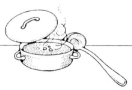

Hot Cereal Nutrient Chart

Cereal, Cooked	Energy Value[1]	Carbo-hydrate	Protein	Dietary Fiber	Sodium[1]	Exchange Value[1]	Approx. Cost[1]
barley, whole, 2/3 cup	159	29 g.	4.6 g.	2.9 g.	178 mg.	2¼ Bread	$.07
brown rice, cream of, 1 cup	127	27 g.	2.6 g.	1.3 g.	533 mg.	2 Bread	$.06
buckwheat, raw whole, 2/3 cup	93	23 g.	3.2 g.	0.6 g.	355 mg.	1¼ Bread	$.10
buckwheat, kasha, 2/3 cup	93	23 g.	3.2 g.	0.6 g.	355 mg.	1¼ Bread	$.21
cornmeal (*Polenta*), 2/3 cup	74	15 g.	1.9 g.	3 g.	355 mg.	1 Bread	$.06
Kamut, cracked, 3/4 cup	191	36 g.	9 g.	2.5 g.	135 mg.	2¾ Bread	$.15
millet, cream of, 1 cup	142	32 g.	4.3 g.	1.4 g.	533 mg.	2 Bread	$.11
millet, whole, 2/3 cup	127	28 g.	3.8 g.	1.0 g.	355 mg.	1¾ Bread	$.10
oat bran, 2/3 cup	90	17 g.	6 g.	4.0 g.	267 mg.	1¼ Bread	$.15
oatmeal (rolled oats), 2/3 cup	100	18 g.	5 g.	2.7 g.	355 mg.	1½ Bread	$.07
oats, whole, 2/3 cup	246	45 g.	7.6 g.	4.3 g.	533 mg.	3½ Bread	$.20

Cereal, Cooked	Energy Value[1]	Carbo-hydrate	Protein	Dietary Fiber	Sodium[1]	Exchange Value[1]	Approx. Cost[1]
quinoa, whole, ⅔ cup	132	23 g.	5.9 g.	3.3 g.	355 g.	2 Bread	$.34
Roman Meal[1], ¾ cup	110	19 g.	4 g.	5 g.	269 g.	1½ Bread	$.15
rye, cream of, ¾ cup	110	22 g.	4 g.	5 g.	400 g.	1½ Bread	$.14
rye, whole, ⅔ cup	197	43 g.	7 g.	6.7 g.	355 g.	2¾ Bread	$.10
spelt, whole, ⅔ cup	168	33 g.	6.3 g.	2.4 g.[1]	355 g.	2½ Bread	$.10
teff, whole, ¾ cup	200	41 g.	7 g.	8.0 g.	200 g.	2¾ Bread	$.58
Wheatena, ¾ cup	100	21 g.	3 g.	4.0 g.	267 g.	1½ Bread	$.10
wheat, whole, ⅔ cup	127	26 g.	4.8 g.	2.0 g.	440 g.	1¾ Bread	$.06

[1]NOTES

Energy Value = Calories (A valuable contribution, not something to avoid!) Sodium is based on salt addition given in recipes; sodium in grains is virtually nil, except for barley which is a good source of high quality organic sodium. *Roman Meal* - Data given is for commercial product only. *Spelt* -Dietary Fiber data not available at this time; amount is estimated from wheat. *Exchange Value* (rounded to nearest ¼): *1 Bread Exchange = 70 Calories. Cost:* 1996 prices.

97

Cereal Cooking Chart

This chart gives the proportion of grain to water, 2 to 4 parts water to 1 part grain, depending on the grain. Use these proportions for any cooking method. Cooking times given are for cooking *whole or cracked grains* by the *Direct Heat Method* (p. 99).

AMOUNT: About 2 Cups Cooked				
Grain	Amt. Dry	Amt. Water	Salt[1]	Cooking Time
barley	½ cup	2 cups	¼ tsp.	40-60 min.
brown rice	⅔ cup	1⅓ cups	½ tsp.	45-60 min.
buckwheat, raw kasha	½ cup	2¼ cups	½ tsp.	30-35 min. 15-20 min.
bulgur (wheat)	1 cup	2 cups	¼ tsp.	15-20 min.
cornmeal	½ cup	2 cups	½ tsp.	30 min.
Kamut (cracked)	⅔ cup	1⅔ cups	¼ tsp.	10 min.
millet	½ cup	2 cups	½ tsp.	40 min.
oats	1 cup	2½ cups	¾ tsp.	40-60 min.
quinoa	⅔ cup	1⅓ cups	½ tsp.	20 min.
rye	1 cup	3 cups	½ tsp.	90 min.
spelt	⅔ cup	1⅓ cups	½ tsp.	40 min.
teff	⅔ cup	1⅓ cups	¼ tsp.	20 min.
triticale	⅔ cup	1⅔ cups	⅝ tsp.	60 min.
wheat	⅔ cup	2⅓ cups	⅝ tsp.	60 min.

Ratio of parts water to grain

2 water to 1 grain:	brown rice, bulgur, quinoa, spelt, teff
2½ water to 1 grain:	oats, triticale, Kamut
3 water to 1 grain:	rye
3½ water to 1 grain:	wheat, wild rice
4 water to 1 grain:	barley, millet, cornmeal, creamed cereals
4½ water to 1 grain:	kasha (buckwheat)

[1]Salt greatly improves the flavor of whole grains! According to Rebecca Wood in *The Whole Foods Encyclopedia* at least ⅛ tsp. per 2 cups grain must be added for assimilation of grains and to reduce their acidic properties. As a standard measure for all grains, to taste, I use ⅛ - ¼ tsp. per ¼ cup grain.

Direct Heat Method

Use the Cereal Cooking Chart (p. 98) for amounts of grain, water, salt, and cooking times. This method is the simplest and can be done with any grain.

1. Place grain and salt in the water, cover and let stand overnight (presoaking may shorten cooking time somewhat).

2. Uncover and bring to a boil.

3. Turn heat down very low or to a simmer (just below boiling).

5. Cover and simmer until done.

6. Do not stir whole grains. Stir cracked or creamed grains only occasionally. Over-stirring causes a gummy texture.

Crock-Pot Method

A great method for families, large and small.. A small crock-pot (about 1 quart) is a good size for 2-4 servings. However, a 3½ quart pot works with as little as 2 cups water.

1. With wax paper grease bottom and sides of the pot with **1 teaspoon butter**. Grease up to where the water level will be. Or you could spray with non-stick spray.

2. Put all ingredients into the pot using room temperature water (see chart, p. 98 for amount of grain and water).

3. Cover and turn on **low**. Cook overnight or for 8 to 9 hours.

4. Stir and serve.

Notes

~Cereals cooked by this method tend to be creamier and some times a bit pasty.

~Ingredients like raisins and nuts will cook up very soft, so if you want their "crunch and chew" add them just a few minutes before serving. Cinnamon will turn the cereal much darker than when cooked over direct heat, so if the recipe calls for it, you will probably be more pleased with the result adding it also just a few minutes before serving.

~An example is *Crock-Pot Oatmeal* (p. 108).

Steamed Method

Steaming is most easily accomplished in a double boiler. This is my favorite method for all whole and cracked grains. Over all it gives the most pleasing texture with the least fuss. When steamed the night before, it is easy to rewarm the cereal in the morning. Use Cereal Cooking Chart (p. 98) for amounts of grain, water, salt. Use cooking times given below.

1. Put grain, water, and salt in top pan of double boiler.

2. Put as much water in the bottom pan as possible without touching the surface of the top pan.

3. Cover top pan with lid and bring water in bottom pan to a boil; reduce heat to maintain a consistent low boil.

4. Check the water level in bottom pan occasionally so that it doesn't boil dry; add more water, as needed.

5. For cooking the night before, turn off heat, leaving the cereal in the pan. In the morning, turn heat back on for 5 or 10 minutes to rewarm the cereal.

COOKING TIMES FOR STEAMED CEREALS

Barley: 1 hr. 45 minutes
Buckwheat: 1 hour
Oats: 1 hour
Millet: 40-45 minutes; parboil[1] 5 minutes over direct heat.
Cornmeal: 1 hour; follow steps #1-3 for *Polenta* (p. 107)
Rye: 2 hours; parboil[1] 5 minutes over direct heat
Spelt: 2 hours
wheat, kamut: 8-10 hours; presoak 2 hours

[1]parboil: boil in advance

Notes

~The limitation of this method is access to a double boiler. It seems the modern trend is toward steamer pans with holes in the bottom instead of a solid bottom. Some p a n sets, such as *Salad Master*, have a solid bottom pan that fits into the steamer pan. Look for *Faberware* in department stores.

~You can improvise a steamer if you have a smaller pan that will fit in a larger one, over a rack. Both pans must have tight fitting lids. The inner pan with the cooking cereal in it must be covered, and the outer pan must be covered to keep the steam inside.

~Examples are *Apple Millet Cereal* (p. 112), *Buckwheat, Kasha* (p. 113)

Oven Method

This method I recommend least for slow cooking since it means heating up a lot of space to cook a pot of cereal. Reserve it for softer grains such as quinoa, buckwheat, oats, barley. Also suitable for spelt (see p. 95).

1. Preheat oven to 150°- 175°.

2. In saucepan bring water to boil; add grain and salt; return to boil for 5 minutes (see *Cereal Cooking Chart*, p. 98, for amounts of grain, water, salt).

3. Pour into casserole dish; cover tightly.

4. Place in oven overnight.

5. To serve, reheat, if desired, over low heat, or in steamer pan.

Thermos Method

If you don't have a double boiler for steaming, I recommend this method. It is very simple to do. I use a wide mouth 40 oz. ceramic thermal carafe (costs about $20). You can also use a thermos, although it is not as easy to get cereal in and out of the narrow mouth. I recommend a 1 qt. stainless steel thermos with stainless steel interior liner such as Gott brand.

1. Fill the thermos or carafe with very hot water to warm it for at least 5 minutes.

2. To insure complete cooking, soak harder whole grains (wheat, rye, millet) the morning before (or 8 to 12 hours) in the amount of water it is to be cooked in (see *Cereal Cooking Chart*, p. 98). Drain, reserving soaking water.

3. Place the drained water into a saucepan and bring to a boil.

4. Add grain and salt (for creamed cereals follow basic directions for *Creamed Cereals*. p. 103).

5. Return to a boil; boil 5 minutes (not necessary for buckwheat, kasha, quinoa, barley).

6. Use a measuring cup with a handle to scoop water and grain into the thermos or carafe.

7. Cap tightly. If a standard thermos bottle, lay it on its side overnight. If a thermal carafe, leave it upright.

8. To serve, reheat over low heat if desired, or in steamer.

Notes Examples are *Thermos Spelt, Barley* (p. 114).

Sprouted Cereal

Omit cooking altogether and sprout whole grain for a hot or cold cereal, or to add to a creamier cereal for crunch. Sprouted grain will have more vitamins and minerals than the original grain, and active enzymes which cooked cereals do not provide (see pp. 256-57). For hot cereal, briefly heat sprouted cereal in a little water or steamer. Don't kill the enzymes!

AMOUNT: 1 Cup Sprouted

1. Soak **½ cup wheat berries, spelt, oats, or rye** in a jar of water overnight or about 12 hours. Cover the top of the jar with a piece of nylon net or screening attached with rubberband.
2. Drain well, Tip jar downward on a slant in a small bowl for good drainage.
3. Let stand for **2 days**, rinsing the sprouts morning and evening. The sprouts should not grow longer than the seeds.
4. Drain off excess water. Serve the sprouts plain or with milk or yogurt, fruit, honey or syrup, or add a small portion to a more creamy cereal such as cooked oatmeal (see *Sue's Breakfast*, p.111).

Per serving: see Hot Cereal Nutrient Chart, p. 96-97 (The volume of sprouted cereal is approximately equivalent to cooked cereal).

ADVANTAGES OF SPROUTING

~ Sprouted grain is more easily digestible than cooked grains.

~ Protein is better assimilated because the complex form is broken down into simpler amino acids during sprouting.

~ Nutrients are increased. Vitamins A, E, and B-vitamins may increase as much as 4 to 10 times; enzymes not destroyed.

~ Sprouting produces vitamin B-12.

~ Some persons allergic or sensitive to certain grains can tolerate the same grains in sprouted form.

Bulgur or Qunioa

Both of these can be eaten for breakfast cereals. *Bulgur* is par-boiled, toasted cracked wheat retaining 75% of the fiber of whole wheat and retaining a worthwhile portion of nutrients. Recipes for cooked bulgur and quinoa are available in **Main Dishes**, p. 111. For *Creamy Quinoa* see p. 106.

Creamed Cereals

Creamed cereals are made with finely ground whole grain. The secret to smoothness is stirring the grain into cold water before cooking. For amounts of grain and salt see the Cereal Cooking Chart, p. 98.

1. Grind the whole grain quite fine in grain mill, a blender or a coffee bean mill (see p. 126). Use the *Grain to Flour Conversion Chart*, p. 85, to produce the amount desired.

2. Measure the total amount of water using **4 parts water to 1 part ground grain.**

3. Reserve a fourth of the water and bring the rest to a boil in a saucepan.

4. Whisk the finely ground grain and salt smoothly into the reserved cold water.

5. Gradually whisk the grain mixture into the boiling hot water. (Optional: cover, remove from heat and let stand overnight for improved nutritional benefits, pp. 50-51).

6. Return to a boil. Cover, reduce heat to low and simmer **10-30 minutes** (depending on the grain), or transfer cereal into another container, as desired (thermos, crock-pot, double boiler). Steaming in double boiler will take about same amount of time to cook as over direct heat, or just a very few minutes longer.

Cream of Millet

AMOUNT: 1 Cup (1 - 2 Servings)

1. Grind fine in grain mill, a blender or a coffee bean mill (see p. 126): **3 tablespoons whole millet** (for ¼ cup finely ground)

2. Measure 1 cup water and pour ¾ **cup water** into saucepan. Bring to a boil.

3. Whisk millet and ¼ **teaspoon salt** into remaining ¼ **cup water.**

4. Gradually whisk grain mixture into boiling water. (Optional: cover, remove from heat and let stand overnight for improved nutritional benefits, pp. 50-51)

5. Return to a boil. Turn heat very low, cover, and simmer until done, about **10 minutes**.

Per serving: see Hot Cereal Nutrient Chart, p. 96.

Cream of Brown Rice

For Cream of Wheat lovers, try this wholesome alternative! Cream of Brown Rice cereal is available in health food stores, or with this recipe you can grind your own rice.

AMOUNT: 1 Cup (1 - 2 Servings)

1. Grind fine in in grain mill, a blender or a coffee bean mill (see p. 126):
   3 tablespoons brown rice (for ¼ cup finely ground)

2. Measure **1 cup water** and pour **¾ cup water** into saucepan. Turn heat on to bring to a boil.

3. Whisk rice and ¼ **teaspoon salt** into remaining ¼ **cup water.**

4. Gradually whisk grain mixture into boiling water (Optional: cover, remove from heat and let stand overnight for improved nutritional benefits, pp. 50-51). return to a boil.

5. Return to a boil. Turn heat very low, cover, and simmer until done, about **10 minutes**.

Per Serving: see Hot Cereal Nutrient Chart, p. 96..

> **ADD A BIT O' BUTTER!** A little butter added to a bowl of hot cereal can transform the flavor--delicious! You only need to add about a teaspoon.

Cream of Rice'n Oat Bran

A tasty variation of cream of brown rice with oat bran! This may be cooked over direct heat, but with the addition of the milk during cooking, I prefer steaming it.

AMOUNT: About 1⅔ Cups (2 - 3 Servings)

1. Follow *Cream of Brown Rice* through step #4 (above).

2. Return to a boil and place mixture in double boiler over boiling water (see *Steamed Method*, p. 100).

3. Whisk in:
   1 cup nonfat (skim) milk *(or non-dairy alternative, p. 29)*
   ⅓ **cup oat bran** *(p. 11)*
   ¼ **teaspoon vanilla**
   ¼ **cup raisins, optional**

4. Cover and steam cook for **10-20 minutes**, or until thickened.

Per ⅔ Cup without raisins
Exchanges: 0.5 Milk, 0.75 Bread, 1 Fruit; 139 Calories, 7 g protein (20%), 1.5 g fat (8%), 25 g carbohydrate (72%; 16 g sugars), 4 g dietary fiber, 2 mg cholesterol, 54 mg sodium, $.25

Cream of Rye

Purchase rye flakes, or boxed Cream of Rye which is merely rye flakes in a round box with a colorful label. Available at health food stores.

AMOUNT: 1½ Cups (Two ¾ Cup Servings)

1. Bring to a boil:
   2 cups water

2. Whisk in:
   ⅔ cup rye flakes
   ⅜ teaspoon salt

3. Boil for **3 minutes**.

4. Turn off heat, cover, and let stand **3 minutes**.

Per Serving: see Hot Cereal Nutrient Chart, p. 97.

> **Special Tip:** Longer cooking will improve the flavor and nutritional benefits of any cereal (pp. 50-51). These boxed cereals can be easily adapted to an overnight cooking or soaking method (pp. 51, 99-101). For longer cooking in the morning, the *Steamed Method* is ideal.

Wheatena

Wheatena is a hearty combination of toasted crushed wheat, wheat bran and wheat germ. Toasting of the grain increases the fiber, but diminishes some of the B-vitamin content. Wheatena is available in some supermarkets and health food stores. For improved nutritional benefits, let cereal soak in the water overnight (see pp. 50-51).

AMOUNT: 1½ Cups (Two ¾ Cup Servings)

1. Combine in saucepan and bring to rapid boil; whisking occasionally:
   1½ cups water
   ½ cup *Wheatena*
   ¼ teaspoon salt

2. Reduce to moderate heat and cook at gentle boil for **4 - 5 minutes**.

3. Cover and remove from heat until ready to serve.

4. Stir before serving.

Per Serving: see Hot Cereal Nutrient Chart, p. 97.

Cracked Kamut Cereal

Cracked kamut cooks much faster than whole grain kamut. The texture will be quite chewy. For improved nutritional benefits, let grain soak in the water overnight (see pp. 50-51).

AMOUNT: 1 - 2 Servings

1. Crack in grain mill, a blender or a coffee bean mill (see p. 126):
   ½ cup kamut grain *(see grains, p. 13)*

2. Bring water to a boil, stir in kamut and salt; lower heat to very low and simmer until done, about **10 minutes:**
   1¼ cups water
   ⅛ teaspoon salt

Per Serving (½ recipe): see Hot Cereal Nutrient Chart, p. 96.

Creamy Quinoa

The added butter gives this cereal an especially pleasing flavor. The rinsing and soaking of the grain is essential to remove bitter flavor (p. 75).

AMOUNT: 2 - 3 Servings

1. The night before, put quinoa in strainer and rinse for 1 minute:
   ½ cup quinoa *(see grains, p. 13)*

2. Set strainer with rinsed quinoa in a bowl filled with water so that it is submerged. Let stand overnight.

3. Discard water and rinse quinoa another 30 seconds.

4. Blend in blender on high speed about 1 minute:
   ½ cup water
   2 tablespoons rinsed, drained quinoa

5. In saucepan bring water to a boil, stir in blender mixture and return to boil; stir in remaining ingredients:
   1 cup water
   blender mixture
   remaining rinsed, drained quinoa
   ¼ teaspoon salt

6. Lower heat, cover and simmer **20-25 minutes** until water is absorbed; stir 2 or 3 times during cooking.

7. To serve, blend in **1 tablespoon butter** for an extra special flavor.

Per Serving of 2 (½ recipe) without butter
  Exchanges: 2.25 Bread; 159 Calories, 5 g protein (13%), 2 g fat (12%), 28 g carbohydrate (75%; 1 g sugars), 6 g dietary fiber, 0 mg cholesterol, 273 mg sodium, $.25

Roman Meal

A creamy blend of rolled oats, wheat, rye, wheat bran, and flaxseed meal. Commercially, Roman Meal has been limited to the western USA. I make my own Roman Meal Blend in quantity and store it in the freezer. I then use ½ cup of it (measured before blending) to make this recipe. For improved nutritional benefits, let grains soak in the water overnight (see pp. 50-51).

AMOUNT: 1½ Cups (2 - 3 Servings)

1. *Roman Meal Blend* Place in blender; blend 30 seconds:
    ¼ cup quick rolled oats
    1 tablespoon whole wheat grain or spelt *(see grains, p. 13)*
    1 tablespoon whole rye grain *(see grains, p. 13)*
    2 tablespoons wheat bran flakes *(p. 11)*
    1½ teaspoons flax seeds *(p. 12)*

2. Bring water to a boil; whisk in salt and *Roman Meal Blend*; boil for **1 minute**:
    1⅓ cups water
    ¼ teaspoon salt
    Roman Meal Blend (step #1)
      or ⅔ cup commercial *Roman Meal*

3. Cover, remove from heat, and let stand **5 minutes.**

Per ½ Cup   Exchanges: 0.75 Bread; 63 Calories, 2.5 g protein (15%), 1 g fat (15%), 12 g carbohydrate (70%; 9 g sugars), 2.5 g dietary fiber, 0 mg cholesterol, 178 mg sodium, $.05

Polenta

Whole kernel corn coarsely ground for a creamy cereal. If using whole corn, grind coarsely in flour mill. Stoneground cornmeal can be purchased at health food store.

AMOUNT: 2 Cups (Three ⅔ cup Servings)

1. Measure **2 cups water** (room temperature). Reserve ½ cup. Bring **1½ cups water** to a boil in saucepan.

2. Whisk smoothly into the remaining **½ cup water:**
    ½ cup stoneground cornmeal *(p. 12)*
    ½ teaspoon salt

3. Whisk cornmeal mixture into boiling water;
    (Optional: cover, remove from heat and let stand overnight for improved nutritional benefits, pp. 50-51).

4. Return to a boil, cover, reduce heat, and simmer about **30 minutes** or continue cooking by an overnight method (pp.99-101).

Per ⅔ Cup: see Hot Cereal Nutrient Chart, p. 96.

Crock-Pot Oatmeal

Crock-Pot breakfast cereal is especially handy for a large family. See basic method, p. 99. Oatmeal will be creamier textured than when cooked over direct heat.

AMOUNT: 4 Cups (6 - 8 Servings)

1. Grease inside of crock-pot up to water level with:
   1 teaspoon butter (or non-stick spray)

2. Add to pot:
   4 cups water, room temperature
   2 cups rolled oats (as *Old Fashioned Quaker Oats*)
   1 teaspoon salt

3. Cover, turn on low. Cook overnight or **8-9 hours.**

4. A few minutes before serving, add other desired ingredients:
   cinnamon, raisins, nuts, etc.

5 Stir and serve.

Per ⅔ Cup: see Hot Cereal Nutrient Chart, p. 96.

Oatmeal Surprise

The old familiar stand-by with added flavor, crunch, and nutrition. For improved nutritional benefits, let cereal soak in the water overnight (see pp. 50-51).

AMOUNT: 2 Servings

1. Bring to boil in saucepan:
   1 cup water

2. Whisk in oats and remaining ingredients:
   ½ cup rolled oats (as *Quick* or *Old Fashioned Quaker Oats*)
   ¼ teaspoon salt
   ¼ teaspoon cinnamon
   2 tablespoons dried apple pieces or ½ diced fresh apple
   2 tablespoons raisins
   2 tablespoons chopped walnuts, optional

3. Reduce heat and cook **5-10 minutes** or to desired consistency.

Per Serving of 2 (½ recipe) with nuts
   Exchanges: 0.25 Bread, 1 Fat, 1 Fruit; 171 Calories, 5 g protein (11%), 6.5 g fat (32%), 25 g carbohydrate (57%; 11 g sugars), 4 g dietary fiber, 0 mg cholesterol, 267 mg sodium, $.20

Oatmeal Bran Cereal

If plain cooked oat bran does not appeal to you, try this tasty modified version! For improved nutritional benefits, let cereal soak in the water overnight (see pp. 50-51).

AMOUNT: 2⅔ Cups (4 - 6 Servings)

1. Bring water to a boil and gradually whisk in remaining ingredients:
   3 cups water
   ½ teaspoon salt
   1 cup rolled oats (as *Old Fashioned Quaker Oats*)
   ⅓ cup oat bran *(p. 11)*

2. Reduce heat to low and cook, stirring occasionally, until thickened, 3-5 minutes for quick oats, 5-10 minutes for old fashioned oats.

Per ⅔ Cup
   Exchanges: 1.75 Bread; 115 Calories, 5 g protein (18%), 2 g fat (15%), 19 g carbohydrate (68%; 0.5 g sugars), 3.5 g dietary fiber, mg cholesterol, 266 mg sodium, $.10

Oat Bran Cereal

You may enjoy Erewhon Oat Bran Cereal with Toasted Wheat Germ, available at health food stores. For improved nutritional benefits, let cereal soak in the water overnight (see pp. 50-51).

AMOUNT: ⅔ Cup (1 Serving)

1. Bring water to a boil and gradually whisk in bran and salt:
   1 cup water
   ⅛ teaspoon salt
   ⅓ cup oat bran
      or *Oat Bran Cereal with Toasted Wheat Germ*

2. Reduce heat and cook **2 or 3 minutes** until thickened, stirring occasionally.

Per Serving with oat bran: see Hot Cereal Nutrient Chart, p. 96.

VARIATION

   Before serving, stir in:
   2 tablespoons raisins   **¼ shredded apple**
   ⅛ teaspoon cinnamon   **1 teaspoon maple syrup**

Per Serving
   Exchanges: 2 Bread, 2.5 Fruit; 245 Calories, 8.5 g protein (14%), 2.5 g fat (9%),48 g carbohydrate (77%; 24 g sugars), 9.5 g dietary fiber, 0 mg cholesterol, 268 mg sodium, $.40

Date Bran Cereal

With this tasty cereal take advantage of both kinds of fiber. Soluble oat bran fiber is helpful for controlling cholesterol and diabetes. Insoluble wheat bran is useful against constipation and colon cancer (see p. 52). For improved nutritional benefits, let cereal soak in the water overnight (see pp. 50-51).

AMOUNT: 1 - 2 Servings

1. Bring water to a boil and gradually whisk in remaining ingredients:
    1⅛ to 1¼ cups water
    ⅛ teaspoon salt
    ⅓ cup oat bran *(p. 11)*
    2 tablespoons wheat bran *(p. 11)*

2. Lower heat. Cook until thickened, stirring occasionally, about **5 minutes.**

3. Stir in:
    2 or 3 chopped dates

Per Serving of 2 (½ recipe)
*   Exchanges: 1.25 Bread, 1.5 Fruit; 143 Calories, 5 g protein (13%), 1.5 g fat (8%), 29 g carbohydrate (79%; 13 g sugars), 6.5 g dietary fiber, 0 mg cholesterol, 133 mg sodium, $.30*

Yummy Oatmeal

A little bit of wheat germ can transform the taste of a bowl of oatmeal. It is rich in B-vitamins and vitamin E (see p. 273). For improved nutritional benefits, let cereal soak in the water overnight (see pp. 50-51).

AMOUNT: 2 Cups (Four ½ cup Servings)

Bring water to a boil and gradually whisk in remaining ingredients:
    2 cups water
    ½ teaspoon salt
    1 cup rolled oats (as *Quick* or *Old Fashioned Quaker Oats*)
    ¼ cup toasted wheat germ *(p. 15)*
    ¼ cup raisins

Per ½ Cup
*   Exchanges: 1.5 Bread, 0.75 Fruit; 130 Calories, 5.5 g protein (17%), 2 g fat (12%), 24 g carbohydrate (71%; 8 g sugars), 3.5 g dietary fiber, 0 mg cholesterol, 267 mg sodium, $.15*

Sue's Breakfast

This is my favorite hot cereal combination. The crunch of spelt is a pleasant contrast to the oats and has been sprouted or cooked in advance for ready addition (pp. 102, 114). A bowlful satisfies and nourishes for the entire morning! I don't measure the amounts, but put them here in order to list the nutrients.

AMOUNT: 1 Serving

1. After cooking oatmeal, combine:
    - **½ cup cooked oatmeal**
    - **1 teaspoon butter**
    - **¼ cup cooked or sprouted spelt** *(pp. 102, 114)*
    - **2 tablespoons raisins**

2. Top with:
    - **1 tablespoon ground flaxseed** *(p. 12)*
    - **1 teaspoon maple syrup**

3. Serve with a little **nonfat milk** and a generous portion of **nonfat plain yogurt.**

VARIATION
In place of spelt, top cereal with ¼ **cup Date-Apple Granola** (p. 119) or other granola.

Per Serving
   Exchanges: 2.25 Bread, 1.5 Fat, 1.75 Fruit; 297 Calories, 8 g protein (10%), 9 g fat (25%), 51 g carbohydrate (64%; 19 g sugars), 8.5 g dietary fiber, 12 mg cholesterol, 26 mg sodium, $.25

Teff

An alternative for persons allergic to a lot of grains. Look for Arrowhead Mills Teff at health food stores. For improved nutritional benefits, let grains soak in the water overnight (see pp. 50-51).

AMOUNT: 1½ Cups (Two ¾ Cup Servings)

1. Place in saucepan:
    - **2 cups water**
    - **³⁄₁₆ teaspoon salt** (⅛ tsp. + half of ⅛ tsp.)
    - **½ cup teff** *(pp. 75-76)*
    - **¼ cup raisins, optional**

2. Bring to a boil; cover and reduce heat; simmer **15-20 minutes,** stirring occasionally, until thickened and water is absorbed.

Per ¾ Cup: see Hot Cereal Nutrient Chart, p.97.

Apple Millet Cereal

A very tasty alternative to plain millet cereal! This may also be prepared over direct heat in a saucepan, but I prefer steaming to prevent boiling the milk.

AMOUNT: 3 Cups (6 - ½ cup Servings)

1. Set top pan of double boiler over direct heat.

2. Bring water to a boil and whisk in salt and millet; boil 5 minutes:
   1 cup water
   ½ teaspoon salt
   ½ cup whole millet *(see grains, p. 13)*

3. (Optional: cover, remove from heat and let stand overnight for improved nutritional benefits, pp. 50-51).

4. Bring water to a boil in lower pan of double boiler.

5. Place top pan with millet over bottom pan; whisk in:
   1 cup nonfat (skim) milk *(or non-dairy alternative, p. 29)*
   1½ teaspoons honey
   1 small or medium tart green apple, grated (unpeeled preferred)

6. Cover and steam **40-45 minutes** or until all liquid is absorbed. Direct heat cooking takes about same length of time.

Per ½ Cup (with peeled apple)
Exchanges: 0.25 Milk, 0.75 Bread, 0.5 Fruit; 81 Calories, 3 g protein (14%), 1 g fat (7%), 17 g carbohydrate (79%; 6 g sugars), 1.5 g dietary fiber, 1 mg cholesterol, 199 mg sodium, $.15

VARIATIONS

1. Omit milk; cook in **2 cups water**.

2. Use nonfat dry milk powder in place of the milk. This will make an enriched, higher protein cereal. Bring water to a boil; pour into blender and blend in milk powder:
   2 cups water
   ½ cup non-instant nonfat dry milk powder *(p. 25)*
   Return to saucepan and proceed with recipe, omitting milk in step #4.

3. To serve, add as desired, per ½ cup serving:
   1 tablespoon chopped walnuts
   1 tablespoon raisins
   ⅛ teaspoon cinnamon, to taste
   1 teaspoon maple syrup, to taste

Per ½ Cup using non-instant nonfat dry milk --Exchanges: 0.5 Milk, 0.75 Bread, 0.5 Fruit; 102 Calories, 5.5 g protein (19%), 1 g fat (6%), 20 g carbohydrate (75%; 9 g sugars), 1.5 g dietary fiber, 2 mg cholesterol, 230 mg sodium, $.20

Orange Banana Kasha

Kasha (toasted buckwheat) has a very soft texture. Orange juice is a perfect compliment to its flavor and banana to its texture.

AMOUNT: 1 Cup (1- 2 Servings)

1. Cook kasha over direct heat or by another method (pp. 99-101). Use chart, p. 98, for proportion of water, kasha, and salt to use.

2. Pour juice over kasha and top with sliced banana:
    1 cup cooked kasha *(see grains, p. 13)*
    ½ - 1 cup orange juice
    1 sliced banana

Per ½ Cup   Exchanges: 1 Bread, 2 Fruit; 148 Calories, 3.5 g protein (9%), 1 g fat (5%), 34 g carbohydrate (86%; 18 g sugars), 3 g dietary fiber, 0 mg cholesterol, 1 mg sodium, $.40

Almond Raisin Buckwheat

I enjoy making this cereal with raw buckwheat (untoasted), but you can make it also with kasha (toasted buckwheat). Untoasted raw buckwheat is milder in flavor and requires a little longer to cook.

AMOUNT: ½ - ¾ Cup (1 Serving)

1. Cook whole buckwheat over direct heat or by another method (pp. 99-101). Use chart, p. 98, for proportion of water, buckwheat, and salt to use.

2. For each **½ cup cooked buckwheat** you have prepared, stir in:
    ¼ cup nonfat (skim) milk *(or non-dairy alternative, p. 29)*
    1 tablespoon raisins

3. Cover and cook about 3 minutes, stirring occasionally until milk is absorbed.

4. Top each serving with:
    1 tablespoon sliced almonds
    1 teaspoon maple syrup

Per ½ Cup   Exchanges: 0.25 Milk, 1 Bread, 0.5 Fat, 1.25 Fruit; 168 Calories, 6.5 g protein (15%), 3 g fat (16%), 31 g carbohydrate (69%; 15 g sugars), 3 g dietary fiber, 1 mg cholesterol, 34 mg sodium, $.30

113

Thermos Barley

Instant hot cereal for breakfast! This comes out perfectly and takes no more than 5 minutes to prepare before bedtime (See Thermos Method, p. 101). Reheat leftover for a minute or two in a little hot water or steamer. Barley contains soluble fiber, as effective in lowering blood cholesterol as oats (see chart p. 52), and natural organic sodium beneficial to the gastrointestinal tract.

AMOUNT: 4 Cups (6 - ⅔ Cup Servings)

1. Pour hot water into 1 qt. thermos or carafe; let stand 5 minutes.
2. Bring to a boil in saucepan:
   2 cups water
3. Stir in and return to a boil:
   1 cup hulled barley *(see grains, p. 13)*
   ½ teaspoon salt
4. Pour hot water out of the thermos or carafe.
5. Scoop water with grain out of saucepan into thermos or carafe with a small measuring cup.
6. Cap tightly; lay thermos on its side overnight; leave carafe upright.

Per ⅔ Cup: see Hot Cereal Nutrient Chart, p. 96.

For Thermos Cooking of other grains, see directions (p. 101).

Thermos Spelt

I make this chewy grain one evening for the entire week to add each morning right from the refrigerator to my hot oatmeal (p. 111), or just eat it by itself with desired accompaniments of fruit, milk, honey, or syrup! Reheat leftover for a minute or two in a little hot water or steamer.

AMOUNT: 3 Cups (4 - 5 Servings)

1. Follow recipe for *Thermos Barley* above. In place of barley, use:
   spelt grain *(see grains, p. 13)*
2. In step #3 boil 5 minutes.

Note: For additional softening, place the spelt and water in saucepan in the morning and let it soak during the day before cooking. This can be done for all the harder grains: rye, millet, triticale, wheat.

Per ⅔ Cup: see Hot Cereal Nutrient Chart, p. 97..

Potpourri of Hot Cereal Additions

Need some idea refreshers? Try these!

nuts & seeds
almonds or walnuts
ground flaxseed *(p. 12)*
ground sesame seeds
  or sunflower seeds *(p. 14)*

dried fruits
diced dried apple
diced dried apricots
raisins or chopped dates

fresh fruit
apple--diced or grated fresh
sliced banana
chopped nectarine
  or peach or apricot
strawberries

flavorings & sweetenings
cinnamon
vanilla (try ½ tsp. per
  1 cup uncooked cereal)
peanut butter and jelly
crushed pineapple tidbits
maple syrup or honey

grains
sprouted or cooked whole grain
  added to creamier cereal
oat bran *(p. 11)*
wheat bran *(p. 11)*
toasted wheat germ *(p. 15)*

milk, cultured milk
yogurt or milk
nut milk or soy milk or soy yogurt
kefir, plain or fruit flavor *(p. 28)*

Swiss Breakfast Cereal

A crunchy and spicy uncooked cereal to be prepared the evening before. This might be thought of as a meusli. But true meusli is predominantly a fresh fruit dish with very little grain, such as our Apple Breakfast Treat (p. 173).

AMOUNT: About 1½ Cups (Three ½ cup Servings)

1. Mix together and store overnight in the refrigerator:
    1 cup nonfat or lowfat milk *(or non-dairy alternative, p. 29)*
    ½ cup rolled oats (as *Quick* or *Old Fashioned Quaker Oats*)
    2 - 3 tablespoons diced dried apricots, unsulfured
    2 tablespoons diced dried apples, unsulfured
    2 tablespoons chopped or slivered almonds
    1 tablespoon sesame seeds *(unhulled preferred, p. 14)*
    ¾ teaspoon vanilla
    ⅜ teaspoon cinnamon
    ⅛ teaspoon salt
    1/16 teaspoon nutmeg

2. Serve hot or cold.

Per ½ Cup with nonfat milk -- Exchanges: 0.25 Milk, 0.75 Bread, 0.75 Fat, 0.5 Fruit; 152 Calories, 7 g protein (17%), 5 g fat (30%), 20 g carbohydrate (53%; 9 g sugars), 2.5 g dietary fiber, 2 mg cholesterol, 134 mg sodium, $.35

Simple Granola

This recipe has many variations (p. 117). This granola is minimally baked to reduce loss of Vitamin B-1. Granola is a rich food. Consider serving a small amount over hot cereal, yogurt, or fruit for crunch, rather than eating an entire bowl of it. Olive oil does not have a taste when baked.

AMOUNT: 8 Cups

Bake: 300°F (150°C) - 20 to 30 minutes, uncovered

1. Preheat oven.

2. Warm honey 40 seconds in microwave or over very low heat; thoroughly blend in oil, vanilla, and cinnamon with wire whisk:
   ½ cup honey
   ½ cup oil *(extra virgin olive oil preferred, p. 14, or light olive oil)*
   2 teaspoons vanilla extract
   1 teaspoon cinnamon, optional

3. Stir honey-oil mixture into oats in a mixing bowl until thoroughly and evenly blended:
   8 cups regular rolled oats

4. Spread evenly in baking pans. I prefer two 9" x 13" baking pans, but you can use cookie sheets, jelly roll pans or any other baking pans available.

5. Bake at 300° for 20-30 minutes, stirring well every 10 minutes.

> **Special Tip:** Granola will continue cooking after removal from oven and will crisp as it cools. Do not overbake it. Time for baking may vary depending on quantity prepared and size of baking pans.

6. Store in tightly closed container in refrigerator or freezer.

Per ½ Cup
   Exchanges: 2.25 Bread, 1.25 Fat, 1 Fruit; 248 Calories, 6.5 g protein (10%), 9.5 g fat (33%), 36 g carbohydrate (57%; 10 g sugars), 4 g dietary fiber, 0 mg cholesterol, 2 mg sodium, $.20

Simple Granola Variations

Add any combination of ingredients listed below to Simple Granola. I suggest 2-4 extra ingredients, ½ - 1 cup of each, unless suggested otherwise. All unfamiliar ingredients can be found at a health food store (see Shopping for Unfamiliar Ingredients, pp. 11-15).

Add with the oats in step #2 of *Simple Granola* (p. 116):
  wheat bran
  coconut, unsweetened
  unroasted nuts
  ¼ cup soy flour
  other grains (to replace part of the oats: rice flakes, rye flakes, barley flakes, wheat flakes, etc.)
  1-2 tablespoons malt
  ¼ cup protein powder *(p. 185)*

Add after baking is completed:
  toasted wheat germ
  toasted coconut *(see below)*
  roasted nuts
  dried fruit pieces (raisins, apples, apricots, pineapple, dates, blueberries, raspberries)
  ground nuts and seeds, raw or toasted *(p. 120)*

Increase, if desired:
  vanilla flavoring

Replace honey with:
  pure maple syrup
  sorghum syrup

Toasted Coconut

Oven: 300°F (150°C) - 5 to 8 minutes

1. Preheat oven.

2. Spread single layer in baking pan. Toast until golden brown:
  unsweetened shredded coconut *(p. 12)*

Special Tip: Watch closely! Coconut browns very fast.

Yummy Granola

*Our favorite variation of Simple Granola
(p. 116). For a Granola Breakfast Company
Buffet, see pp. 227-228.*

AMOUNT: 10 Cups

Bake: 300°F (150°C) - 20 to 30 minutes, uncovered

1. Preheat oven.

2. Warm honey 40 seconds in microwave or over very low heat;
   thoroughly blend in oil, vanilla, and cinnamon with wire whisk:
   ½ cup honey
   ½ cup oil *(extra virgin olive oil preferred, p. 14)*
   2 teaspoons vanilla extract
   1 teaspoon cinnamon, optional

3. Stir honey-oil mixture into remaining ingredients in a mixing bowl
   until thoroughly and evenly blended:
   8 cups regular rolled oats
   ½ cup chopped or sliced almonds[1]
   ½ cup shredded coconut[1]

4. Spread evenly baking pans. I prefer two 9" x 13" baking pans,
   but you can use cookie sheets, jelly roll pans or any other
   baking pans available.

5. Bake at 300° for 20-30 minutes, stirring well every 10 minutes.

6. Store in tightly closed container in refrigerator or freezer.

[1]Add roasted nuts or toasted coconut after baking.

Per ½ Cup (includes cinnamon)
   *Exchanges: 1.75 Bread, 1.5 Fat, 0.5 Fruit; 225 Calories, 6 g protein (10%), 10 g fat (38%),
30 g carbohydrate (52%; 8 g sugars), 4 g dietary fiber, 0 mg cholesterol, 2 mg sodium, $.20*

VARIATION

Makes 12 Cups
Stir into baked granola (or add unroasted seeds before baking):
   ½ cups wheat bran *(p. 11)*
   ½ cup toasted wheat germ *(p. 15)*
   ½ cup raisins
   ¼ cup roasted ground sesame seeds *(p.14)*
   ¼ cup roasted ground sunflower seeds *(p. 14)*

Per ½ Cup
   *Exchanges: 0.5 Meat, 2 Bread, 2.25 Fat; 287 Calories, 10 g protein (13%), 15.5 g fat (45%),
32 g carbohydrate (42%), 5 g dietary fiber, 0 mg cholesterol, 3 mg sodium, $.30*

Date Apple Granola

A very tasty no-honey, no-oil granola with a firm crunch!

AMOUNT: 12 Cups

Bake 200°F (95°C) - 2 to 3 hours

1. Combine juice concentrate and vanilla; add dates and apples; let stand for several hours or overnight to soften fruit:

    3 - 6 oz. cans frozen unsweetened apple juice concentrate (thawed)

    1 teaspoon vanilla

    1 cup date dices or chopped dates, packed

    1 cup dried apples, unsulfured *(p. 13)*

2. Finely grind in blender:

    1 cup whole or sliced raw almonds

3. Pour ground almonds into large mixing bowl. Blend the softened fruit with juice in the blender and pour it into the almonds; mix together thoroughly.

4. With a large mixing spoon gradually blend into liquid mixture:

    10 cups regular rolled oats

> **Special Tip:** Use your hands to do the final mixing in of the oats.

5. Spread single layer in baking pans, cookie sheets, or pans with shallow sides, such as pizza or jelly roll pans. Bake at 200° for 2-3 hours until fairly dry, stirring every 30 minutes for even baking. This will crisp up as it cools.

6. Stir in during last 30 minutes:

    1 cup diced dates

7. Store in refrigerator or freezer.

Per ½ Cup   Exchanges: 2 Bread, 0.5 Fat, 2 Fruit; 240 Calories, 7 g protein (11%), 5.5 g fat (20%), 42 g carbohydrate (69%; 17 g sugars), 4.5 g dietary fiber, 0 mg cholesterol, 10 mg sodium, $.30

VARIATION

Makes 14 Cups

Add after baking (or untoasted, unroasted items before baking):

1 cup toasted wheat germ *(p. 15)*

1 cup toasted shredded coconut *(p. 117)*

½ cup roasted ground sesame seeds *(p. 14)*

½ cup roasted ground sunflower seeds *(p. 14)*

Per ½ Cup   Exchanges: 0.25 Meat, 2 Bread, 1 Fat, 1.5 Fruit; 258 Calories, 8 g protein (12%), 8 g fat (27%), 40 g carbohydrate (61%; 16 g sugars), 5.5 g dietary fiber, 0 mg cholesterol, 10 mg sodium, $.30

Roasted Nuts & Seeds

Roasting improves the flavor of nuts and seeds, but they are hard to find roasted without oil and without salt. It only takes moments to pop raw unsalted ones into the oven. Chop or grind them after roasting to minimize exposure of the surface area to heat.

> **Special Timesaving Tip:** Roast a quantity of nuts or seeds sometime when you are not involved in other food preparation; store for ready use at busier moments.

Bake: 300°F (150°C) - about 30 to 35 minutes

1. Preheat Oven.

2. Spread desired nuts or seeds in single layer in a shallow baking pan:
   sesame seeds
   sunflower seeds
   peanuts
   almonds
   cashews
   pumpkin seeds

3. Bake at 300° until lightly golden, stirring occasionally.

4. Cool and store in tightly covered container in freezer or refrigerator.

Ground Nuts & Seeds

*Nuts and seeds are better assimilated by the body when ground up. Seeds (**sunflower, sesame, and flax seeds**) are especially appealing when ground.*
   ¼ cup seeds = ½ cup ground
   1 tablespoon seeds = 2 tablespoons ground

1. Grind just the portion of nuts or seeds you need for a recipe in blender, or grind seeds in a small coffee bean mill.

2. If grinding extra, grind no more than 1 week's supply and store in the freezer. Once ground, nuts and seeds turn rancid more quickly.

> **Special Tip:** If you grind many seeds, a small coffee bean mill is ideal. It is faster, more efficient, and easier to clean than a blender. Seeds are perfectly ground in 15 seconds. Coffee bean mills available from $12-$20.

Toast for Breakfast?

Mother[1] always told us children that the crust of the bread was the most nutritious part. I liked to pull the crusts off my bread. She was also one of those that especially enjoyed almost-burnt toast. Toast for breakfast certainly is an American tradition. I hate to speak against toast, especially when it's whole grain! But a caution is in order. Toasting destroys about 12-20% of vitamin B-1. Even more can be destroyed if the bread is toasted dark, and some folic acid is also lost. Therefore:

TOAST LIGHTLY!

Try slices of delicious *Spelt* or *Kamut Bread* without toasting (pp. 122-123). Vary the breakfast breads with English muffins, muffins, biscuits, bagels, or tortillas. Don't overlook sourdough English muffins, biscuits, and bread (pp.284-85).

[1] In honor of my mother, she set an example as a true home cook! Several of my favorite recipes from childhood are found in **SueGreggCookbooks**

Spelt Bread

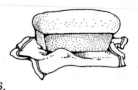

Very soft, delicious bread! It has completely replaced my wheat bread.[1] *To use this recipe with sourdough for Sourdough Bread see p. 286.*

AMOUNT: 2 Medium Loaves (8½" x 4½" Pans)
Bake: 350°F (175°C) - 35 to 45 minutes

1. Blend in a glass measuring cup in order given and allow to stand 5 - 10 minutes until it bubbles up:
   ¼ cup very warm (but not hot) **water**
   2 teaspoons (1 package) **active dry yeast**
   ½ teaspoon honey
2. Blend in mixing bowl:
   2 cups cool water
   3 cups spelt flour
   yeast mixture
3. Cover bowl with damp cloth and let stand several hours or overnight at room temperature (away from drafts and heat).
4. Mix in with wooden spoon and beat vigorously for 200 strokes or on medium speed in electric mixer for 5 minutes:
   2 teaspoons salt
   ⅓ cup olive oil
   ⅓ cup honey
   ⅛ teaspoon vitamin C powder, optional (helps rising)
   a portion of 6-7 remaining cups spelt flour (no more than keeps batter easy to beat vigorously)
5. Blend in remaining flour while workable to stir, reserving about 1 - 1½ cups to add while kneading just to prevent sticking (add no more flour than needed to prevent sticking to hands or working surface even if total flour measurement is different from the recipe.
6. Knead 20 minutes or 600-800 strokes until smooth and resistant to kneading action, adding as little flour as needed to prevent sticking.
7. Set in bowl greased with butter, turning over to grease the top; cover with a damp cloth and let stand until double in size, about 1½ hrs.[1]
8. Gently press down in center and from sides to center, turn dough over and set to rise again until double, about 45 minutes.[1]
9. Gently press down, knead a few times, cover; let rest 10-15 min.

SHAPING LOAVES

1. Divide dough in half and shape each into a loaf (see illustrations, p. 123). Place in well greased or sprayed loaf pans (p. 271).
2. Cover loaves with a damp towel and set in a warm corner to rise until almost double, about 25 minutes (cont'd next page).

[1]Time is a rule of thumb. Test for adequate rise by poking finger in dough about 1/2 inch. If indentation remains, dough has sufficiently risen.

3. Bake at 350° for 35-45 minutes until golden brown on the bottom (tapping it with the finger also will give hollow sound). Turn loaves out and cool on sides on a cake rack; brush with melted butter for a soft crust.

Per Slice (16 slices per loaf)
   Exchanges: 1.5 Bread, 0.5 Fat, 0.25 Fruit; 146 Calories, 4.5 g protein (11%), 3 g fat (16%), 31 g carbohydrate (73%; 3 g sugars), 6 g dietary fiber, 0 mg cholesterol, 133 mg sodium, $.20

Kamut Bread

A very soft, heavier loaf, yet still light textured. A unique color and flavor! I like to use ½ cup honey and oil in this recipe. For additional help in making yeast breads, see references listed at bottom of p. 122.

AMOUNT: 2 Medium Loaves (8½" x 4½" Pans)
Bake: 350°F (175°C) - 35 to 45 minutes

Use recipe for *Spelt Bread*, p. 122, with following changes:
   use ½ cup honey and ½ cup olive oil
   use about 2 - 2½ cups less flour (add no portion of remaining flour in step #4 if it makes batter too stiff to beat vigorously)
   knead 10 minutes or 400 strokes

Per Slice (16 slices per loaf) using ½ cup honey and oil
   Exchanges: 1.5 Bread, 0.5 Fat, 0.25 Fruit; 131 Calories, 3.5 g protein (8%), 3 g fat (15%), 26 g carbohydrate (78%; 3 g sugars), 3.5 g dietary fiber, 0 mg cholesterol, 133 mg sodium, $.20

VARIATION Substitute **1½ cups kamut flour** with **1½ cups oat flour** (blend 2 cups rolled oats in blender about 1 minute or mill 1 cup + 2 tablespoons whole oat groats).

Shaping a Loaf

1. press into ¾" thick rectangle   fold ⅓ dough towards center   fold other ⅓ over that

2. fold each end in towards center

3. turn seamed edge down   lift into loaf pan   ready to bake

4. delicious loaves!

English Muffins

Delicious toasted and topped with scrambled eggs or with unsweetened jam, butter, or peanut butter. For Sourdough English Muffins, see p. 284.

AMOUNT: Makes 10 - 12 Muffins
Bake: 325° Electric Fry Pan *(or medium heat range top)*

> **Tip:** An electric fry pan preheated to 325° will give a more controlled, even temperature. If not available, bake on griddle or fry pan over medium heat.

1. Mix yeast and honey into water until begins to bubble, about 10 minutes: stir in flour; cover with damp cloth; let stand overnight:
   1¾ cups warm water
   4 teaspoons (2 packages) **active dry yeast**
   1 teaspoon honey or crystalline fructose *(p. 12)*
   3 cups whole wheat or spelt flour

2. Blend in remaining ingredients and knead about 8 minutes; blend in oat flour and knead 2 minutes longer:
   2 tablespoons olive oil *(extra virgin olive oil preferred, p. 14)*
   3 tablespoons honey or crystalline fructose *(p. 12)*
   2 teaspoons salt
   about 2 cups whole wheat or 2½ cups spelt flour *(see grains, p. 13)*
   (adjust flour amounts to prevent sticking while kneading)
   ½ cup oat flour (rolled oats may be ground quite fine in blender)

3. Cover bowl with damp towel and let dough rise in warm place until double, about 45 minutes.

4. Press dough down gently, turn over in bowl, cover and let rise again until double, about 25 minutes.

5. Knead dough into a ball with hands, pat out on lightly floured pastry sheet to about ½" thick.

6. Cut muffins with floured rim of glass (about 3½" diameter).

7. Set muffins on cookie sheet; let stand 15 minutes.

8. Bake muffins in ungreased fry pan, 10 minutes on each side until golden brown, turning once.

9. To serve, split muffins in half by piercing around the sides with a fork; toast lightly.

Per ½ Muffin (of 10 Muffins)
  Exchanges: 1.25 Bread, 0.25 Fat, 0.25 Fruit; 109 Calories, 3.5 g protein (12%), 2 g fat (16%), 21 g carbohydrate (72%; 3 g sugars), 3 g dietary fiber, 0 mg cholesterol, 213 mg sodium, $.10

Breakfast Biscuits

Make biscuits for breakfast as a refreshing change from toast on occasion. These have a tender, soft crumb. Especially enjoyable with eggs or a la King with tuna or chicken. Bake with or without wheat! To use this recipe with sourdough for Sourdough Biscuits see p. 285.

AMOUNT: 9 - 10 Biscuits
Bake: 425°F (220°C) - 12 to 15 minutes

1. Place flour in medium mixing bowl:
    2 cups whole wheat pastry or barley flour *(see grains, p. 13)*
    or 2⅓ cups spelt

2. Whisk together in a 2 cup measure or small bowl:
    1 cup buttermilk *(p. 11; or non-dairy alternative, p. 29)*
    3 tablespoons olive oil *(extra virgin olive oil preferred, p. 14)*

3. Stir liquid ingredients into flour just until mixed.

4. Cover bowl; let stand at room temperature overnight *(pp. 50-51).*

5. Preheat Oven to 425°.

6. Mix into dough evenly while beating 10 strokes:
    2½ teaspoons baking powder   "sift" these through a small
    ½ teaspoon baking soda   strainer with a spoon to break
    ½ teaspoon salt   up any lumps.

7. Drop spoonfuls of dough on lightly greased cookie sheet.

8. Bake 425° for 12-15 minutes until lightly golden on the bottom.

> **Tip:** Do not expect these biscuits to be "round" and high like white flour biscuits that are rolled and cut. They are likely to be large and quite flat, and more flavorful.

Per Biscuit of 10 (with 2% fat buttermilk)
   Exchanges: 1.25 Bread, 0.75 Fat; 136 Calories, 3 g protein (9%), 4.5 g fat (30%), 20 g carbohydrate (60%; 1 g sugars), 2 g dietary fiber, 1 mg cholesterol, 148 mg sodium, $.15

Sunflower Biscuits

Different, but tender and flavorful. No need to spread butter on these to enjoy! The unsaturated fat of the seeds will balance the fat of the butter. To refresh your memory on the value of sunflower seeds, see **Main Dishes**, *pp. 24-25. Make sure the seeds are fresh!*

AMOUNT: 12 Large Biscuits
Bake: 375°F (190°C) - 15 to 20 minutes

1. Preheat Oven.

2. Grind in blender or in a coffee been mill (see tip below):
   ½ cup sunflower seeds (to make 1 cup ground seed)

3. In mixing bowl blend together thoroughly:
   1 cup ground sunflower seeds *(p. 15)*
   1 cup whole wheat pastry flour *(p. 15)*
      (see tip below for grinding in a coffee bean mill)
   3½ teaspoons baking powder *(low sodium preferred, p. 11)*
   1 teaspoon salt

4. Blend and stir into dry ingredients with a fork, just until blended:
   ⅔ cup buttermilk *(p. 11; or non-dairy alternative, p. 29)*
   4 tablespoons unsalted butter, melted

5. Drop by large spoonfuls onto greased cookie sheet.

6. Bake at 375° for 12-15 minutes until golden on bottom.

Per Biscuit
   Exchanges: 0.25 Meat, 0.75 Bread, 2.25 Fat; 180 Calories, 6 g protein (13%), 12.5 g fat (60%), 13 g carbohydrate (27%; 2 g sugars), 3 g dietary fiber, 11 mg cholesterol, 178 mg sodium, $.15

Coffee Bean Mill: See special tip for grinding seeds in a coffee bean mill, p. 120. Small amounts of grain also grind well in a coffee bean mill, especially whole wheat pastry berries. Place ⅓ cup grain at a time in the mill. Mill for 15 seconds, then give it a rest. Repeat 2 or 3 more times until the flour is the fineness you want. One cup flour takes about ⅔ cup grain.

The Egg Breakfast

Which of you fathers, if your son asks for . . . an egg, will give him a scorpion? Luke 11:12

THE EGG BREAKFAST

SUBJECTS

RECIPES

The Egg Breakfast

Fruit Juice or Fresh Fruit
Eggs (Soft-cooked, Scrambled, Fried, Omelet, Frittata, or Tofu Scramble)
Potatoes or Beans
and/or
Hot Bread
(English Muffin, Toast, Bagels, Biscuits, or Tortillas)
Spread (Jam, Butter)

Nutrition Goals Menu[1]

6 - 12 oz. Fresh Orange Juice
2-Egg Vegetable Patch
Omelet (pp.142, 144)[1]
1-2 English Muffins (p. 124)
1-2 Tbsps. Jam

[1]*Small: $1.40*	*36% Fat*	*502 Calories*
[1]*Large: $2.05*	*28% Fat*	*734 Calories*

---

[1]This menu is included in the "Average of 7 Breakfasts" Column on the *Nutrition Goals Chart*, pp. 16-17. Small servings represent menu for adult female; large servings represent menu for adult male. Omelet includes 2 tbsps. green onion, 2 tbsps. diced zucchini, ¼ c. green pepper, ⅛ tsp. basil, and is topped with ½ tomato, 1 tsp. salsa, 2 tbsps. fat free sour cream, ¼ cup alfalfa sprouts.

Give Eggs a Break!

*As an inexpensive source of good nutrition,
there is nothing more glorious than the egg.*
Edward Ahrens, Time Magazine, March 26, 1984

This billboard slogan caught my attention: "Give Eggs a Break!" Apparently eggs are actually 32% lower in cholesterol content than once believed. That's a worthy drop in percentage to note! Yet there is even more to the story of cholesterol and the egg than this.

Extensive research has led authorities away from the popular notion that blames the cholesterol content in foods for high blood cholesterol. This is especially good news for the egg which contains more cholesterol than any other food. More attention, for example, is now being given to the amount of total fats consumed, saturated fat in particular. In addition, other dietary considerations that may contribute to heart disease are under investigation, such as the lack of vitamin E, and the effects of trans-fatty acids.[1]

Yet, I am still frequently asked, "Are your recipes low in cholesterol?" Most of us, influenced by food advertising, are still convinced cholesterol in food will inevitably raise our blood cholesterol. Here is the reason, I believe, that we have fixed our minds on this idea: The food industry usually responds to the latest nutritional bandwagon before it has stood the test of time and further research. As a result, "contains no cholesterol" printed on thousands of food labels, for example, and advertised on TV have convinced us that cholesterol in foods must be bad. Few of us have been exposed to a more scholarly approach. The major research studies on cholesterol and diet have been reviewed extensively in "The Cholesterol Myth," by Thomas J. Moore in the *Atlantic Monthly*, September, 1989. This 33-page article is well worth reading.[1]

For about 85% of the population there is no apparent relationship between eating eggs and blood cholesterol levels. In research studies the human body has shown a remarkable capacity to establish its own cholesterol-producing level in spite of the diet. Some people apparently have a genetic problem that does not allow their bodies to correctly metabolize cholesterol. For these there may be some benefit in eliminating egg yolks from the diet. Only periodic blood cholesterol testing will reveal if a person with high blood cholesterol falls in this group.

[1]See **The 15 Minute Meal Planner**, pp. 105; 119-122.

The consequence of the food cholesterol theory has resulted in a multitude of recipes that call for egg whites in place of the whole egg. Yet, most of these recipes continue to call for other ingredients of inferior nutritional quality, such as white flour and refined sugars. Wouldn't it be wiser to use the whole egg moderately while improving the nutritional quality of the other ingredients, as well? For example, increasing scientific evidence points to the importance of an adequate vitamin E and essential fatty acid intake for healthy hearts. Yet the wide use of depleted and altered foods such as white flour and margarine reduces the intake of these nutrients. By using a wide variety of ingredients of high nutritional value these elements will also be included in our diets.

Let me illustrate on the following charts that you can use whole eggs in moderation, yet maintain the recommended daily nutrition goal of 250-350 milligrams cholesterol (see *Nutrition Goals*, p. 17).

Cholesterol Averages of Meals - *SueGreggCookbooks*

Breakfasts (**Breakfasts**, p. 17)	85-103 mg.
Lunches (**Lunches & Snacks**, p. 147)	59-89 mg.
Main Dish Menus (**Main Dishes**, p. 11)	90 mg.
Casserole Menus (**Meals in Minutes**, p. 73)	100-102 mg.
Soup Menus (**Soups & Muffins**, p. 7)	79 mg.

Daily Cholesterol Average - *SueGreggCookbooks*

	Female	Male
Breakfast	85	103
Lunch	59-89	59-89
Dinner	90[1]	90[1]
Total Cholesterol	**234-264 mg.**	**252-282 mg.**

[1]An average of combined menus from **Main Dishes, Meals in Minutes**, and **Soups & Muffins** (see box above).

Eggs have been a time-honored food for generation after generation. The Bible reflects the historical perspective on eggs when Jesus said,

Which of you fathers, if your son asks for a fish, will give him a snake instead? Or if he asks for an egg, will give him a scorpion? If you then, though you are evil, know how to give good gifts to your children, how much more will your Father in heaven give the Holy Spirit to those who ask him! Luke 11:11-13

The Anatomy of An Egg

If you are ready to "give eggs a break," let's get on to the more intriguing part: the anatomy of an egg and how it affects the way to best purchase, store, and cook eggs.

If you have children, gather them together along with an egg from the refrigerator when reading this section.[1]

As you get the egg, notice which end is up in the box. You've got the egg? Don't break it yet! Prick a small pinhole in the wide end of the egg. Does anything drip out? Nothing noticeable escapes from the pinhole because there is an *air space* in the wide end of the egg. The air provides for the developing chicken and also receives waste gasses from it. This space will grow larger as the egg ages, and is also a possible place for bacteria to enter. Keeping the wide end of the egg up during storage keeps the yolk centered away from the air space.

Heat will cause the air in the air space to expand and escape too rapidly. This is why eggs sometimes crack while cooking them in the shell. If you make the small pinhole before you cook it, this will help prevent the egg from cracking. Next time you cook an egg with a pinhole, you might notice the air bubbles escaping from it as you first put it into very hot water to cook. Another way to prevent cracking is to allow the eggs to come to room temperature before putting them into very hot water. A better way, however, is to start the eggs in cold water from the tap, allowing them to heat gradually. This usually makes the pinhole unnecessary.

We all know how easily eggs break! The shell is a protection for the developing chicken, but it is also very porous. It has a *semipermeable* wall. A semipermeable wall or membrane will allow certain substances in and keep others out. This occurs through a process called *osmosis*. Osmosis occurs with either liquids or gasses. To best understand how osmosis works, look it up in an encyclopedia. Through osmosis, gasses and water pass through the wall to aid the chicken's development. Thus the egg will absorb refrigerator odors in a similar manner (one good reason for keeping all foods covered). This is why eggs are best kept in the carton. The egg shell also has a thin film covering it, called *bloom* which reduces the loss of water and gasses from the egg. Washing eggs before you store them would remove this bloom, diminishing a major portion of the eggs' natural protection.

[1] If reading this with your children, you might ask them reasons for their observations before reading the answer. For example, "Why do you think nothing is coming out of the pinhole?"

The shell also has two membranes that can give added protection from invading bacteria. You don't need to worry about harmful bacteria getting into an egg unless it is cracked. If you crack an egg, store it in a tightly covered container if not to be used immediately.

Now break the egg into a flat dish, without breaking the yolk. Do the white and yolk seem to spread out or do they seem to stand up quite firmly? Very fresh eggs will tend to stand up firmly. As the egg ages, carbon dioxide escapes into the air space causing the yolk and white to  flatten. As this carbon dioxide escapes, air begins to replace the space between the shell and the egg. This makes a hard-cooked egg easier to peel. That's why not-so-fresh eggs are easier to peel than fresh eggs.

Look carefully on top of the egg yolk for a small spot that is lighter yellow in color. This the *blastodisc* or *germ spot*. The blastodisc will develop into the chicken embryo if kept under the right conditions. Blood vessels are developed in the blastodisc to transfer protein and nutrients from the yolk for the development of the chicken embryo. Food for the developing chick is stored in the yolk.

The white of the egg is called *albumin*, consisting of four layers. Within the innermost layer, you may notice the thicker twisted stringy bits of white on either end of the yolk. This is called the *chaleza*. The chalezas anchor the yolk, keeping it suspended in the center of the white, protecting it from damage. The chaleza is not usually visible in poor quality eggs.

The egg is a very high protein food. As an egg cooks, the protein traps moisture, causing it to *coagulate*. That is, it becomes a solid mass. The albumin, or white of the egg, will coagulate at a lower temperature than the yolk. Cooking at low temperatures will allow the yolk to cook sufficiently before the white becomes overcooked. Overcooking also toughens the egg protein because water begins to be drawn out of it. Toughened protein is not only less pleasant to eat, but harder for the body to digest. Likewise, overcooking or cooking at too high a temperature will cause sulfur in the white to escape and combine with iron in the yolk, forming the green ring that sometimes appears around the outside of the yolk. This does not make the egg inedible, but it is a sign of overcooking.

Since a lot of heat is trapped inside an egg cooked in the shell, it will continue to cook after you remove it from the heat. To immediately stop the cooking, the eggs should be put into cold water from the tap. This will prevent the green ring from forming and also make it easier to peel the eggs--that is, if the eggs aren't too fresh.

The characteristic of egg protein to coagulate helps to provide structure for leavened baked goods. The egg acts as a *binder*. Since both the yolk and the white have about equal amounts of protein, two egg whites work as effectively as a binder in baking as one whole egg.

Egg whites also have the capacity to collect and hold air when they are beaten. The egg white molecules are naturally curled. When they are agitated by vigorous beating the molecules uncurl, forming an interconnection of stretched-out molecules that trap air. Egg whites must be carefully separated from the yolks so that no yolk gets into the white. The fat of the yolk will completely inhibit the egg whites from trapping air. Since the yolk becomes more vulnerable to breakage the warmer it gets, an egg can be separated more successfully if it is refrigerator cold. On the other hand, egg whites will more effectively trap air if beaten at room temperature. Beaten egg whites add lightness when folded into baked goods. They can help to lighten the texture of whole grain waffles and pancakes that may seem too heavy and, of course, are what give an angel food cake its lightness.

Now for the most important part of the egg that you cannot observe--the nutrient value. The quality of the egg's nutrient value is best understood by realizing that the egg is structured to feed a developing chicken. Therefore, it contains highest quality balanced nutrition to meet this need. Egg protein is of such quality that all other protien foods are measured against it. Egg protein has the highest *biological value*. That is, egg protein is the most usable by the human body. 94-95% of the egg protein is easily digested, assimilated, and utilized. A 2 oz. standard large egg (about 56 grams) contains 6 grams of complete protein, and about 5.6 grams fat. The types of fat are in healthy proportion of 30% saturated, 33% monounsaturated, and 37% polyunsaturated fat. The yolk has a full range of nutrients, except for vitamin C, to nourish the developing chicken: vitamins A, B-complex, D, E, K, and iron, calcium, potassium, phosphorous, zinc, magnesium, and so on. Egg cholesterol is about 213 mg. (less than previously thought) and balanced by lecithin. There is considerable debate, however, whether the lecithin is effective in human digestion to assist proper break down of the cholesterol.

Eggs also have a substance called avidin that combines with biotin, one of the B-vitamins, when eggs are eaten raw. This prevents the biotin from being utilized by the body. For this reason, some warn not to eat too many raw eggs. This should not be of concern with occasional use of raw eggs, especially since biotin is available in other foods, especially in whole grains.

The use of eggs has a long history. We know that Job, who probably lived around 2000 B.C., ate eggs... *is there flavor in the white of an egg? I refuse to touch it; such food makes me ill (Job 6:6).* I pause to wonder when nutritionists announce that you can eat all the egg whites that you want, as if that were a privilege--they ARE tasteless! When Roman legions attacked Britain in 55 B.C. they were surprised to find that less civilized peoples there were raising chickens. Egg cookery had already been well established in Roman society.

Egg Buying Wisdom

You wouldn't think much wisdom would be needed to buy a dozen eggs, but these days we seem to need wisdom for everything we do, given all the inferior choices we have. You can buy sizes from peewee to jumbo, but most recipes calling for eggs refer to large eggs. In most of my recipes medium or large can be used. Eggs are graded AA, A, and B. These grades are of little use in determining the nutritional value of eggs. A better measure, perhaps, is whether the eggs are battery eggs or fertile eggs.

Battery eggs are produced from hens that are kept factory-style in very crowded quarters. As a result, the hens must be fed an assortment of hormones, antibiotics, dyes, tranquilizers, and drugs so that they can survive these conditions and produce quality eggs. Consequently battery eggs are at risk for containing chemical residues. In addition, the unfortunate conditions to which the laying hens are subjected may be fairly questioned. *A righteous man cares for the needs of his animal, but the kindest acts of the wicked are cruel (Proverbs 12:10).* Most supermarket eggs are battery eggs.

Eggs labeled as *fertile eggs* may or may not be raised under better conditions and may or may not have superior nutrient value. A fertile egg is simply an egg that has been fertilized by a rooster. That means the egg does contain many natural hormones that battery eggs do not have. The nutritional value of these hormones is not yet understood. Fertile eggs are also more likely to have been free range fed. Free range fed chickens are allowed the space to move about on the ground as chickens were designed to do in order to thrive. They don't need chemical treatment for survival. Consequently, their eggs are not at risk for containing chemical residues.

Usually free range fed chickens are given feeds of higher nutrient quality. Udo Erasmus in *Fats & Oils* suggests that egg nutrient value depends on what the hens have been fed. That is logical. He further explains that hens that lay battery eggs generally receive more stable oleic acid fat in their diet than feeds with higher essential fatty acids, which free range chickens are more likely to receive. The implications, then, are that eggs from free range fed chickens may contain more of the essential fatty acids needed to assist the body's proper utilization of the cholesterol.

Other claims made for fertile eggs (not substantiated) include: they are higher in lecithin which balances the cholesterol, they contain less cholesterol, they may be higher in vitamin B-12 and folic acid, they may be considerably higher in vitamin A, and the albumin is of higher quality. Beatrice Trum Hunter in *Consumer Beware* claims that some persons who have allergic reaction to battery eggs do not react to fertile eggs. Free range fed eggs are usually better tasting.

Fertile eggs are readily available in many health food stores and at Trader Joe Markets. That they are free range fed is not guaranteed, so it would be wise to make inquiry unless "cage-free" or "free range" (or similar statement) also appears on the label. Fertile eggs are usually more expensive than battery eggs. Yet they are still an economical buy. For example, the protein of 2.2 eggs is equal to the protein in 2 oz. of cooked boneless chicken. at $3.99 per lb. for boneless chicken, 2 oz. chicken costs $.92. At $.99 per lb. for whole chicken, 2 oz. chicken costs about $.41. At $1.89 per dozen, 2.2 fertile eggs cost $.35.

When buying eggs be sure they have been kept in the refrigerator case, not just near it. Battery eggs in some supermarkets are more likely to be unrefrigerated than fertile eggs in health food stores. Check inside the egg box to make sure none of them are cracked.

Storing & Caring for Eggs

~ Immediately refrigerate eggs in the box at 45° or cooler. The wide ends are normally already up. Eggs stored at room termperature will lose more quality in one day than in a week under refrigeration.

~ Eggs are best used within 1 or 2 weeks but will keep without loss of nutrient value for up to 5 weeks. Hard-cooked eggs, likewise.

~ A cracked egg carries risk of bacteria, *salmonella* in particular. Do not eat it raw. Salmonella can be destroyed by sufficient cooking. Baking is the safest way to use a cracked egg. If you have misgivings, don't use it.

~ Gently wash, rinse, and dry eggs that are to be used raw to remove any surface contamination. Thoroughly wash hands and utensils after handling eggs.

~ Immediately refrigerate leftover cooked eggs or egg-based recipes such as custard or cream pie. Bacteria begins to grow rapidly at room temperature. Such food items should not be left unrefrigerated more than 2 hours maximum.

To receive a USDA-reviewed booklet prepared by the egg board, *Egg Handling & Care Guide*, send a self-addressed, stamped business or large sized envelope to: The Incredible Edible Egg 33, Box 733, Park Ridge, IL. 60068. Another helpful brochure to write for is *Answers to Often Asked Questions About Eggs*, American Egg Board, 1460 Renaissance Drive, Park Ridge, IL 60068.

THE SALMONELLA PROBLEM - WHAT TO DO?

There are two ways that salmonella can get into eggs, 1) through a crack, and 2) through the hens' ovaries. In recent years salmonella found in eggs by the latter means has given rise to public concern and the following recommendations: 1) Do not consume raw eggs, and 2) Cook eggs very well. These cautions are especially important for people most at risk for being seriously affected by salmonella--the very young, the elderly, pregnant women, and those whose immune systems have been compromised by a recent illness.

A well cooked egg, according to Michael E. St. Louis, MD, researcher at the Center for Disease Control in Atlanta, GA, means 7 minutes of boiling, 5 minutes for poaching, and 3 minutes on each side for frying. In other words, cook until both yolk and white are firm. What is the actual risk to using not such well cooked eggs? In 1990 Americans consumed 55 billion eggs. It is reported that one person died that year from salmonella-infected eggs. In 1994, although cases of sickness from salmonella from eggs was small, the increase from previous years has been dramatic, suggesting increased caution, especially for those most at risk.

Egg Cookery

Now that we have discussed the anatomy of an egg you'll know all the reasons for the directions given in egg recipes. Two words summarize egg cookery:

COOK GENTLY!

Do not cook eggs in the shell, or eggs with unbroken egg yolks in a microwave oven. Exploding hot eggs can cause serious harm! In fact I recommend you don't cook eggs at all in the microwave.

Soft or Hard Cooked Eggs

Start eggs in cold water from the tap to prevent cracking and do not boil. See Anatomy of an Egg, p. 132.

1. Optional: Prick a pinhole in large end of each egg to prevent cracking.

2. Place eggs in saucepan and cover completely with cold water from the tap.

3. Over high heat bring water just to a boil (bubbles will break the surface of the water).

4. Cover and remove from heat.

5. For **Soft cooked**: Let stand for **3-5 minutes**.
   Immediately remove from water.

   For **Hard cooked**: Let stand for **15-minutes**.
   Immediately place in cold water.

Serving Tip: To open a soft cooked egg, tap it around the center of shell and through the cooked egg with a table knife. Scoop the egg out of each half with the knife or a spoon.

Peeling Tip: The white of very fresh hard-cooked eggs will cling to the shell making them very hard to peel. Store them in the refrigerator a couple of days after cooking and they will be easy to peel.

Storage Tip: Lightly mark an X with a pencil on the wide end of each hard-cooked egg. Return to the egg box in refrigerator with the wide ends up. You'll know exactly which eggs are the cooked ones.

Per Large Egg (56 grams)
Exchanges: 1.5 Meat; 89 Calories, 7 g protein (32%), 6 g fat (65%), 240 mg cholesterol, 73 mg sodium, $.20 (@ $1.89 per doz.)

Poached Eggs

It is not neccesary to have an egg poacher to poach an egg. In fact, it is more work to wash the little egg poacher cups after removing the eggs, than it is to poach them in a pan of water. Fresh eggs will hold together better when poached than less fresh eggs.

Poach: To cook in simmering, but not boiling water or other liquid, so that the food does not lose its shape.

1. Fill saucepan with enough water to cover eggs about 1 inch.

2. Add **1 tablespoon apple cider vinegar.**

Why the vinegar? It will set the white so that it will hold together and can be easily scooped around the yolk. It will not discolor the eggs or give them any unpleasant taste.

3. Bring to a boil; turn heat down to keep water simmering.

4. Break an egg into the water holding shell close to the water and facing the side of the pan.

5. As the white begins to cook and turn white, scoop it together toward the yolk with a slotted spoon and toward the side of the pan.

6. Repeat with additional eggs; do not crowd the eggs.

7. Simmer eggs in water **3-5 minutes** until yolk is cooked as much as desired.

8. Remove eggs with slotted spoon.

Boil: To heat water or another liquid until bubbles rise up to break the surface continuousy and vigorously.

Simmer: To heat water or another liquid until tiny bubbles gradually rise from the bottom of the pan to the top without, or just barely, breaking the surface. This is just below boiling.

WAYS TO SERVE POACHED EGGS

~Over **buttered toast**
~On **English muffin** topped with **salsa** and **Parmesan cheese**
~On **toast or English muffin** with large **tomato slice, chives, green onion, or sweet basil leaves**
~Over **cooked asparagus or broccoli spears** on **toast**, topped with **cheese sauce** (*Main Dishes*, p. 155)

Scrambled Eggs

After experimenting with non-stick pans for
a couple of years, I have returned to my
"durable for a lifetime, guaranteed safe for health"
stainless steel pans. Scrambled eggs should be a delicately light
golden mass, moist, and not browned.

AMOUNT: 2 - 3 Eggs

1. Add to shallow saucepan or fry pan over moderately low heat:
   1½ teaspoons olive oil or butter *(extra virgin olive oil preferred, p.14)*

2. Whisk together thoroughly with a fork in a bowl:
   2 or 3 eggs
   1 tablespoon water or milk per egg
   ⅛ teaspoon salt, optional

   > The liquid whisked into the egg will "stretch"
   > the protein and make it more tender.

3. Evenly distribute heated oil or melted butter over surface of
   the pan and pour in the eggs. Be sure oil/butter is heated high
   enough before adding egg. Otherwise, the egg will replace the
   fat, moving it to the side of the pan, and the egg will stick.

4. When the eggs begin to set, push the cooked eggs to one
   side with edge of spatula to let uncooked eggs run underneath.
   You can also gently turn the eggs over, if you like, but don't stir
   the eggs; stirring scrambled eggs breaks them up into hard and
   unpleasant little lumps and pieces.

5. Remove eggs from heat when just barely set on the top--even
   a bit undercooked. Do not let the egg brown on the bottom.

6. Cover with lid until ready to serve.

Per 1 Egg using olive oil and water (salt and lecithin not included)
Exchanges: 1.25 Meat, 0.5 Fat; 99 Calories, 6 g protein (25%), 8 g fat (73%),
214 mg cholesterol, 65 mg sodium, $.20

Quantity cooking tip: For 2-3 eggs I use an 8" pan. If eggs are too
shallow in the pan, they cook too fast; if too thick (over 1¼" deep) they
cook too slowly requiring too much stirring. To scramble in a large
quantity, spray a baking pan with non-stick spray, cover bottom of pan
with melted butter or oil, add eggs and bake in 350° oven. When they
begin to cook around the outside edge, gently loosen them up and
carefully distribute. Continue, distributing the cooked eggs occasionally, until all are scrambled.

Gourmet Scramble

Light and very flavorful. So special, yet a cinch to make!

AMOUNT: 4 Eggs

1. Add to shallow saucepan or fry pan over moderately low heat:
   1 tablespoon unsalted butter *(p. 11)*

2. Whisk together thoroughly with a fork in a mixing bowl until evenly blended and evenly yellow:
   4 eggs
   ¼ cup sour cream *(fat-free preferred, p. 14)*
   ⅜ teaspoon salt
   ⅛ teaspoon dried tarragon leaves
   2 green onions with green tops, chopped diagonally

3. Scramble (see *Scrambled Eggs*, p. 140, if needed).

Per Egg with fat-free sour cream
   Exchanges: 1.25 Meat, 0.5 Fat; 115 Calories, 7 g protein (25%), 8.5 g fat (66%), (10%), 222 mg cholesterol, 265 mg sodium, $.25

Cheesy Egg Muffin

AMOUNT: 1 Serving

1. Top muffin with egg and cheese:
   toasted whole grain English muffin half *(p. 12 or 124)*
   scrambled egg *(p. 140)*
   2 tablespoons grated cheddar or jack cheese

2. Warm in oven, under broiler, or in toaster oven until cheese melts.

3. Garnish with a **dash of paprika** and/or **minced parsely** or with **chives, dried or fresh.**

Per Serving with 1 egg (garnish not included)
   Exchanges: 2.25 Meat, 1.25 Bread, 0.5 Fat; 239 Calories, 13 g protein (22%), 13 g fat (50%), 17 g carbohydrate (28%; 1 g sugars), 2 g dietary fiber, 229 mg cholesterol, 340 mg sodium, $.45

VARIATIONS
For added flavor, add **diced green chiles, chopped green onion, sliced mushooms,** or whatever you desire when cooking the egg or on top of the egg before melting cheese over the top.

Breakfast Burritos

AMOUNT: 4 Burritos

1. Grate **½ cup cheddar cheese**; set aside.

2. Optional (or do #6 below); wrap tortillas in foil and warm in 300-350° oven just to heat through, about 10 minutes (not too long):
   4 whole wheat or corn tortillas *(see breads, p. 11)*

3. Cook until just tender in oil over moderately low heat:
   1 tablespoon olive oil
   ½ cup chopped green pepper
   ½ cup chopped onion
   1 cup sliced fresh mushrooms, optional

4. Whisk together with a fork in mixing bowl until evenly mixed:
   4 eggs
   3 tablespoons sour cream *(fat-free preferred, p. 14)* **or nonfat milk**
   ⅜ teaspoon salt

5. Scramble the eggs (p. 140). As eggs are cooking sprinkle **¼ teaspoon cumin powder** over the top (If added to egg before cooking, cumin will clump together and not blend). Cover eggs to keep warm.

6. Optional (or do #2 above): Warm tortillas, one at a time in a hot fry pan or directly over gas burner, flipping them over to prevent burning or over-browning.

7. Put the ingredients in bowls on the table for self-assembly, or assemble in advance, dividing vegetables, cheese, and eggs onto the tortillas. Add **salsa** if desired. Fold up as for burritos.

8. Serve with **sour cream, plain yogurt**, or *Guacamole* (*Main Dishes*, p. 229), if desired.

See Menu Suggestions, p. 143.

Per Burrito with mushrooms (ingredients in #8 not included)
Exchanges: 1.25 Meat, 1.75 Bread, 0.75 Fat, 0.5 Vegetable; 250 Calories, 10.5 g protein (17%), 12 g fat (43%), 25 g carbohydrate (40%; 1.5 g sugars), 3 g dietary fiber, 214 mg cholesterol, 377 mg sodium, $.50

VARIATION
Omit mushrooms. Prepare **½ lb.** *Breakfast Sausage* (p. 230); brown and crumble it in fry pan; assemble in Burritos.

Scrambled Egg Enchiladas

As well as a hearty breakfast, these will serve for an economy dinner.

AMOUNT: 4 Enchiladas
Bake 450°F (235°C) -10 to 12 minutes, uncovered

1. Grate ½ **cup jack or cheddar cheese**; set aside.

2. Combine in mixing bowl for sauce:
   8 oz. can (1 cup) tomato sauce
   half 4 oz. can diced green chiles, drained,
   or ¼ cup chopped green pepper
   2 green onions with tops, chopped
   ¼ cup toasted wheat germ *(p. 15)*

3. Whisk together thoroughly with fork in separate bowl; scramble briefly in fry pan:
   4 eggs
   ¼ cup sour cream *(fat-free preferred, p. 14)* **or nonfat (skim) milk**
   half the grated cheese (¼ cup)
   ¼ teaspoon dried oregano leaves
   ⅛ teaspoon salt

4. Fill **4 whole wheat tortillas**, placing on one side of each:
   2 tablespoons sauce
   ¼ of the scrambled eggs (about ⅜ cup)

5. Roll up and place seam side down in 8" or 9" square baking dish, sprayed or greased (p. 271). Top with **remaining sauce.**

6. Bake uncovered in oven at 450° for 10-12 minutes to warm through. Top the last 5 minutes of baking with **remaining grated cheese (¼ cup).** Serve with **remaining chiles**, if desired.

Per Enchilada   Exchanges: 2.25 Meat, 2 Bread, 1 Vegetable; 306 Calories, 16 g protein (22%), 13 g fat (38%), 31 g carbohydrate (40%; 3 g sugars), 4 g dietary fiber, 229 mg cholesterol, 617 mg sodium, $.70

Menu Suggestions

Breakfast
   Scrambled Egg Enchiladas
   Pineapple Wedges
   Optional: Breakfast Beans (p. 156)
      or Refried Beans (**Main Dishes**, p. 64)
Dinner
   Scrambled Egg Enchiladas
   Refried Beans
   Tossed Salad

143

Sun-Up Fried Eggs

I prefer to use stainless steel rather than non-stick pans for eggs (see comment on Scrambled Eggs, p.140). I use as little fat as possible to prevent sticking, so the eggs will need to be loosened carefully from the bottom of the pan. This method of cooking fried eggs allows less fat and a lower temperature for even cooking. Use a pan with a proper fitting lid so that steam may be created inside.

1. Warm oil or butter in a shallow sauce-pan or fry pan over moderate heat (do not let butter brown):
   ½ teaspoon olive oil *(preferred, p. 14)*
   or unsalted butter

2. Tilt pan to evenly distribute fat. Break eggs into pan, or break one at a time into a bowl first, if desired.

3. Turn heat to low. As soon as white begins to cook, add **½ teaspoon water** to the pan for each egg.

4. Cover pan. Cook **3-5 minutes** to desired doneness.

Per Egg with ¼ teaspoon olive oil   Exchanges: 1.25 Meat, 0.5 Fat; 99 Calories, 6 g protein (25%), 8 g fat (73%), 214 mg cholesterol, 65 mg sodium, $.20

Egg Frames

A fun recipe for kids! A fried egg in the toast.

1. For 1 serving lightly toast the bread; butter on both sides:
   1 slice whole grain bread, toasted lightly
   1½ teaspoons *Butter Spread* *(p. 264)* **or butter** (half on each side)

2. Cut a 2" circle or cookie cutter shape out of center of toast (a non-stick spray can lid works perfectly for a circle); set aside.

3. Heat oil or butter in fry pan over moderately low heat. Place buttered toast in pan; break egg into cut-out center of toast; cover pan with lid and cook egg to desired doneness:
   ¼ - ½ teaspoon olive oil *(preferred, p. 14)* **or butter** (allow to melt)
   1 egg

4. Blend and serve over the top of egg:
   reserved toast circle, crumbled
   1½ teaspoons Parmesan cheese
   sprig of parsley, minced

Per Serving with ¼ teaspoon olive oil
   Exchanges: 1.5 Meat, 1.25 Bread, 1.5 Fat, 0.25 Vegetable; 247 Calories, 11 g protein (18%), 15 g fat (54%), 17 g carbohydrate (28%; 1 g sugars), 2 g dietary fiber, 223 mg cholesterol, 316 mg sodium, $.35

Omelets

Omelets are my favorite way to serve eggs even though I am not an expert omelet maker. Therefore, I know you can do it too! Here are a few tips to give you a successful beginning. And don't worry over achieving perfection. They'll taste good anyway.

Purchasing an Omelet Pan

1. An omelet pan should have curved sides about 1½" high.

2. Special non-stick omelet pans are available everywhere. Choose a 7" or 8" omelet pan, good for cooking 2 or 3-egg omelets. Some pans are hinged for folding over the omelet. If you want to use your omelet pan for crepes as well, you won't want a hinged one.

3. I prefer a stainless steel omelet pan over non-stick for durability and for health reasons (It isn't exactly clear how non-stick finishes affect the food). Stainless steel omelet pans are harder to find. I bought mine at a restaurant supply company (easily located in the city). An oven-proof handle will allow for making fritattas (p. 150).

4. Reserve your omelet pan just for making omelets or crepes. This preserves the seasoned surface. Cooking other foods in it will interfere with the smooth transition of omelet or crepes from pan to serving plate.

Seasoning the Omelet Pan (Not necessary for non-stick pans)

This is a one-time process as long as you don't use the pan for anything else except crepes, and don't wash it out.

1. Wash the pan well in hot water with detergent; rinse.

2. Dry pan over low heat.

3. Add **1 tablespoon oil** *(I prefer using extra virgin olive oil)*

4. Heat over low heat until oil begins to smoke.

5. Distribute the oil over the inside of the pan with paper towel.

6. Remove pan from heat to cool.

7. Wipe away excess oil with paper towel.

8. After making omelets wipe pan out with a paper towel. Do not wash the pan. Rub surface with a little salt if egg gets stuck on.

2-Egg Omelet

These are the basic instructions for making a successful omelet. Once you've got the idea you'll only need to remember the basic proportions of the ingredients. For nutrient data, see p. 149.

AMOUNT: 2-Egg Omelet

Basic Ingredients:

    2 eggs
    2 teaspoons water
    ⅛ teaspoon pepper or drops Tabasco sauce, to taste
    ⅛ teaspoon salt
    1½ teaspoons to 1 tablespoon oil or unsalted butter
    2 tablespoons filling, as desired *(pp. 147-149)*

1. Prepare filling ingredients, cover, and set aside (see *Omelet Fillings,* pp.147-48).

2. Combine eggs, water, and seasonings; beat vigorously with a fork for 30 strokes.

3. Melt the oil or butter over medium high heat in omelet pan until butter is barely brown (oil won't brown). Heat serving plate.

4. Add eggs quickly and all at once.

5. Gently move the pan back and forth over burner while eggs cook. This will only be a minute or so.

6. When edges of omelet are cooked enough to lift, lift edge on one side tipping the pan to allow uncooked egg to run underneath the cooked edge. Keep doing this, shaking the pan a bit between each lift.

7. When practically no more runny egg remains on top, spread filling over center of omelet.

8. To fold the omelet (this step is best fully understood by doing):
   a) Tilt right side of pan off the heat with left hand holding pan handle.
   b) With metal spatula in right hand lift tilted side of omelet about ⅓ over other side with spatula.
   c) Rotate handle to right side and grasp with right hand.
   d) With quick flip of wrist turn omelet out onto hot plate; as you do this the omelet should automatically fold over the un-covered portion. Don' t worry if it doesn't come out exactly right; this takes repeated practice.

9. Spoon over the top any remaining filling or other ingredients desired. Keep warm in oven until ready to serve.

Omelet Fillings

To fold an omelet easily only a very little filling can be added--about 2 teaspoons filling per egg. This seems pretty chintzy to me, so I always make more, sneak in a little extra, and top the finished omelet with the rest. First for basic instructions, then some filling choices.

1. Choose **2 - 4 vegetables** you have on hand.

2. Chop vegetables into small pieces.

3. Lightly cook chopped vegetables in **1 tablespoon oil or water.**

4. Cover and set aside.

5. Have on hand some **grated cheddar or Parmesan cheese,** if desired, to sprinkle over finished folded omelet (or it can be added before folding).

For 2 or 3-Egg Omelet

Choose 2 - 4 vegetables such as:
    cooked leftover potato - ½ to 1 small
    tomato - 1 small or ½ large
    zucchini - ⅓ small
    a green onion, including green tops
    green or red pepper - a ring or two chopped
    fresh mushrooms, 3 small or 2 large
    celery - ⅓ to ½ rib
    onion - 2 - 3 tablespoons minced
    parsley sprig, minced, or chopped fresh chives
    cooked spinach - up to ½ cup, drained, chopped
    asparagus spears - 2 or 3 cooked
    avocado - ¼ - ⅓ diced (a few wedges for garnish are elegant)
    salsa, to taste

Choose ⅛ - ¼ **teaspoon herbs or seasoning (1 or 2)**; add to vegetables while cooking, or sprinkle over egg while cooking:
    sweet basil leaves
    dried chives
    dried parsley
    dill weed
    Spike Seasoning *(p. 14)*
    Salad Herbs
    Italian Seasoning
    cumin
    curry powder
    garlic powder
    chili powder

Omelet Fillings

Follow the basic suggestions for amount and cooking, p. 147.

Spinach Mushroom *Our favorite!*

cooked spinach
fresh mushrooms
1-2 tablespoons light cream cheese
  or kefir cheese *(p. 13)*

Mexicana *Zippy!*

diced green or jalepeño chiles (I use canned)
diced tomato
minced onion
Top finished omelet with:

  grated cheddar cheese
  avocado wedges
  hot salsa

Potato Hearty *A good way to use a bit of leftover potato.*

leftover cooked potato, diced
diced celery
minced onion
sweet basil, curry, or *Spike Seasoning* *(p. 14)*

Vegetable Patch

zucchini
green or red pepper or pimiento
green onion
celery
your favorite herbs
Top finish omelet, if desired, with:

  tomato wedges
  mound of alfalfa sprouts
  salsa or sour cream *(fat-free or light preferred, p. 14)*

Sausage Pizzeria

cooked *Breakfast Sausage* *(p.234)***, crumbled**
diced green pepper
diced onion
chopped mushrooms
chopped or sliced ripe olives, optional
Top finished omelet with:

  grated cheddar cheese
  warmed tomato sauce seasoned with *Italian Seasoning*
Set in hot oven a minute or two to melt cheese.

148

Chinese

mung bean sprouts
celery (thinly sliced on diagonal)
green onion
shredded chicken or beef, or tuna, optional
Serve with **soy sauce**.

Sea-Going Salmon

canned salmon
green onion
1-2 tablespoons light cream cheese
 or kefir cheese *(p. 13)*

Strawberry Surpise

Omit pepper or Tabasco from egg; Add:
fresh strawberries, thinly sliced
sprinkle crystalline fructose *(p. 12)* **over berries**
Top finished omelet with:
dollop of light sour cream or blended yogurt-sour cream

A Dab 'll Do Ya!

Don't overlook main dish leftover dabs to fill an omelet. You might even get a second main meal from just a little leftovers with egg. Here are a few good leftover choices to get your imagination working:

Chili (Main Dishes, pp. 60, 190)
Sloppy Joe Sauce (Main Dishes, p. 200)
Chicken Curry (Main Dishes, p. 110; **Meals in Minutes**, p. 26)
Chicken or Tuna a la King (Main Dishes, p. 116)
Breakfast Beans (p. 156)
Lentil Rice Casserole (Main Dishes, p. 68)

OMELET NUTRIENTS

Per 2-Egg Plain Omelet made with 1½ teaspoons olive oil
 Exchanges: 2.75 Meat, 1.25 Fat; 219 Calories, 12 g protein (23%),
18 g fat (75%), 0 g dietary fiber, 428 mg cholesterol, 395 mg sodium, $.40
 ½ cup Vegetables: Add 1 Vegetable Exchange, 25 Calories
 1 tablespoon Oil to cook vegetables: Add 2 Fat Exchanges, 100 Calories
 1 tablespoon Grated Cheese: Add 0.25 Meat Exchange, 27 Calories
 ¼ cup each: Salmon - Add 1.25 Meat Exhange, 81 Calories; Chicken - Add 1 Meat Excange,
 63 Calories; Ground Turkey - Add 1.75 Meat Exchange, 108 Calories
 1 tablespoon each.: Nonfat Sour cream - Add 0.25 Fat Exchange, 9 Calories;
 Light Sour Cream - Add 0.5 Fat Exchange, 23 Calories
 1 tablespoon Light Cream Cheese: Add 0 .75 Fat Exhange, 36 Calories
 1 tablespoon Kefir Cheese: Add 1.5 Fat Exchange, 70 Calories

Zucchini Fritatta

"Frittata" is the Italian word for omelet. All the ingredients are blended together with the eggs. The egg mixture is then cooked and served without folding. The top of the eggs are cooked either by covering the pan with a lid or setting the pan, uncovered, under the broiler for 5-10 minutes until lightly browned.

AMOUNT: 2 - 4 Servings (4 Eggs[1])

1. Cook vegetables in oil until tender, about 5-7 minutes in fry pan or omelet pan; add to eggs (#2 below):
   1 tablespoon olive oil
   ¼ cup chopped onion
   1 small zucchini, unpeeled, diced
   1 clove garlic, minced

2. Whisk together thoroughly with a fork:
   4 eggs
   ¼ cup Parmesan cheese
   ¼ cup toasted wheat germ *(p. 15)* **or bread crumbs**
   1 tablespoon minced parsley
   ½ teaspoon sweet basil leaves
   cooked vegetables (#1 above)

3. In the same pan you cooked the vegetables, add:
   1 tablespoon olive oil

4. Heat pan over moderate heat and add egg mixture. When
   bottom of the eggs begin to cook firmly enough to lift edges
   without tearing, tilt pan and lift edges with a metal spatula to let
   uncooked egg run underneath.

5 When most of the egg is cooked, lower heat and cover the pan
   about 3 minutes to finish cooking the top just until set. Eggs on
   the bottom will be browned.

6. Loosen the egg from the pan and slide onto a plate. Cut
   in wedges to serve.

[1]For best results use 8-8½" pan for 3 eggs, 9-9½" pan for 4 eggs, 10-10½" pan
for 6 eggs. Adjust other ingredient amounts accordingly. A pan with curved
sides facilitates easy removal of fritatta. See *Omelet Pans*, p. 145.

Per 1 Egg Serving
   *Exchanges: 1.75 Meat, 0.25 Bread, 1.25 Fat, 0.25 Vegetable; 194 Calories, 10 g protein (22%),
14 g fat (67%), 6 g carbohydrate (12%; 1 g sugars), 2 g dietary fiber, 218 mg cholesterol,
160 mg sodium, $.40*

VARIATIONS
1. Substitute very small **broccoli pieces** for zucchini.
2. Use any of the **Omelet Fillings**, *pp. 148-49.*

150

Tofu Scramble

*Even if not allergic to eggs, this is a
tasty alternative! Please don't expect
it to look like scrambled eggs, however.
Tofu contains no cholesterol.*

AMOUNT: 4 Servings

1. Drain thoroughly, at least 30 minutes, between paper towel
   on a large dinner plate:
   1 lb. firm or regular tofu *(p.15)*

2. Mash tofu coarsely with a fork on a clean, dry plate; place in
   a mixing bowl; blend in:
   2 - 4 tablespoons *Liquid Aminos,*[1] *to taste*
   ½ teaspoon dry mustard
   4 sliced fresh mushrooms
   1 chopped green onion
   1 green chile, canned, finely diced

3. Heat fry pan over moderate heat; add and coat bottom of
   pan with:
   1 tablespoon olive oil or butter (do not allow to brown)

4. Add tofu mixture. Cover and cook over medium heat about
   15 minutes or until a bit set.

5. Top with:
   ½ cup grated cheddar, jack, or mozzarella cheese
   paprika garnish

6. Serve, as desired, with:
   ketsup
   barbecue sauce
   salsa

Per Serving of 4
  *Exchanges: 2 Meat, 0.25 Bread, 1.25 Fat, 0.25 Vegetable; 166 Calories,
13.5 g protein (29%), 12.5 g fat (60%), 5 g carbohydrate (11%; 1 g sugars),
15 mg cholesterol, 439 mg sodium, $.70*

[1]**Bragg liquid Aminos** is a liquid similar to soy sauce derived from
fermented soybeans but has no added salt. It is a tasty seasoning high in
protein. Purchase at a health food store. See also under Sue's Kitchen
Magic Seasoning, p. 15.

Lumberjack Potatoes 'n Kasha

For active workers who like a he-man breakfast of eggs and hash browns. Serve with poached or fried eggs for perfect compliment (along with the ketsup).

AMOUNT: 6 Servings

1. Bring to boil and cook at low boil for **5-6 minutes:**
   2¾ cups water
   1½ cups diced raw potatoes (unpeeled preferred)

2. Add:
   1 cup uncooked kasha (toasted buckwheat)
   (*see grains, p. 13, or to make your own kasha, see p. 74*)
   1 teaspoon salt

3. Cover, reduce heat to low and simmer **10-15 minutes** or until all the water is absorbed and kasha is tender.

4. Meanwhile, saute onion and garlic in oil until tender and add seasonings:
   ¼ cup oil (*extra virgin olive oil preferred, p. 14*)
   1 medium onion, slivered or chopped
   1 clove garlic, minced, or 1/8 teaspoon garlic powder
   2 teaspoons dill weed
   ½ teaspoon paprika

5. Fold in potato-kasha mixture and cook about **5 minutes** longer.

6. Optional--To serve, mound on plates, make a well in the center and set a poached or fried egg in it; garnish with:
   paprika
   minced parsley or chives, fresh or dried

Per serving (of 6)
    Exchanges: 1.75 Bread, 1.75 Fat, 0.25 Vegetable; 212 Calories, 4.5 g protein (8%), 10 g fat (40%), 29 g carbohydrate (52%; 2 g sugars), 3 g dietary fiber, 0 mg cholesterol, 359 mg sodium, $.40

Fried Sweet Potatoes or Yams

A refreshing change from fried potatoes! High in vitamin A.

AMOUNT: Allow ½ medium potato per serving
Bake: 400°F (205°C) - 1 hour

> **Timesaver Tip:** Bake potatoes, peel, place in covered container and refrigerate a day in advance. Also a great way to use leftover baked potatoes.

1. Scrub potatoes, pierce with fork, and bake on oven rack at 400° for 1 hour or until tender.

2. Cool potatoes enough to handle and peel. Refrigerate until cold.

3. Slice cold potatoes about ¼" thick or as desired.

4. Over moderate heat, melt in fry pan (do not brown):
   1½ - 2 tablespoons unsalted butter

5. Fry potato slices in single layer until lightly golden.

Per ½ Medium Sweet Potato (4.2 oz) with 2 teaspoons butter
  Exchanges: 3.25 Bread, 1.5 Fat; 302 Calories, 4 g protein (5%), 7.5 g fat (22%),
55 g carbohydrate (73%; sugar grams-NA), 6 g dietary fiber, 20 mg cholesterol, 24 mg sodium, $.55

Easy Fried Potatoes

Compared to hash browns, these require less fat and are much faster to make. Use leftover baked potatoes, or bake a couple extra when baking potatoes for dinner just to have on hand for breakfast.

AMOUNT: Allow 1 medium potato per serving

Melt butter in fry pan over moderate heat; add potatoes and fry, turning as they brown lightly:

   1 tablespoon butter (for a large amount of potatoes use more)
   cooked potatoes, peeled or unpeeled, ¼" slices (or as desired)

Per 1 Medium Unpeeled Potato (7 oz.) with 2 teaspoons butter
  Exchanges: 3.25 Bread, 1.5 Fat; 287 Calories, 5 g protein (6%), 7.5 g fat (23%),
51 g carbohydrate (70%; 7 g sugars), 4 g dietary fiber, 20 mg cholesterol, 16 mg sodium, $.45

Potato Tostadas

A great dish for a dinner as well as breakfast. Use leftover baked potatoes, or bake a couple extra when baking potatoes for dinner to have on hand for this recipe.

> **Timesaver Tip:** Prepare a day ahead and refrigerate: chopped cooked potatoes & onions, turkey sausage, blended sour cream and milk.

AMOUNT: 6 Tostadas

Bake Tortillas: 350°F (175°C) - 10 minutes

1. Preheat oven to 350°.

2. To crisp tortillas: rub each tortilla on both sides with oil using a piece of wax paper:
   6 stoneground corn tortillas *(see breads, p. 11)*
   ½ teaspoon canola or olive oil for each tortilla
   Set tortillas directly on oven rack and bake to desired crispness, about 10 minutes.

3. Steam the onion to cook it; add potatoes to heat through:
   ⅓ cup chopped onion
   2 cooked medium potatoes, peeled, chopped

4. Season and brown:
   ½ lb. *Breakfast Sausage* *(p. 234)*

5. Blend together:
   ½ cup sour cream *(fat-free preferred, p. 14)*
   2 tablespoons lowfat milk

6. Mix together
   1 medium avocado, mashed or chopped small
   2 teaspoons lemon juice
   ⅛ teaspoon salt, to taste

7. To serve, place ingredients in serving containers for self assembly. Layer in following order:
   tortilla
   mashed avocado
   breakfast sausage, crumbled
   potato-onion
   sour cream & salsa

See Menu Suggestions, p. 155.

Per Tostada with fat-free sour cream and 1 tsp. salsa -- Exchanges: 1 Meat, 0.25 Milk, 1.5 Bread, 1.25 Fat; 231 Calories, 12 g protein (19%), 10 g fat (35%), 29 g carbohydrate (46%; 4 g sugars), 3 g dietary fiber, 24 mg cholesterol, 263 mg sodium, $.50

154

Sweet Potato Sausage Bake

An unusual dish. Very tasty with eggs.

AMOUNT: 6 - 8 Servings
Bake covered: 375°F (190°C) - 50 to 60 minutes

1. Prepare the following ingredients:
   1 lb. *Breakfast Sausage*, browned *(p. 234)*
   1 - 1½ lbs. sweet potatoes or yams (thin ones),
   cut in small rounds
   3 red apples (Jonathan are good), **unpeeled, sliced**

2. Layer potatoes, apples, and browned breakfast sausage in a
   lightly greased 9" x 13" baking pan.

3. Combine and pour evenly over all:
   2 tablespoons honey
   4 teaspoons whole wheat pastry flour (other flour may be used)
   ½ teaspoon cinnamon
   ¼ teaspoon salt
   ½ cup water

4. Cover and bake at 375° for 50-60 minutes or until potatoes and
   apples are tender.

Per Serving of 8
Exchanges: 1.25 Meat, 0.5 Bread, 1.25 Fruit; 174 Calories, 12 g protein (27%), 4 g fat (21%), 24 g carbohydrate (52%; 12+ g sugars--sugar grams for sweet potatoe not available), 3 g dietary fiber, 35 mg cholesterol, 366 mg sodium, $.50

Menu Suggestions

Breakfast
Sweet Potato Sausage Bake
or Potato Tostadas
Scrambled Eggs
Pineapple Wedges
or Tomato Slices with Tostadas

Dinner
Sweet Potato Sausage Bake
or Potato Tostadas
Tossed Salad

155

Breakfast Beans

Cooked the day before, these only need to be reheated at breakfast. Beans with eggs is a very tasty combination. For alternative cooking methods using the pressure cooker or crock-pot, and for "degassing" beans see Main Dishes, pp. 58-59.

AMOUNT: 4 Cups

1. Soak beans in water several hours or overnight:
   2 cups uncooked pinto or black beans
   8 cups water

2. Drain beans and add as much fresh water as drained,   Bring just to a boil; reduce heat and simmer until tender, 2-3 hours. Add more water, if needed.

3. Meanwhile, cook in a little water:
   1 onion, chopped small

4. Drain beans, saving liquid and add:
   cooked onion
   1½ tablespoons chili powder
   2 teaspoons cumin powder
   1 teaspoon salt
   ⅛ teaspoon garlic powder

5. Blend part of the beans with some of the reserved bean liquid in electric mixer. Blend with unblended beans and as much extra reserved bean liquid as desired. Heat through thoroughly.

6. Optional: For added flavor, melt into beans:
   up to 4 tablespoons unsalted butter

Per ½ cup without optional butter
   Exchanges: 0.5 Meat, 1.5 Bread, 0.25 Vegetable; 144 Calories, 8 g protein (22%), 1 g fat (5%), 27 g carbohydrate (73%; 1 g sugars), 10 g dietary fiber, 0 mg cholesterol, 283 mg sodium, $.20

The Fruit Breakfast

On each side of the river stood the tree of life, bearing twelve crops of fruit, yielding its fruit every month. Revelation 22:2

THE FRUIT BREAKFAST

SUBJECTS

RECIPES

The Fruit Breakfast

Mixed Fresh Fruit Bowl
Toppings
(Yogurt, Granola or Nuts)
Hot Bread
(Muffin, Coffee Cake, Scone, Bagel)
Spread
(Jam, Butter)
Hot Beverage
(Herb Tea, Tea, Coffee, Hot Carob or Cocoa)

Nutrition Goals Menu[1]

1-1½ Servings Mixed Fruit Bowl (p. 172)
½-¾ cup Nonfat Plain Yogurt
(sweetened with ½ - 1 tbsp. honey)
1-2 tbsps. Chopped Almonds
1-2 Good Morning Muffins (p.104)

[1]*Small: $1.15*	*14% Fat*	*520 Calories*
[1]*Large: $1.85*	*16% Fat*	*899 Calories*

[1]This menu is included in the "Average of 7 Breakfasts" Column on the *Nutrition Goals Chart*, pp. 16-17. Small servings represent menu for adult female; large servings represent menu for adult male.

What are the Benefits of Fruits?

On each side of the river stood the tree of life, bearing twelve crops of fruit, yielding its fruit every month. Revelation 22:2

Vitamin A

(Beta carotene)

Infection fighter; healthy skin and body tissues; eye health; cancer and heart protection; promotes growth; shortens duration of diseases.

Vitamin C

Strengthens immune system; speeds healing; may lower cholesterol; strengthens blood vessels; regenerates collagen; improves brain function; builds resistance to environmental pollution.

Fruit Fibers

Beneficial for bowel regularity and maintaining appropriate blood cholesterol levels.

Water

Fruits have highest content of organic, chemically pure water, acting as cleansing foods.

160

What are the Benefits of Fruits?

Contain beneficial fruit acids

Fruit Acids

Citric, malic, tartaric, and oxalic acids act as powerful germicides, assisting the body in the elimination of toxins and impurities.

Wholesome natural sugar packs

Sugar

Fruits provide sugars in the most wholesome way possible, accompanied by appropriate fiber and a wide range of nutrients. To get these sugars in their health-giving form, all fruits should be eaten ripe.

Many high n mineral, potassium

Potassium

Maintains water balance with sodium; aids clear thinking; lowers blood pressure; promotes healthy heart muscle, kidneys, and nervous system.

Leave an alkaline-ash in the blood

Alkaline

Most Americans eat an over-abundance of acid producing foods. An appropriate balance of acid and alkaline producing foods maintains the proper pH balance in the body to prevent illness and disease.

What's in the Fruit?

FRUIT	PEAK SEASON	VIT. C	VIT. A[1]	DIETARY FIBER	OTHER MAJOR CONTRIBUTIONS
apple (1 med. w/skin) apple (1 med. peeled)	Sept. - May	L - 8 mg.	L - 70 I.U.	**3.3 gr.** 2.7 gr.	pectin; some B-vitamins; malic acid
apricots (3)	June - July	L - 2 mg.	**H - 2,770 I.U.**	2.0 gr.	potassium; malic acid
avocado (½ med.)	year round	L - 7 mg.	M - 534 I.U.	2.2 gr.	potassium, some B-vitamins, phosphorus, high quality unsaturated fat
banana (1 med.)	year round	M - 12 mg.	M - 230 I.U.	2.5 gr.	most easily digested and assimilated of all fruits; potassium, magnesium; fair source of calcium, phosphorus, iron, B-1, B-2, pectin
blackberries (½ cup)	July - Sept.	**H - NA**	M - NA	3.0 gr.	potassium; pectin: fair source of calcium, phosphorus, vitamin E; some B-vitamins, malic acid
blueberries (½ cup)	May - Aug.	M - 10 mg.	L - 75 I.U.	1.8 gr.	iron, manganese; pectin: some potassium: calcium: phosphorus: some B-vitamins
cherries, sweet (10)	May - Aug.	L - 3 mg.	L - 150 I.U.	1.3 gr.	iron, copper, manganese: some potassium, calcium. phosphorus: malic, citric acids
coconut, dried (1 Tbsp.)	year round	none	none	1.4 gr.	2.5 grams fat

Food (serving)	Season				Comments
cranberries (½ cup)	Sept. - Jan.	M - 10 mg.	none	0.4 gr.	citric acid
dates (2)	year round	none	L - 8 I.U.	1.5 gr.	high energy value: potassium, iron; some B-vitamins, calcium
figs, dried (3)	year round	L - 0.23 mg.	L - 114 I.U.	**9.5 gr.**	restorative in recovery from illness; contributes to healthy muscles, strength; potassium, calcium, iron, magnesium; some B-vitamins, zinc, copper
grapefruit, pink (½ med)	Oct. - April	**H - 47 mg.**	M - 318 I.U.	1.6 gr.	5 times more vit. A than white grapefruit; fair source of potassium; some calcium, phosphorus; malic acid
grapes (½ cup)	June - Nov.	L - 3 mg.	L - 75 I.U.	0.5 gr.	some potassium, calcium, phosphorus, B-vitamins
kiwi (1)	June - Dec.	**H - 174 mg.**	L - 70 I.U.	2.0 gr.	citric acid
mango (½ med.)	June - July	H - 29 mg.	**H - 4,030 I.U.**	1.2 gr.	potassium, iron, niacin; fair source of calcium, phosphorus
melon casaba (1/10 med.) honeydew (1/10 med.) cantaloupe (1/6 med.) watermelon (1 cup)	May - Oct. June - Oct. June - Sept. May - Sept.	H - 26 mg. M - 11 mg. **H - 30 mg.** M - 15 mg.	L - 49 I.U. L - 70 I.U. **H - 3,066 I.U.** M - 590 I.U.	0.5 1 1.1 1.4	potassium; 90% water

Abbreviation key: mg=milligrams; I.U.=International Units; gr.=grams; L=low; M=moderate; H=high; NA=Not available

FRUIT	PEAK SEASON	VIT. C	VIT. A[1]	DIETARY FIBER	OTHER MAJOR CONTRIBUTIONS
nectarine (1 med.)	June - Sept.	**H - 74 mg.**	L - 148 I.U.	**3.3 gr.**	potassium; some calcium; phosphorus
orange (1 med.)	Dec. - April	**H - 70 mg.**	L - 270 I.U.	2.4 gr.	potassium, calcium, phosphorus, folic acid; pectin; citric acid
papaya (½ med.)	year round	**H - 94 mg.**	**H - 3,060 I.U.**	1.4 gr.	enzyme papain aids digestion; potassium; some calcium, phosphorus, iron; some B-vitamins
peach (1 med.)	May - Oct.	L - 7 mg.	**H - 1,300 I.U.**	1.4 gr.	potassium, niacin; malic acid
pear, unpeeled (1 med.)	Aug. - Oct.	L - 7 mg.	L - 30 I.U.	**4.1 gr.**	high fiber; pectin
persimmon (1 med.)	Oct. - Dec.	M - 13 mg.	**H - 3,640 I.U.**	2.5 gr.	calcium, potassium, phosphorus
pineapple (½ cup)	year round	M - 12 mg.	L - 17 I.U.	1.2 gr.	potassium; enzyme bromelain aids digestion; some B-vitamins; malic, tartaric acids
plum (1 med.)	June - Sept.	L - 6 mg.	M - 210 I.U.	1.6 gr.	potassium, calcium, iron; small amounts B-vitamins; malic, oxalic acids
prunes (3)	year round	L - 1 mg.	M - 420 I.U.	1.6 gr.	potasssium, iron; good source of B-vitamins

raisins (¼ cup)	year round	L - 1 mg.	L - 3 I.U.	1.9 gr.	high energy food; potassium, iron, B-vitamins
raspberries (½ cup)	June - July	M - 15 mg.	L - 80 I.U.	**3.2 gr.**	some B-vitamins; malic, citric acids
strawberries (½ cup)	May - June	**H - 42 mg.**	L - 20 I.U.	1.4 gr..	potassium, calcium, iron, phosphorus, some B-vitamins; malic, citric acids
tangerine (1)	Oct. - Jan.	**H - 26 mg.**	M - 770 I.U.	1.7 gr.	potassium; small amounts of calcium, phosphorus
tomato (1 med.)	May - Oct.	**H - 25 mg.**	**H - 1,278 I.U.**	2.0 gr.	potassium, phosphorus, some B-vitamins; malic, oxalic acids

[1]VITAMIN A Plant foods do not contain vitamin A in the form required by the human body. They contain provitamin A, called beta carotene. The body converts beta carotene into vitamin A.

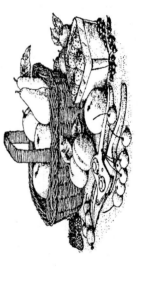

165

Fruit Nutrient Summary

 ### Highest *Vit. C* Fruits

kiwi, 174 mg.[1]
papaya, 94 mg.
nectarine, 74 mg.
orange, 70 mg.
grapefruit, 47 mg.
strawberries, 42 mg.

cantaloupe, 30 mg.
mango, 28 mg.
casaba melon, 26 mg.
tangerine, 26 mg.
tomato, 25 mg.
blackberries, NA

 ### Highest *Vit. A* Fruits

(Beta carotene)

mango, 4,030 mg.
persimmon, 3,640 mg.
cantaloupe, 3,066 mg.
papaya, 3,060 mg.

apricots, 2,770 mg.
peach, 1,300 mg.
tomato, 1,278 mg.

 ### Highest *Fiber* Fruits

2+ grams dietary fiber per average serving[1]

apple
apricots
avocado
banana
blackberries
figs

kiwi
nectarine
orange
pear
persimmon
raspberries

 ### Available *Year Round*

(Not necessarily peak season)

apples
bananas
dates
coconut, dried
figs, dried
papaya

pineapple
prunes
raisins
oranges
avocado

[1]Milligrams per average serving (see chart, pp. 162-165 for serving size)

Fruit Trivia

Answers on p. 170.   Fruits may be repeated.

1 A homely brown fuzzy fruit on the outside, but gorgeous on the inside, this fruit is a good illustration of *1 Samuel 16:7.*

2 A fruit whose name means *an apple with many seeds.*

3 90-95% of this fruit crop is produced by cutting bunches of grapes from the vine and laying them on paper mats between the vineyard rows, a process called sun-drying.

4 The ripening of this fruit is inhibited if put in the refrigerator although the peeling will turn black.

5 250 varieties of these are grown in the U.S.A.   14 of them provide 90% of the commercially available supply. Name some varieties.

6 A fruit the prophet *Isaiah* used to heal Hezekiah of a fatal boil (*2 Kings 20:7*).

7 This fruit, which is half the size of an orange, contains more than twice the vitamin C, and more potassium than a banana.

8 A high energy food historically loved by sportsmen.

9 A fruit that must have been in the Garden of Eden (*Genesis 3:7*).

10 A citrus fruit that is actually riper and often sweeter if its peeling is slightly green because when ripe on the tree it pulls some of the chlorophyll from the tree stems and leaves into its peeling--a process called *regreening.*

11 Two fresh fruits that are not best eaten tree-ripened.

12 This fruit is actually an edible leaf that is classified as an herb.

13 The best selling fruit in America.

14 The fruit most accused of coming from the *tree of the knowledge of good and evil,* but not mentioned in *Genesis 2:16, 2, 6.*

15 A high fat fruit with a hard and hairy shell.

167

Fruit Trivia

Answers on p. 170. Fruits may be repeated.

16 This fruit contains the highest amount of *levulose*, the sweetest of all sugars.

17 A beautiful yellow-orange tropical fruit that is soft and juicy when ripe and easier eaten off the seed than to cut it off.

18 A type of fig that gets its name from California and from Smyrna in Turkey where it came from.

19 Three fruits the desert-wandering Israelites brought back from an exploration trip to the land of Canaan (*Numbers 13:23*).

20 An enzyme, *papain*, that digests protein is extracted from this fruit when it is unripe.

21 A fig whose ancestor fig was brought to the New World by the mission fathers.

22 A fruit that appears prominantly in the temple furnishings built by King Solomon (*1 Kings 7:18, 20, 42*).

23 The only four fruits (with the exception of a few minor berries) native to the continental United States.

24 The edible part of this fruit is its seeds. This fruit will keep whole about 1 week, but if the seeds are removed and stored in the freezer they will keep indefinitely.

25 This tree bears 12 crops of fruit, and its leaves are for the healing of the nations (*Revelation 22:2*).

26 This fruit grows on a giant herb plant that can grow 25 feet tall, but it does not grow on trees.

27 98% of the American crop of this fruit is grown in California, but originally it came from Southwest France in 1856.

28 The fiber of this fruit helps to clean the teeth and massage the gums.

29 These 2 fruits grow on palm trees.

30 Among this wonder fruit's multiple benefits is its usefulness in treating colds, sore throats, coughs, heartburn, rheumatism, diptheria, scurvy, and asthma.

31 This apple variety is America's favorite--75 million bushels a year.

Fruit Trivia

Answers on p. 170.   Fruits may be repeated.

32 In parts of Africa and the Caribbean this fruit comes from a plant called *The Medicine Tree*. All parts of the plant, including the fruit, have many health-giving properties.

33 This fruit has the highest content of natural sugar of all dried fruits.

34 Classified as a berry, the word, *berry*, is not found in its name.

35 A fresh fruit that contains the enzyme, *bromelin*, that aids in digestion.

36 A mere 8% of this fruit crop is sold fresh. Unless fully ripened on the tree when harvested, it will not have good flavor.

37 The most perishable of fruits, these need to be eaten within a day or two of picking or purchase.

38 Like fresh pineapple, this fresh fruit contains an enzyme that will prevent gelatin from gelling.

39 A fruit that was unripe yesterday, will be overripe tomorrow, and perfectly ripe today.

40 Health enthusiasts who advocate food combining suggest that this watery, fast-digesting group of fruits be eaten alone.

41 Two fruits that are seldom eaten by Americans for breakfast. One of them is a popular breakfast item in Great Britain, served cut in half and broiled.

42 *An _____ a day keeps the doctor away* is not a bad saying!

Fruit Trivia - Answers

1 kiwi
2 pomegranate
3 raisins
4 bananas
5 apples
6 fig
7 kiwi
8 figs
9 figs

10 oranges
11 bananas
   pears
12 pineapple
13 bananas
14 apple
15 coconut
16 pear
17 mango
18 Calimyrna Fig

19 figs, grapes
   pomegranates
20 papaya
21 Black Mission Figs
22 pomegranate
23 blueberries, concord
   grapes, cranberries
   American persimmons
24 pomegranate
25 tree of life

26 banana
27 prunes
28 apples
29 coconuts
   dates
30 lemons
31 red delicious
32 papaya
33 dates
34 orange

35 pineapple
36 apricots
37 berries
38 kiwi
39 pear

40 melons
41 avocado
   tomato
42 apple

What to Do About Those Chemicals

According to most authorities, much of the pesticides used on unwaxed fruits can be removed by washing under running water and, when appropriate, scrubbing with a good vegetable brush. Some also recommend using detergent, but I don't recommend it, unless an all-purpose cleaner such as *Amway LOC* or *Shaklee Basic H* is used. Be sure to rinse thoroughly. It is a good policy to wash off fruits with inedible peelings, as well, before peeling them.

Waxed fruits and vegetables are best peeled since the wax tends to seal pesticides and chemicals into the skin, and the wax itself is almost impossible to entirely remove. Health food stores carry natural cleaners to reduce waxes, chemicals, and pesticides, such as *Dr. Donsbach's Superoxy Food Wash* or *Nature Clean All Purpose Dr. Donsbach's Superoxy Food Wash* or *Nature Clean All Purpose*

4 Ways . . . . . .
to minimize the pesticide and chemical
residues in fruits and vegetables

● Grow your own fruit.

● Purchase domestically grown fruit.
Generally less treated than imported produce.

● Purchase in-season and locally grown fruits.
The shorter the distance to the consumer, generally
the less treated with chemicals to preserve freshness.

● Purchase organically grown fruit.
Sources include some health food stores, food co-ops,
some supermarkets, local organic farms, and fruit stands.

Mixed Fruit Bowl

*Combine year-round bananas and apples
with in-season fruits.*

2 Servings

Combine:

> **1 banana, sliced**
> **1 peeled or unpeeled apple, chopped**
> **1 cup seasonal fruit, or 1 piece, chopped**
>   (orange, pear, peach, pineapple, grapes, etc)
> **2 - 4 tablespoons raisins or chopped dates**
> **1 teaspoon honey blended with a little lemon juice, optional**

Per Serving with 1 orange as the seasonal fruit
  *Exchanges: 4.25 Fruit; 150 Calories, 2 g protein (4%), 38 g carbohydrate (92%; 35 g sugars),
4.5 g dietary fiber, 0 mg cholesterol, 2 mg sodium, $.35*

Grape preparation tip: We enjoy seedless grapes
more in a fruit bowl if they are cut in half.

Melon Ball Bowl

*To get the full cleansing and nutritional benefit of
melons, it is best to eat them alone, or 20-30
minutes before the rest of the meal.*

Combine any in-season variety of melon, cut in balls or chunks:

> **watermelon**
> **cantaloupe**
> **honeydew melon**
> **casaba melon**
> **crenshaw melon**
> **a little lime or lemon juice**

Per 1 Cup
  *Exchanges: 1.25 Fruit; 51 Calories, 0.5 g fat (5%), 12 g carbohydrate (87%; 10.5 g sugars), 2
g dietary fiber, 0 mg cholesterol, 16 mg sodium, $.25*

Mint Leaf Garnish: Fresh mint leaves add an
elegant touch to any fruit bowl. Get a starter
mint plant from friend or nursery and plant
it in a corner of your yard. You will soon have
a plentiful supply of mint leaves. They need
no attention to grow except sun and soil.

Apple Breakfast Treat

This is a true meusli - more fruit than cereal, and is surprisingly filling. It is one of our favorite warm weather breakfasts.

1 Serving

1. Soak oats in water overnight:
   1 tablespoon rolled oats, uncooked
   3 tablespoons water

2. Just before serving blend in remaining ingredients except almonds; top with almonds:
   3 tablespoons nonfat or lowfat yogurt
   1 teaspoon lemon juice
   1 teaspoon honey
   1 tart apple, grated (unpeeled or peeled, as desired)
   2 teaspoons almonds (chopped, slivered, or sliced)

Per Serving with unpeeled apples
Exchanges: 0.25 Milk, 0.25 Bread, 0.5 Fat, 3 Fruit; 190 Calories, 4.5 g protein (9%), 3.5 g fat (16%), 36 g carbohydrate (74%; 31 g sugars), 5.5 g dietary fiber, 0 mg cholesterol, 28 mg sodium, $.45

VARIATION

Use **1 cup fresh berries** in place of grated apple.

Citrus Ambrosia

A vitamin C gold mine.
Use a well-sharpened knife!

2 Servings

Mix together:
   1 orange (peel, section, cut into chunks)
   1 small grapefruit (peel, section, cut into chunks)
   1 tablespoon coconut (shredded, unsweetened, toasted (optional)
   1 tablespoon almonds (chopped, slivered, or sliced)

Per Serving (½ Recipe)
Exchanges: 0.5 Fat, 1.25 Fruit; 82 Calories, 2 g protein (8%), 3 g fat (29%), 14 g carbohydrate (63%; 11 g sugars), 3 g dietary fiber, 0 mg cholesterol, 1 mg sodium, $.30

Papaya Pineapple Delight

A delectably creamy blend. Kefir cheese is a creamy spread similar to cream cheese with a little tang. Purchase at a health food store.

2 Servings

Blend first two ingredients and fold into the fruit:
> **½ cup nonfat or lowfat plain yogurt**
> **½ cup kefir cheese** *(p. 13)* **or sour cream** *(p. 14)*
> **1 cup fresh pineapple chunks**
> **½ cup papaya** (peeled, seeded, cut into chunks)

Per Serving (½ Recipe) with kefir cheese
> *Exchanges: 0.25 Milk, 3 Fat, 1.25 Fruit; 218 Calories, 6 g protein (11%), 14 g fat (60%), 16 g carbohydrate (30%; 17 g sugars), 2 g dietary fiber, 53 mg cholesterol, 85 mg sodium, $.70*

Nutrient Rich Papaya! Papaya is one of the few fruits rich in both vitamins A and C (61% RDA of A and 3 times RDA of C in half medium papaya). It is especially tasty with a sprinkle of lemon or lime juice.

VARIATIONS

Add fresh or frozen **blueberries** or chopped **dried figs**.

Berry Delicious

The time to especially enjoy this simple elegant fruit is when you can pick it off the vines without cost!

1 Serving

Mix yogurt and sweetener and fold in the berries:
> **½ cup nonfat or lowfat yogurt**
> **1 tablespoon honey or maple syrup, to taste**
> **1 cup fresh berries**

Per Serving with raspberries
> *Exchanges: 0.5 Milk, 3 Fruit; 174 Calories, 8 g protein (16%), 38 g carbohydrate (80%; 33 g sugars), 8 g dietary fiber, 2 mg cholesterol, 71 mg sodium, $1.30*

Apple Nuggets

A tasty breakfast dish served plain, hot or cold, topped with yogurt, raisins, or topped with granola or an unsweetened wholegrain cold cereal.

7 Cups

1. In large saucepan combine:
    10 apples - Jonathan or McIntosh red apples especially good; preferably unpeeled, 8 wedges each cut in 3 chunks
    2¼ cups water
    1 tablespoon lemon juice
    2 teaspoons apple pie spice or:
        1½ teaspoons cinnamon
        ½ teaspoon nutmeg
        ½ teaspoon cloves
        ¼ teaspoon allspice
        ¼ teaspoon ginger

2. Bring to a boil; boil gently until apple pieces are soft, but still keeping their shape and not mushy.

Per ½ Cup
Exchanges: 1.75 Fruit; 70 Calories, 18 g carbohydrate (97%; 15 g sugars), 3 g dietary fiber, 0 mg cholesterol, 1 mg sodium, $.25

Quick Apple Yogurt

1 Serving

Stir together:
    ½ cup nonfat or lowfat plain yogurt
    2 - 4 tablespoons apple butter, to taste
        (unsweetened from health food store)

Per Serving with 2 tablespoons unsweetened apple butter
Exchanges: 0.5 Milk, 1.75 Fruit; 124 Calories, 7 g protein (21%), 25 g carbohydrate (79%; 27 g sugars), 2 mg cholesterol, 67 mg sodium, $.55

VARIATION

In place of apple butter add:
    apple or apricot fruit concentrate, to taste *(p. 12)*

Delicious Fruit Compote

Stewed dried fruit provides a tasty alternative when in-season fresh fruit is scarce. Enjoy this fruit feast high in potassium, vitamin A, fiber, and fruit acids. Use unsulfured fruit (see fruit, dried, p. 12). Yummy with yogurt!

3 Cups

1. Soak fruits in water overnight:
   ¼ cup dried prunes
   ¼ cup dried apples
   ¼ cup dried apricots
   ¼ cup dried peaches
   ¼ cup dried pears
   ¼ cup raisins
   3 cups water

2. Chop softened fruit in smaller pieces, as desired.

3. Add, to taste:
   cinnamon
   allspice
   lemon juice

Per ½ Cup without seasonings
   Exchanges: 2.5 Fruit; 95 Calories, 25 g carbohydrate (95%; 20 g sugars),
4 g dietary fiber, 0 mg cholesterol, 2 mg sodium, $.40

Prune Compote

A rich source of dietary fiber, potassium, and vitamin A.

1 Serving

Combine ingredients to soak overnight:
   6 large dried prunes, pitted (about ¼ cup packed)
   Choice of:
      ½ cup strong herb tea (1 tea bag steeped in ½ cup water;
         such as *Orange Spice* or *Cinnamon Stick*)
      or **½ cup apple juice** (or 6 oz. can)
      or **½ cup water**
   1 tablespoon honey or other natural sweetener
   thin slice of lemon, optional
   1 cinnamon stick, optional

Per Serving with tea, honey, lemon slice
   Exchanges: 4.75 Fruit; 187 Calories, 50 g carbohydrate (96%; 42.5 g sugars),
7 g dietary fiber, 0 mg cholesterol, 3 mg sodium, $.60

176

Festive Cantaloupe Boat

Simple, but elegant, Emilie Barnes served this for our annual summer breakfasts (see company menu, p. 231).

4 Servings

1. With a sharp knife wedge around the middle of cantaloupe; scoop out and discard seeds. Peel and cut enough of 3-4 fruits to generously fill centers of cantaloupe:
   - **2 cantaloupe**
   - **about 2 - 3 cups fresh fruit**
     (peaches, banana, strawberries, kiwi, grapes, berries, pineapple, blueberries, etc.)

2. Place filled cantaloupe halves in cereal bowls of appropriate size with a liner plate underneath each bowl.

Per Serving with 2 peaches, 1 banana, 1 kiwi, 1 cup strawberries for the 4 servings
    Exchanges: 5.5 Fruit; 214 Calories, 4 g protein (7%), 53 g carbohydrate (89%; 43.5 g sugars), 10 g dietary fiber, 0 mg cholesterol, 54 mg sodium, $.85

VARIATION
Fill centers with **Gourmet Fruit Bowl** (below), and/or top with **Whipped Cream**, p. 218, or **Whipped Fluff Topping**, p. 219.

Gourmet Fruit

Serve over waffles or by itself. Especially good with Whipped Fluff Topping (p. 219). Or serve in Festive Cantaloupe Boats (above).

5 Cups

Mix together:
- **1 large banana, sliced (1 cup)**
- **2 peaches or nectarines, chopped**
- **1 cup fresh or frozen blueberries**
- **2 cups halved strawberries**

Per ½ Cup
    Exchanges: 1.25 Fruit; 45 Calories, 11 g carbohydrate (90%; 9 g sugars), 2 g dietary fiber, 0 mg cholesterol, 2 mg sodium, $.25

Alice's Fruit Soup

A super-quick 5 minute recipe and so-o-o refreshing! A fruit dessert, snack, or topping especially handy when little fresh fruit is available. Serve as is or with a dollop of whipped cream. Delicious for waffle topping with a little of the juice drained off. I often use the leftovers for a yummy Fruit Smoothie (see Variations, p. 191). Vary any of the fruits except the raspberries, but substitute frozen for frozen, and canned for canned.

11 Cups (without Bananas)

1. Place in a large bowl:
    12 oz. package frozen raspberries
    16 oz. package frozen strawberries
    12 oz. package frozen blueberries, boysenberries,
       or blackberries

2. Add and stir to combine:
    20 oz. can pineapple chunks, unsweetened, undrained
    16 oz. can peach slices, unsweetened, undrained (cut up)
    16 oz. can pear halves, unsweetened, undrained (cut up)

3. Let stand about 2 hours at room temperature or overnight in refrigerator to let frozen fruit thaw and juices to mingle.

4. Refrigerate until ready to serve. Add to portion to be served:
    sliced bananas, as desired, optional

Special Tip: This will keep several days in the refrigerator. Add sliced bananas only to the portion to be used immediately, as they will turn brown in leftover fruit soup.

Per 1 Cup (without bananas)
  Exchanges: 1.75 Fruit; 67 Calories, 17 g carbohydrate (98%; 9 g sugars), 2 g dietary fiber, 0 mg cholesterol, 6 mg sodium, $.40 (reflects high price of frozen fruit, especially raspberries; see cost saver tip below)

Cost Saver Tip: Freeze your own home grown fresh berries; or purchase fresh seasonal berries when the price is low and freeze them.

178

On-the-Go
Shakes 'n Muffins

He brought you . . . *into a good and spacious land,
a land flowing with milk and honey. Exodus 3:8*

SHAKES 'N MUFFINS

SUBJECTS

RECIPES

Shakes

Blender Muffins

On-the-Go
Shakes 'n Muffins

Breakfast Shake
Bread, optional
(Muffin, Bagel, English Muffin)
Spread, optional
(Jam, Butter)

Nutrition Goals Menu[1]

*1-2 servings Basic Breakfast
Shake (p. 185)*

1-2 Molasses Muffins (p. 193)

[1]*Small: $ .85   4% Fat   324 Calories*
[1]*Large: $1.65   4% Fat   649 Calories*

[1]This menu is included in the "Average of 7 Breakfasts" Column on the *Nutrition Goals Chart*, pp. 16-17. Small servings represent menu for adult female; large servings represent menu for adult male.

Take a Shake - A Meal-in-a-Glass!

Maximum nutritional value can be packed into a shake to satisfy hunger and provide alertness and energy throughout the morning or afternoon. Shakes are perfect for people on the go, whether at home or away from home. Most can be whipped up in the blender in 5 minutes or less and carried to school or work in a thermos. Don't gulp down a shake on the run; sip it slowly for good digestion.

This section includes my favorite shake recipes, but do your own experimenting too. Combinations are endless! A basic shake usually contains 3 ingredients: 1) liquid: milk, yogurt, juice, water, ice, or non-dairy alternative (p. 29), 2) fresh fruit or vegetable, or frozen fruit (see tip below), 3) sweetener and/or other flavoring as desired to enhance taste. See, for example the recipe for *Basic Shake,* p.185.

I prefer shakes with a protein base, such as yogurt, to balance the high amount of carbohydrate. If you prefer to use juice or water, you might add one of the other protein ingredients listed on p.184. For totally non-dairy shakes, *Carrot Shake* and *Fruit Smoothies* (p. 191), are most delicious and filling alternatives. Bananas, fresh or frozen, make an excellent thick non-dairy base. For "crunch" in your shakes, blend in ingredients such as ice cubes, nuts, seeds, date dices, or raisins just long enough to achieve a texture to suit you.

Use the *Optional Ingredients for Extra Nutrients* (p. 184) to fortify basic shakes with additional nutrient value. I have also listed several *Alternative Ingredients for Shakes* (p. 183) for creating your own variety of flavor and taste.

Using a commercial powdered supplement product is another option. While not inexpensive, these products, generally available at health food stores, provide power-packed nutrition and recipe suggestions for their use. Taste and ingredients vary widely. I recommend *The Ultimate Meal*, a powdered blend of 16 food and nutrient ingredients. It is low-fat, salt-free, dairy-free, wheat and soy-free, and high in fiber.

For even heartier quick breakfasts, bake and freeze individually wrapped muffins to add to your shake meals. See recipes, pp.194-198.

Fresh Fruit Tip: Whenever you have ripe fresh fruit that will not be used right away, peel or chop it as needed and freeze in ziploc freezer bags for an instant supply of frozen fruit for your shakes!

Alternative Ingredients for Shakes

Ingredient	Add to 1 Serving	Nutrient Value
Liquid nonfat milk nonfat/lowfat yogurt kefir *(p. 28)* non-dairy *(p. 29)* fruit juice water ice cubes	1 - 1½ cups 3 or 4 ice cubes	protein calcium vit. C (citrus juices)
fruits/juices banana orange lemon/lime grapefruit pineapple melons papaya apple/pear peach berries dried fruits raisins dates	1 piece or ½ - 1 cup ½ cup or 6 oz. juice ¼ c. dried fruit 2 - 4 tbsps.	vit. C citric acid (enhances protein absorption) soluble fibers minerals vit. A pectin
vegetables/juices sprouts carrots tomato leafy greens	½ - 1 cup	vit. C vit. A minerals

Sweeteners, to taste *(p. 15)*
honey
maple syrup
crystalline fructose
molasses (high iron)
stevia
Sucanat
dates or figs, chopped
raisins
barley malt
rice syrup
sorghum

Flavorings/Spices
vanilla extract
almond extract
peppermint extract
nutmeg
cinnamon
mint, dried or fresh
orange or lemon peel
instant decaffeinated coffee
fruit concentrates *(p. 12)*
frozen fruit juice concen-
    trates *(Fruit Juices, p. 13)*

Optional Ingredients for Extra Nutrients

Ingredient	Add to 1 Serving	Nutrient Value
Grains wheat germ *(p. 15)* wheat bran *(p. 11)* oat bran oats	1 tbsp. - ¼ cup	dietary fiber vit. E B-vitamins vits/minerals
nuts/seeds, ground *(p. 14)* flax seeds *(p. 12)* sunflower seeds sesame seeds pumpkin seeds almonds nut butters nut milk *(p. 34)*	1- 2 tbsps. ½-1 cup	as vegetable oils below

vegetable oils *(p. 14)*
flaxseed oil *(p. 12)*
olive oil
wheat germ oil *(p. 15)*
almond oil
walnut oil
a blend of oils
	1 tsp. - 1 tbsp.	monounsaturated fat
		essential fatty acids
		assist absorption of
		    vits. A, D, E, K
		prevents hunger
		    3-4 hours
		assist regularity
		assist burning
		    body fat
		maintain skin/hair

protein egg protein powder *(p. 185)* nonfat dry milk powder *(p. 14)* carob powder *(p. 12)*	1 egg 1-2 tbsps. 2 tbsps. 1-2 tbsps.	extra protein extra calcium
other brewer's yeast *(p. 275)* lecithin, liquid/granules *(p. 13)*	¼ tsp. - 3 tbsps. 1 tbsp. liquid 1-2 tbsps. granules	B-vitamins regulate cholesterol

About Protein Powder

Many brands of commercial protein powders are available at health food stores. They are usually made from soy or milk and egg, and are often fortified with vitamins and minerals, and sometimes dietary fibers. Taste appeal and cost vary widely. Some don't taste good at all. They are an easy way to increase protein content, especially if you don't use dairy products. I prefer not to use protein powder, as I get plenty of protein without it. Serving size on containers usually specifies "rounded tablespoons." Two rounded tablespoons actually measure about ¼ cup. Therefore, if the label states that 2 rounded tablespoons contain 12 grams protein, be aware that it may actually require ¼ cup to provide 12 grams protein.

Basic Breakfast Shake   1 Serving

Use these basic ingredients to create your own simple, flavorful shakes!

Blend in blender until smooth:
½ cup nonfat milk, plain yogurt, or fruit juice
½ cup nonfat plain yogurt or fruit juice
1 piece chopped fresh fruit or fruit combination
**   or ¼ - ½ cup fresh or frozen berries**
1 teaspoon - 1 tablespoon honey, to taste
**   or crystalline fructose** *(p. 12)*
optional ingredients for extra nutrients *(p. 184)*
4 ice cubes, optional

Per Serving (with ½ cup each nonfat milk and yogurt; optional ingredients not included)   Exchanges: 1 Milk, 2 Fruit; 178 Calories, 12 g protein (26%), 34 g carbohydrate (71%; 33 g sugars), 3 g dietary fiber, 5 mg cholesterol, 132 mg sodium, $.65

Sue's Apple Bran Shake   1 Serving

This is very thick and satisfying!

Blend in blender until smooth:
1 cup nonfat yogurt *(p. 15)*
1 apple, unpeeled, chopped
¼ cup uncooked oat bran *(p. 11)*
1½ teaspoons honey or crystalline fructose *(p. 12)*
1 teaspoon flaxseed oil, optional *(p. 12)*
2 teaspoons brewer's yeast, optional *(p. 275)*

Per Serving with all ingredients
*   Exchanges: 0.5 Meat, 1 Milk, 1.75 Bread, 1 Fat, 3.25 Fruit; 375 Calories, 29 g protein (29%), 2 g fat (4%), 69 g carbohydrate (67%; 47 g sugars), 12 g dietary fiber, 4 mg cholesterol, 157 mg sodium, $1.25*

Orange Refresher

So-o-o good! The citric acid in orange juice enhances calcium absorption from the yogurt or from milk.

4 Servings

Blend in blender until smooth:

1 cup nonfat plain yogurt *(p. 15)*
1 cup water
6 oz. can frozen orange juice concentrate, unsweetened
⅓ cup honey
1½ teaspoons vanilla
optional ingredients for extra nutrients *(p. 184)*
8 to 10 ice cubes

Per Serving of 4 (optional ingredients for extra nutrients not included)
Exchanges: 0.25 Milk, 4.25 Fruit; 200 Calories, 4 g protein (8%),
48 g carbohydrate (92%; 48 g sugars), 1 mg cholesterol, 35 mg sodium, $.50

Apple Shake

1 Serving

Blend in blender until smooth:

1 cup nonfat plain yogurt *(p. 15)*
1 medium apple, unpeeled (Jonathan is good)
½ teaspoon honey or crystalline fructose, to taste *(p. 12)*
¹⁄₁₆ teaspoon cinnamon
optional ingredients for extra nutrients *(p. 184)*

Per Serving (optional ingredients for extra nutrients not included)
Exchanges: 1 Milk, 2.75 Fruit; 207 Calories, 13 g protein (24%), 41 g carbohydrate
(75%; 41 g sugars), 5 g dietary fiber, 4 mg cholesterol, 135 mg sodium, $.85

Strawberry Milk Shake

1 Serving

Blend in blender until smooth:

⅓ cup nonfat plain yogurt *(p. 15)*
⅓ cup nonfat (skim) milk
⅓ cup fresh strawberries or other berries
1 tablespoon honey or crystalline fructose, to taste *(p. 12)*
optional ingredients for extra nutrients *(p. 184)*

Per Serving (optional ingredients for extra nutrients not included)
Exchanges: 0.75 Milk, 2 Fruit; 142 Calories, 7.5 g protein (20%), 29 g carbohydrate
(77%; 30 g sugars), 1 g dietary fiber, 3 mg cholesterol, 89 mg sodium, $.50

Banana Smoothie

1 Serving

Blend in blender until smooth:
- **1 cup nonfat (skim) milk**
- **1 banana, peeled**
- **1 tablespoon honey or crystalline fructose** *(p. 12)*
- **¼ teaspoon vanilla**
- **optional ingredients for extra nutrients** *(p. 184)*

Per Serving (optional ingredients for extra nutrients not included)
    Exchanges: 1 Milk, 4 Fruit; 255 Calories, 10 g protein (15%), 1 g fat (4%), 55 g carbohydrate (82%; 53 g sugars), 3 g dietary fiber, 5 mg cholesterol, 132 mg sodium, $.55

Pineapple Froth

1 Serving

Light and refreshing!

Blend in blender until smooth:
- **½ cup plain nonfat or lowfat yogurt or kefir** *(p. 28)*
- **6 oz. canned pineapple juice, unsweetened**
- **2 tablespoons nonfat dry milk powder** *(p. 14)*
- **1 tablespoon honey**
- **¹⁄₁₆ teaspoon nutmeg**
- **optional ingredients for extra nutrients** *(p. 184)*
- **4 ice cubes**

Per Serving with nonfat yogurt (optional ingredients for extra nutrients not included)
    Exchanges: 1 Milk, 3.5 Fruit; 249 Calories, 12 g protein (18%), 54 g carbohydrate (81%; 54 g sugars), 5 mg cholesterol, 158 mg sodium, $.80

Date Shake

3 Servings

Rich and filling!

Blend in blender about 2 minutes:
- **1 cup nonfat or lowfat plain yogurt**
- **1 cup nonfat (skim) or lowfat milk**
- **2 tablespoons nonfat dry milk powder** *(p. 14)*
- **15 pitted dates, cut in half**
- **4 almonds, unroasted, unsalted**
- **¼ teaspoon vanilla**
- **optional ingredients for extra nutrients** *(p. 184)*
- **4 ice cubes**

Per Serving of 3 with nonfat milk and nonfat yogurt (optional ingredients not included)
    Exchanges: 0.75 Milk, 8 Fruit; 384 Calories, 10 g protein (10%), 1 g fat (3%), 89 g carbohydrate (88%; 74 g sugars), 9 g dietary fiber, 3 mg cholesterol, 89 mg sodium, $1.30

Sunshine Shake

1 - 2 Servings

Wake up your day with this satisfyingly
scrumptious potassium and vitamin C rich drink!

Blend in blender until smooth:
- **1 medium orange, peeled and cut in chunks**
- **1 medium banana, peeled**
- **½ cup lowfat vanilla or nonfat or lowfat plain yogurt** *(p. 15)*
  (add honey, to taste with plain yogurt, if desired)
- **¹⁄₁₆ teaspoon cinnamon**
- **¹⁄₁₆ teaspoon nutmeg**
- **optional ingredients for extra nutrients** *(p. 184)*

Per Recipe with lowfat vanilla yogurt (optional ingredients for extra nutrients not included)
Exchanges: 0.5 Milk, 4 Fruit; 214 Calories, 9 g protein (15%), 1 g fat (4%), 48 g carbohydrate (81%;
45 g sugars), 5.5 g dietary fiber, 2 mg cholesterol, 68 mg sodium, $.70

Carob-Banana a la Mint

1 Serving

Rich and creamy!

Blend in blender until smooth:
- **¾ cup nonfat (skim) milk**
- **2 tablespoons nonfat dry milk powder** *(p. 14)*
- **1 tablespoon carob powder** *(p. 12)*
- **1 medium banana, peeled**
- **1 teaspoon honey or crystalline fructose** *(p. 12)*
- **¼ teaspoon dry mint flakes or 1 drop mint flavoring**
- **optional ingredients for extra nutrients** *(p. 184)*

Per Serving (optional ingredients for extra nutrients not included)
Exchanges: 1.25 Milk, 3 Fruit; 259 Calories, 13 g protein (19%), 1 g fat (4%),
54 g carbohydrate (78%; 47 g sugars), 4 g dietary fiber, 7 mg cholesterol, 182 mg sodium, $.65

Carob Milkshake

1 Serving

Carob is a good calcium source, containing 4 times that of chocolate.
1 tbsp. contains 30 mg. calcium.

Blend until smooth:
- **1 cup nonfat (skim) or lowfat milk**
- **1 tablespoon carob powder** *(p. 12)*
- **1½ teaspoons honey, to taste**
- **⅛ teaspoon vanilla, to taste**

Per Serving with nonfat milk
Exchanges: 1 Milk, 0.75 Fruit; 137 Calories, 9 g protein (24%), 27 g carbohydrate
(72%; 22 g sugars), 1 g dietary fiber, 5 mg cholesterol, 134 mg sodium, $.35

Coffee Shake
1 Serving

Coffee lovers, get your protein, fiber, and coffee, too--in one quick drink! If you like regular coffee, this is a good way to minimize its negative effects on the stomach.

Briefly blend each ingredient into the milk one at a time; add ice cubes and blend until smooth:

¾ cup nonfat (skim) milk
¼ cup uncooked rolled oats or oat bran
2 tablespoons nonfat dry milk powder *(p. 14)*
¾ teaspoon instant decaffeinated or regular coffee
⅜ teaspoon vanilla
1½ teaspoons honey or crystalline fructose *(p. 12)*
3 ice cubes

Per Serving -- Exchanges: 1.25 Milk, 1 Bread, 0.75 Fruit; 234 Calories, 15 g protein (26%), 2 g fat (7%), 39 g carbohydrate (67%; 26 g sugars), 2 g dietary fiber, 7 mg cholesterol, 179 mg sodium, $.55

Egg Nog
1 Serving

For information about using eggs raw, see pp. 134, 137.

Whisk together or blend in blender:

1 cup nonfat (skim) milk
3 tablespoons nonfat dry milk powder *(p. 14)*
1 egg *(fertile egg preferred, p. 12)*
1½ tablespoons honey, to taste
¼ teaspoon nutmeg
¹⁄₁₆ teaspoon cloves
¼ teaspoon vanilla, to taste

Per Serving   Exchanges: 1.25 Meat, 1.75 Milk, 2.5 Fruit; 350 Calories, 23 g protein (26%), 6.5 g fat (17%), 51 g carbohydrate (57%; 50 g sugars), 224 mg cholesterol, 317 mg sodium, $.80

Molasses Protein Shake
1 Serving

Blend until smooth in blender:

1 cup nonfat (skim) milk
2 tablespoons nonfat dry milk powder *(p. 14)*
2 tablespoons molasses, unsulfured *(blackstrap preferred, p. 14)*
pinch of salt
pinch of nutmeg

Per Serving
Exchanges: 1.5 Milk, 2.25 Fruit; 231 Calories, 14 g protein (25%), 42 g carbohydrate (73%; 42 g sugars), 8 mg cholesterol, 312 mg sodium, $.55

Blueberry Shake

2 Cups

Blend in blender until smooth:
- ½ cup nonfat (skim) milk
- ½ cup nonfat plain yogurt *(p. 15)*
- 2 tablespoon nonfat dry milk powder *(p. 14)*
- ½ cup frozen or fresh blueberries
- 1 tablespoon honey or crystalline fructose *(p. 12)*
- ¼ teaspoon vanilla
- 4 ice cubes
- optional ingredients for extra nutrients *(p. 184)*

Per 1 Cup (optional ingredients for extra nutrients not included)
Exchanges: 0.75 Milk, 1.5 Fruit; 134 Calories, 8.5 g protein (25%), 23 g carbohydrate (70%; 25 g sugars), 1.5 g dietary fiber, 3 mg cholesterol, 107 mg sodium, $.45

Oat Bran Protein Shake

1 Serving

A quick way to get cholesterol-regulating high fiber in the morning without cooking it or without quite so much tasting it!

Blend in blender until smooth:
- 1 cup nonfat (skim) milk
- 1 tablespoon carob powder *(p. 12)*
- 1 tablespoon nonfat dry milk powder *(p. 14)*
- 3 tablespoons uncooked oat bran *(p. 11)*
- 1 banana
- ¾ teaspoon honey or crystalline fructose *(p. 12)*
- ⅛ teaspoon vanilla
- ¹⁄₁₆ teaspoon nutmeg

Per Serving   Exchanges: 1.25 Milk, 1.25 Bread, 3 Fruit; 336 Calories, 17 gm protein (17%), 3 g fat (7%), 65 g carbohydrate (74%; 45 g sugars), 8 g dietary fiber, 7 mg cholesterol, 174 mg sodium, $.70

Peanut Butter Shake

1 Serving

For kids and peanut butter lovers!

In blender blend a small amount of milk with the peanut butter; blend in remaining ingredients:
- 2 - 3 tablespoons peanut butter, to taste *(p. 14)*
- 1 cup nonfat (skim) milk
- 2 tablespoons nonfat milk powder, optional *(p. 14)*
- 1½ teaspoons honey
- ⅛ - ¼ teaspoon vanilla, to taste

Per Serving (nonfat milk powder included)
Exchanges: 0.5 Meat, 1.5 Milk, 0.25 Bread, 3.25 Fat, 0.75 Fruit; 377 Calories, 22 g protein (24%), 17 g fat (40%), 34 g carbohydrate (37%; 31 g sugars), 2 g dietary fiber, 8 mg cholesterol, 321 mg sodium, $.60

Wake-Up Carrot Shake   1 Serving

Dairyless. Sunflower seeds give this a very special flavor.

Blend ingredients in blender until smooth; rinse blender with the water and add to the shake:
- **1 tablespoon sunflower seeds** (grind in blender before adding other ingredients or see p. 120)
- **6 oz. can pineapple juice or 1 cup fresh pineapple juice**
- **1 medium carrot, cut in 1" chunks**
- **1 - 2 teaspoons honey, to taste**
- **2 ice cubes**
- **2 - 4 tablespoons water**

Per Serving -- Exchanges: 0.25 Meat, 0.75 Fat, 2.5 Fruit, 1.25 Vegetable; 183 Calories, 3 g protein (7%), 4.5 g fat (20%), 37 g carbohydrate (74%; 31 g sugars), 3 g dietary fiber, 0 mg cholesterol, 36 mg sodium, $.40

Fruit Smoothie   2-4 Servings

Dairyless, delicious, filling! Cut recipe in half for 1 sumptuous serving.

Place all in blender and blend until smooth:
- **2 bananas, broken in chunks** (may be frozen, if desired)
- **2 oranges, peeled, cut in chunks** (or about 4 tangerines)
- **1 apple, cut in chunks**
- **6 dates, chopped**
- **¼ cup frozen juice concentrate, flavor desired, optional for added sweetness** *(as Dole Pine-Orange-Banana; see Fruit Juices, p. 13)*
- **3 ice cubes** (use 2 for half a recipe)
- **water filled to the 1 cup mark**

Per Serving of 4 Exchanges: 5.75 Fruit; 233 Calories, 2 g protein (4%), 59 g carbohydrate (94%; 48 g sugars), 7 g dietary fiber, 0 mg cholesterol, 6 mg sodium, $.65

VARIATIONS

1. In place of 1 orange, the apple, the dates, and frozen concentrate, add **1 cup *Alice's Fruit Soup*,** p.178. Reduce to **½ cup water.**

2. In place of 1 orange and the apple, add **about 1½ cups fresh pineapple,** peeled and chopped.

3. Use up to **⅓ cup frozen fruit juice concentrate.** Combine 2 different kinds, if desired--*Banana-Pineapple* with *Apple-Pear-Cherry* are good.

Tip: Purchase 12 oz. cans frozen juice concentrate (see p. 13); Store unused portion in tupperware or cover top of original container securely with foil.

191

Blender Bran Muffins

The blender version of my Bran Muffins, our first muffin recipe to be converted from white flour and sugar to whole grain flour and honey. It is still a favorite! Grain in this recipe equals **1 ½ cups flour**. See pp. 82-83 for additional blending in blender tips, our recommended procedure to improve nutritional benefits (as in Blender Banana Muffins, p. 196) or for standard mixing with flour.

AMOUNT: 12 Muffins
Bake: 350°F (175°C) - 20 minutes

1. Preheat oven to 350°. Spray or grease muffin pan *(p. 271)*.

2. In large mixing bowl thoroughly stir water into bran; stir in raisins and nuts, as desired; let stand 5 minutes:

    1½ cups wheat bran (not boxed cereal flakes) *(p. 11)*
    ½ cup boiling hot water
    ½ cup raisins, optional (soak in water 5 minutes to soften; drain)
    ½ cup chopped walnuts, optional

3. Place in blender; blend at high speed 3-5 minutes until smooth:

    1 cup buttermilk *(p. 11; or non-dairy alternative, p. 29)*
    1 egg *(or alternative, p. 269)*
    ⅓ cup honey (warmed 20 seconds on high in microwave)
    1 cup whole wheat pastry berries (grain, not flour) *(p. 13)*

4. Blend in briefly, but thoroughly (use spoon or rubber spatula, as needed, if blender fails to catch hold of the batter):

    1 teaspoon salt   "sift" these through a small strainer
    1¼ teaspoons baking soda with a spoon to break up any lumps.

5. Pour batter into **softened bran mixture**; blend all thoroughly, but briefly. Do not overmix!

6. Evenly fill muffin cups almost full. Bake 20 minutes at 350°. Cool muffins in pan for 3-5 minutes for easy removal with slight tug on side of each muffin.

Per Muffin of 12 without raisins, nuts -- Exchanges: 1 Bread, 0.75 Fruit; 110 Calories, 3.5 g protein (12%), 24 g carbohydrate (81%; 9 sugars), 4 g dietary fiber, 19 mg cholesterol, 269 mg sodium, $.15

Carrot or Zucchini Muffins   14 Large Muffins

Increase to **2 eggs, ½ cup honey, 1½ tsps. baking soda**; add **1 tsp. cinnamon**; fold in **1 cup grated carrots or zucchini** with raisins and walnuts.

Per Muffin of 14 with raisins, walnuts, carrots   Exchanges: 0.25 Meat, 0.75 Bread, 0.5 Fat, 1.25 Fruit, 0.25 Vegetable; 138 Calories, 4 g protein (11%), 3.5 g fat (21%), 25 g carbohydrate (68%; 13 g sugars), 3.5 g dietary fiber, 27 mg cholesterol, 218 mg sodium, $.20

Blender Molasses Muffins

These dark, rich, and moist muffins are a little sweeter with cinnamon-sugar topping, but are also very tasty without it. Pastry wheat grain in this recipe is equal to 2¼ cups flour. See pp. 82-83 for additional blending in blender tips, our recommended procedure to improve nutritional benefits (as in Blender Banana Muffins, p. 196) or for standard mixing with flour.

AMOUNT: 10 - 12 Muffins
Bake: 350°F (175°C) - 20 to 25 minutes

1. Preheat oven to 350°. Spray or grease muffin pan *(p. 271)*.

2. Optional--Mix together for *cinnamon-sugar topping*; set aside:
   1 tablespoon crystalline fructose *(p. 12)* **or sugar**
   ¼ teaspoon cinnamon

3. Place in blender; blend at high speed 3-5 minutes until smooth:
   ¾ cup water
   1 egg *(or alternative, p. 269)*
   3 tablespoons honey
   ½ cup molasses *(p. 14)*
   1 teaspoon vanilla extract
   1½ cups whole wheat pastry grain (not flour) *(see grains, p. 13)*
   or other grain alternative (see list below)

4. Mix in thoroughly, but briefly, using blender and/or rubber spatula, as needed:
   2 teaspoons baking powder *(p. 11)*   "sift" these through a small
   ½ teaspoon baking soda   strainer with a spoon to break
   ¾ teaspoon salt   up any lumps.

5. Fill muffin cups almost full.

6. Optional: Sprinkle evenly over top of each muffin:
   ¼ teaspoon cinnamon-sugar topping (expect some leftover)

7. Fill any empty cups half full of water. Bake 20 minutes at 350°. Cool muffins in pan for 3-5 minutes for easy removal with slight tug on side of each muffin.

Per Muffin (of 12) with wheat, cinnamon-sugar topping   Exchanges: 1.25 Bread, 1.25 Fruit; 140 Calories, 2.5 g protein (9%), 1 g fat (5%), 30 g carbohydrate (86%; 15 g sugars), 2 g dietary fiber, 18 mg cholesterol, 186 mg sodium, $.20

GRAIN ALTERNATIVES *(see grains, p. 13)*
   1¼ cups barley grain (2¼ cups flour)
   1½ cups + 3 tablespoons kamut grain (2¼ cups flour)
   1½ cups spelt grain (2¾ cups flour)
   1½ cups + 1 tablespoon rye grain (2¼ cups flour)

Good Morning Blender Muffins

These have a cake donut flavor! Pastry wheat grain in this recipe equals
2¼ cups flour. *See pp. 82-83 for additional blending in blender tips, our recommended procedure to improve nutritional benefits (as in Blender Banana Muffins, p. 196) or for standard mixing with flour.*

AMOUNT: 10 - 12 Muffins

Bake: 350°F (175°C) - 20 minutes

1. Preheat oven to 350°. Spray or grease muffin pan *(p. 271)*.

2. Mix together for *cinnamon-sugar topping* and set aside:
   1 tablespoon crystalline fructose *(p. 12)* **or sugar**
   ¼ teaspoon cinnamon

3. Place in blender; blend at high speed 3-5 minutes until smooth:
   ¾ cup buttermilk *(p. 11; or non-dairy alternative, p. 29)*
   2 eggs *(or alternative, p.269)*
   ⅓ cup honey
   2 tablespoons olive oil *(extra virgin preferred, p. 14)*
   1½ cups whole wheat pastry grain (not flour), *(see grains, p. 13)*
   or other grain alternative (see list below)

4. Mix in thoroughly, but briefly, using blender and/or rubber spatula, as needed:
   2 teaspoons baking powder *(p. 11)*   "sift" these through a small
   ¾ teaspoon baking soda   strainer with a spoon to
   ½ teaspoon salt   break up any lumps.
   1 teaspoon cinnamon

5. Fill muffin cups evenly, almost full.

6. Sprinkle evenly over top of each muffin:
   ¼ teaspoon cinnamon-sugar topping (expect some leftover)

7. Fill any empty cups half full of water. Bake 20 minutes at 350°. Cool muffins in pan for 3-5 minutes for easy removal with slight tug on side of each muffin.

Per Muffin (of 12) with wheat, 2% fat buttermilk, oil, topping
  Exchanges: 0.25 Meat, 1.25 Bread, 0.5 Fat, 0.75 Fruit; 157 Calories, 4 g protein (10%),
3.5 g fat (20%), 28 g carbohydrate (70%; 9.5 g sugars),
2 g dietary fiber, 36 mg cholesterol, 152 mg sodium, $.20

GRAIN ALTERNATIVES *(see grains, p. 13)*
   1¼ cups barley grain (2¼ cups flour)
   1½ cups spelt grain (2¾ cups flour)
   1½ cups + 3 tablespoons kamut grain (2¼ cups flour)

194

Blender Sunshine Muffins

*Deliciously moist, sweet, and tender. Pastry wheat grain in this recipe equals **2 cups flour**. See pp. 82-83 for additional blending in blender tips, our recommended procedure to improve nutritional benefits (as in Blender Banana Muffins, p. 196) or for standard mixing with flour.*

AMOUNT: 12 - 15 Muffins

Bake: 350°F (175°C) - 20 minutes

1. Preheat oven to 350°. Spray or grease muffin pan *(p. 271)*.

2. Prepare *cinnamon-sugar topping* and orange peel, setting them aside in separate containers:
   1 tablespoon crystalline fructose *(p. 12)* **or sugar**
   ¼ teaspoon cinnamon
   grated peel of 1 orange (about 1 tablespoon)

3. Place in blender; blend at high speed 3-5 minutes until smooth:
   ¾ cup orange juice (use juice from grated orange + thawed frozen orange juice concentrate, not reconstituted, as needed)
   1 egg *(or alternative, p. 269)*
   ½ cup honey
   1 tablespoon olive oil *(extra virgin preferred, p. 14)*
   1 teaspoon vanilla extract
   1⅓ cups whole wheat pastry grain (not flour), *(see grains, p. 13)*
   or other grain alternative (see list below)

4. Pour batter into mixing bowl; whisk in just until blended:
   1½ teaspoons baking powder *(p. 11)* "sift" these through a small
   ½ teaspoon baking soda strainer with a spoon to
   ½ teaspoon salt break up any lumps.
   1 teaspoon cinnamon
   grated orange peel (step #2)
   1 cup grated carrot
   ½ raisins (soften in water 5 minutes; drain)
   ½ cup chopped walnuts

5. Fill muffin cups evenly; top each with:
   ¼ teaspoon cinnamon-sugar topping (expect some leftover)

6. Bake at 350° for 20 minutes; let cool in pan 3-5 minutes.

Per Muffin (of 15) with wheat   Exchanges: 0.25 Meat, 1 Bread, 0.75 Fat, 1.5 Fruit, 0.25 Vegetable; 165 Calories, 3 g protein (7%), 4 g fat (23%), 29 g carbohydrate (70%; 16 g sugars), 2.5 g dietary fiber, 14 mg cholesterol, 106 mg sodium, $.20

GRAIN ALTERNATIVES *(see grains, p. 13)*
   1⅛ cups barley grain (2 cups flour)
   1½ cups kamut grain (2 cups flour)
   1⅓ cups spelt grain (2⅓ cups flour)

Blender Banana Muffins

The flavor of these go especially well with breakfast foods. For more blender tips or to mix by hand with flour see pp. 82-83) use **2 cups pastry, kamut or barley flour** *or* **2 ⅓ cups spelt flour** *for hand mixing.*

AMOUNT: 14 - 16 Muffins

Bake: 325°F (175°C) - 25 minutes

1. Place in blender and blend, starting at lower speed and increasing to highest speed for 3 minutes (keep batter churning):
   ¾ cup buttermilk *(p. 11; or non-dairy alternative, p. 29)*
   1 - 2 tablespoons olive oil *(extra virgin preferred, p. 14)*
   1 - 2 tablespoons melted butter (or more olive oil)
   ⅓ cup honey (warmed slightly if too cold and thick)
   1½ very ripe bananas, broken pieces (for ⅔ cup mashed)
   1 teaspoon cinnamon
   ¼ teaspoon nutmeg
   grain choice (not flour)of
   1⅓ cups whole wheat pastry grain
   or 1½ cups spelt or kamut
   or 1¼ cups barley grain

2. Cover blender; let stand at room temperature overnight *(pp. 50-51).*

3. Grease or spray muffin pans *(p. 271).*

4 Preheat oven to 325°.

6. Just before baking, add and reblend on highest speed for 1 minute:
   1 egg *(or alternative, p. 269)*

6. Mix into blender batter thoroughly, but briefly, using blender and/or rubber spatula, as needed:
   1½ teaspoons baking powder *(p. 11)*   "sift" these through a small
   ½ teaspoon baking soda   strainer with a spoon to break
   ½ teaspoon salt   up any lumps.

7. Optional--Fold in with rubber spatula:
   ½ - ¾ cup chopped walnuts

   Mixing Tip: If desired, fold in half the nuts in top half of batter in blender. After pouring first half of batter into muffin cups, fold remaining nuts into remaining batter in blender.

8. Evenly fill muffin cups almost full. Fill any empty cups half full of water. Bake 20 minutes at 350°. Cool muffins in pan for 3-5 minutes for easy removal.

Per Muffin (of 16) with pastry wheat, 1 tbsp. oil, 1 tbsp. butter, ½ cup nuts
  Exchanges: 0.25 Meat, 0.75 Bread, 1 Fat, 0.75 Fruit; 137 Calories, 3.5 g protein (10%), 5 g fat (32%), 20 g carbohydrate (58%; 8 g sugars), 2 g dietary fiber, 14 mg cholesterol, 97 mg sodium, $.20

Blender Wheat Germ Muffins

*Enjoy the taste and nutritional benefits of wheat germ (p. 273). Pastry wheat grain in this recipe equals **1 cup flour**. See pp. 82-83 for additional blending in blender tips, our recommended procedure to improve nutritional benefits (as in Blender Banana Muffins, p. 196) or for standard mixing with flour.*

AMOUNT: 10 - 12 Muffins
Bake: 400°F (205°C) - 20 minutes

1. Preheat oven to 400°. Spray or grease muffin pan *(p. 271).*

2. Place in blender; blend at high speed 3-5 minutes until smooth
   1 cup buttermilk *(p. 11; or non-dairy alternative, p. 29)*
   1 large egg *(or alternative, p. 269)*
   2 tablespoons olive oil *(extra virgin preferred, p. 14)*
   1 teaspoon vanilla
   ⅔ cup whole wheat pastry grain (not flour), *(see grains, p. 13)*
   or other grain alternative (see list below)

3. Stir or fold in with rubber scraper or mixing spoon:
   6 tablespoons *Sucanat* *(p. 15)* **or other sweetener**
   1 cup toasted wheat germ *(p. 15)*
   2 teaspoons baking powder *(p. 11)*   "sift" these through a small
   ½ teaspoon baking soda   strainer with a spoon to
   ½ teaspoon salt   break up any lumps.

4. Fill muffin cups almost full. Fill any empty cups half full of water. Bake at 400° for 20 minutes; let cool in pan 3-5 minutes. Cool muffins in pan for 5-10 minutes for easy removal with a slight tug on side of each muffin.

Per Muffin (of 12) with wheat, 2% fat buttermilk
 Exchanges: 1 Bread, 0.5 Fat, 0.5 Fruit; 127 Calories, 5 g protein (16%), 4 g fat (27%), 17 g carbohydrate (57%; 6 g sugars), 2 g dietary fiber, 19 mg cholesterol, 143 mg socium, $.20

GRAIN ALTERNATIVES *(see grains, p. 13)*
   ½ cup + 1 tablespoon barley grain (1 cup flour)
   ¾ cup kamut grain (1 cup flour)
   ¾ cup spelt grain (1¼ cups flour)

Blender Orange Date Muffins

*Pastry wheat grain in this recipe equals **1½ cups flour.** See pp. 82-83 for additional blending in blender tips, our recommended procedure to improve nutritional benefits (as in Blender Banana Muffins, p. 196) or for standard mixing with flour.*

AMOUNT: 10-12 Muffins
Bake: 400°F (205°C) - 20 to 25 minutes

1. Preheat oven to 400°. Spray or grease muffin pan *(p. 271).*

2. Place in blender; blend at high speed 3-5 minutes until smooth:
   ¾ cup buttermilk *(p. 11; or non-dairy alternative, p. 29)*
   1 egg *(or alternative, p. 269)*
   ¼ cup honey
   1½ tablespoons olive oil *(extra virgin preferred, p. 14)*
   1 teaspoon vanilla extract
   1 cup whole wheat pastry grain (not flour), *(see grains, p. 13)*
   or other grain alternative (see list below)

3. Mix in thoroughly, but briefly, using blender and/or rubber spatula, as needed:
   1⅛ teaspoons baking powder *(p. 11)*   "sift" these through a small
   ⅜ teaspoon baking soda   strainer with a spoon to
   ⅜ teaspoon salt   break up any lumps.

3. Fold in (for even mixing, see *Mixing Tip*, p.196):
   1 orange, peeled, diced
   ¾ cup diced dates

4. Fill muffin cups almost full. Fill any empty cups half full of water. Bake at 400° for 20 minutes. Cool muffins in pan for 3-5 minutes for easy removal with a slight tug on side of each muffin.

Per Muffin (of 12) with wheat   Exchanges: 0.75 Bread, 0.25 Fat, 1.5 Fruit; 143 Calories, 3 g protein (8%), 2.5 g fat (15%), 28 g carbohydrate (77%; 14 g sugars), 3 g dietary fiber, 18 mg cholesterol, 102 mg sodium, $.20

GRAIN ALTERNATIVES *(see grains, p. 13)*
   ¾ cup + 2 tablespoons barley grain (1½ cups flour)
   1 cup + 2 tablespoons kamut grain (1½ cups flour)
   1 cup spelt grain (1¾ cups flour)

The Waffle/Pancake, French Toast Breakfast

He makes grass grow for the cattle, and plants for man to cultivate--
bringing forth food from the earth. . . and bread that sustains his heart.
Psalm 104:14, 15

WAFFLE/PANCAKE, FRENCH TOAST

SUBJECTS

RECIPES

 # The Waffle/Pancake, French Toast Breakfast

Fruit Juice, optional
Waffles, Pancakes, or French Toast
Toppings
(Fruit or Fruit Topping, Syrup,
Yogurt or Whipped Cream)
Spread, optional
(Butter or Butter Spread)

Nutrition Goals Menu[1]

6 oz. Orange Juice
1-1½ Servings Blender Waffles (p. 206)
½-1 cup Fresh Fruit Topping (p. 220)
2-4 tbsps. Maple Syrup (p. 217)
½ - ¾ cup Lowfat Vanilla Yogurt

[1]*Small: $1.50   19% Fat   656 Calories*
[1]*Large: $2.15   19% Fat   1,014 Calories*

---

[1]This menu is included in the "Average of 7 Breakfasts" Column on the *Nutrition Goals Chart*, pp. 16-17.   Small servings represent menu for adult female; large servings represent menu for adult male.

Waffle/Pancake Making Tips

Become an expert in whole grain waffle/pancake making in no time! Here's how:

1. Use the recipe for *Blender Waffles/Pancakes*, p. 204.
2. Acquaint yourself with *Whole Grain Blender Magic*, pp. 83-84.
3. Take advantage of the additional tips below.

● **Waffle iron** Purchase a Belgian waffle iron. Select a small round one (about 7"). The grid has deeper perforations, making the lightest whole grain waffles. Pancakes are great, but nothing beats a waffle for family eating pleasure!

● **Grain** Since practically any whole grain or grain combination works great in this recipe, minimize the use of wheat. Wheat makes waffles and pancakes heavier than with any other grain, and is used in many other recipes where a wide variety of grains don't work well. This is your opportunity to use variety and to also to meet allergy needs. The strangeness of some grains used in other ways (millet, for example) is hardly noticed in waffles.

● **Liquid** Buttermilk is our first choice of liquid for lightness and flavor, but thinned yogurt, sour milk or kefir can be substituted with equally good results. Use fresh (for best texture) or powdered buttermilk (see p. 11). For non-dairy alternatives, see p. 29 (Nut milk is especially recommended, p. 34). Different liquids and flours will alter the batter consistency. Keep it quite pourable--better thin than too thick. A vortex (large hole in the center of churning batter) insures best consistency for waffle batter. Adjust batter consis-tency to your preference (you may want your batter a little thicker for pancakes). To substitute juice, stay away from those with high sugar content (strawberry, for example) that will cause the batter to stick in the waffle iron. Apple or orange juice are fairly safe.

● **Egg** The egg is optional so there is no need for a substitute, but we always use it. Two egg whites will also work fine in place of 1 egg.

● **Oil** Fat is for crispy waffle lovers, but it also adds nutritional value if you add the right kind. Therefore, we don't omit it even if the fat percentage looks more attractive. Fat also makes the waffles more golden brown. Use olive oil (for its health benefits, see p. 262). We use extra virgin olive oil and cannot detect its strong flavor. If not satisfied with that, use light or extra light olive oil. If you omit the fat, special care must be taken to prepare the waffle iron or griddle so the batter does not stick, even with a non-stick surface. Give the iron or griddle one good spray with non-stick olive oil spray before baking the first waffle or pancakes and thereafter as needed.

● **Vanilla Extract** Many waffle and pancake recipes call for a little sugar. Vanilla acts somewhat similar as sugar in adding that "certain something" to the flavor. I call it the secret ingredient for especially tasty waffles, except in buckwheat waffles.

● **Salt** Use salt, to taste. For most persons food will taste flat without it. At least a small amount should be added to improve nutritional value (see [1]note, p. 98). Use a quality sea salt (p. 14).

● **Sweetener** Traditional recipes call for a bit. We don't add any. Who needs it with all that sweet stuff on top! Besides, added sugar in the batter will just mean more sticking problems in the waffle iron.

● **Baking powder** leavens and there are several alternatives (see pp. 278-80). It may be omitted, if desired, with beaten egg whites, or replaced with baking soda (½ teaspoon soda to replace 1 teaspoon baking powder). We use *Rumford* or low sodium baking powder (p. 11). Leavening should be fresh and active for good results (see p. 279 for testing its freshness). Be prepared for the batter to start rising toward the top of the blender when the leavening is added. Have the waffle iron hot for ready pouring or pour part of the batter   i n t o another container.

● **Baking soda** gives a wonderful lightness when combined with cultured milk (buttermilk, yogurt, sour milk, kefir). It is also needed to react with the acid of fruit juices. It may be omitted when using water or regular non-cultured sweet milk.

● **Mixing in advance** There are important nutritional benefits (see pp. 50-51) and other advantages to mixing up the batter several hours in advance, preferably overnight. Reserve the egg and leavenings to add just before baking :

~*Nutritional Value* Advance mixing allows the breakdown of the *phytates* in the flour that bind valuable nutrients, thus preventing their assimilation by the body--especially calcium, phosphorus, manganese, iron and zinc, and better protein absorption.

~*Smooth Batter* Not all blenders grind the grain equally smooth during initial blending and not all grains are ground equally smooth. Softening of the initially blended grain overnight will facilitate complete grinding of about any grain with a second blend of about 1 minute.

~*Convenience* Premixed batter is a great last minute timesaver, as well as breaking the preparation into two quick 5 minute steps.

Continued on p. 206

203

Blender Waffles/Pancakes

Surprisingly light, crispy, appetite arousing whole grain waffles without an expensive grain mill. A Belgian waffle iron is our favorite for these. Great for pancakes, too! Maximized whole grain nutrition at minimum cost. Versatile allergy alternatives with grain variations (single grains or combinations). Requires less than 10 minutes to mix. Caution: a good blender that can crush ice cubes is essential (See pp. 82-83). Experiment with the smaller recipe first (first listed ingredients in parentheses). For additional success tips see pp. 202-204, 206.

AMOUNT: 2 (2½ - 3 waffles) or 4 (4 - 5 waffles) or 20-24 Pancakes

1. Place in blender; blend at highest speed 3 minutes:
   - **(¾) 1½ - 1¾ cups buttermilk** (or non-dairy alternative)
   - **(1) 2 tablespoons olive oil**, **optional** (for crispness)
   - **(½) 1 teaspoon vanilla extract**, **optional** (omit with buckwheat)
   - **(⅔) 1½ cups raw brown rice or uncooked rolled oats**
     (or other grain variation--see suggestions, p. 205)

   The batter should always swirl about a vortex in the blender. If it doesn't, slowly add more liquid until the hole reappears. This is the secret to light and tender waffles. Batter for pancakes may be thicker, but keep batter relatively thin and keep it churning.

2. Cover blender; let stand at room temperature overnight (see p. 203).

3. Preheat waffle iron at highest temperature, or griddle on medium-high.

4. Just before baking, add and reblend on highest speed for 1 minute:
   - **1 egg, optional**
   - **additional liquid** (if batter needs thinning for vortex or churning)

5. Blend in thoroughly, but briefly (assisted with rubber spatula, if needed):
   - **(1) 2 teaspoons baking powder** *(p. 11)*   "sift" these through a small
   - **(¼) ½ teaspoon baking soda**   strainer with a spoon to
   - **(½) 1 teaspoon salt, to taste**   break up any lumps.

6. Pour batter onto hot waffle iron (or griddle for pancakes), sprayed with olive oil non-stick spray. Bake about 4 minutes in waffle iron until crispy (Don't peek!) or until light goes off. For pancakes, bake on first side until bubbles on unbaked side begin to break; turn once nd bake on second side.

Per Serving of 4 (all ingredients with brown rice)
   Exchanges: 0.25 Meat, 0.5 Milk, 3.5 Bread,
1.5 Fat; 376 Calories, 10 g protein (11%),
10 g fat (26%), 59 g carbohydrate (63%; 5 g sugars)
 2.5 g dietary fiber, 57 mg cholesterol, 657 mg
sodium, $.40

204

Blender Waffles/Pancakes Variations

As a general rule, use ⅔ cup (for 2 servings) or 1½ **cups** (for 4 servings) of any grain or grain combination in recipe, p. 204. The following are suggestions and we like them all:

brown rice or millet
Wonderfully light, these look like white flour waffles! Batter will be very thin. Fill waffle iron almost completely to edges. These two grains also make a great combination using equal parts of each grain.

kamut, spelt, wheat
Kamut is a favorite. Wheat we seldom use because this recipe is our chance to use so many non-wheat grains. Wheat will make the heaviest waffles or pancakes of all the whole grains and many persons are either sensitive or allergic to wheat.

buckwheat Reduce to **1 cup** (for 4 servings). It expands.
Sprouting buckwheat is our favorite and it is much less costly than toasted or raw buckwheat. Sprouting buckwheat includes the dark outer hull. My husband's favorite. I like this grain best not combined with other grains.

barley Hulled, not pearled. Reduce to **1 cup** (for 4 servings). It expands.

corn Dry whole corn, not cornmeal
Usually provides some crunch and distinct corn flavor appealing to most tastes.

quinoa
Thoroughly rinse quinoa in strainer night before 1-2 minutes; let stand in bowl of water overnight; drain and rinse about 1 more minute. This raemoves bitter flavor (see p. 75). Batter will be very thin. Fill waffle iron almost completely to edges.

oats Uncooked rolled oats or oat groats
Especially good in combination with other grains. Use ½ **cup** (in recipe for 4) in combination. Sue's favorite is ½ **cup rolled oats + 1 cup kamut.** The same measurement of rolled oats will make a thinner batter than that of oat groats.

For a super health bonus (pp. 266-268) add **1 tablespoon flax seed.** Blend it with the egg (step 4, p. 204) in the blender.

Other optional ingredients
Sprinkle nuts or seeds over the top of the batter after pouring it into the waffle iron as **chopped pecans, walnuts, sunflower seeds.** Stir into batter such ingredients as **nonfat dry milk, wheat bran, wheat germ, lecithin granules** (p. 184).

Baking the Waffles/Pancakes

● Turn waffle iron to hottest setting and allow it to heat up fully. Turn pancake griddle medium-high (drops of water should sizzle on the griddle surface).

● Spray the surface with non-stick spray just before adding the first batter.

● Do not pour batter quite to edges of iron--3/4 cup batter is about right to fill a 7" waffle iron.

● Allow waffles to bake until light goes off (or about 4-5 minutes for most of the newer waffle irons). Gently test lifting the lid. If the waffle is done, the lid will lift easily without the waffle sticking to both surfaces of the iron. If it does not come up easily, give it a little more baking time. To bake pancakes, turn the cakes when the bubbles on the top side start to break.

● The best way to prevent scratching the waffle iron while removing the waffle is to loosen and lift the edge up with a party kabob stick.

Keeping Waffles or Pancakes Hot

● Serving them directly from the iron is best. Otherwise, set each person's waffle plate in the oven to get hot, with an extra waffle serving plate for the extras. Turn the oven to 200-300°. As waffles b a k e place a waffle on each plate. Waffles will crisp up a bit more in the oven. To serve, have syrup or at least some other topping hot.

● To keep pancakes hot, overlap them on one hot serving plate in the oven or on a plate covered with a large inverted metal mixing bowl on top of the range next to the griddle. As hot baked pancakes are added to the serving plate covered with the bowl, they warm the bowl which in turn keeps the cakes hot until ready to serve.

Freezing & Reheating Leftover Waffles/Pancakes

● Allow to thoroughly cool. Wrap snugly in saran, then firmly in foil. Use within 2 weeks. There are several methods to reheat waffles. For waffles I use the first method:

~Turn the waffle iron on medium heat setting. Match the waffles with the iron grid and reheat. If waffles are still frozen use lower heat.

~Toast in toaster on lightest setting. Great for a snack!

~Warm on oven rack 3-5 minutes at 350°. Heat pancakes covered.

International Waffles

3 - 4 Servings

Our favorite waffle recipe before we discovered Blender Waffles. Bake as for Blender Waffles. For benefits of advance mixing see pp. 50-51.

1. Blend dry ingredients in large mixing bowl:

    ⅔ cup rice flour (grind ½ cup brown rice)
    ⅔ cup oat flour (grind ½ cup whole oat groats or rolled oats)
    ⅓ cup millet flour (grind ¼ cup millet)
    ⅓ cup buckwheat flour (grind ¼ cup buckwheat or kasha)
    2 teaspoons baking powder   "sift" these through a small strainer
    ½ teaspoon baking soda   with a spoon to break up any lumps.
    ½ - 1 teaspoon salt, to taste

2. Separate **4 eggs**; beat egg whites stiff, but not dry.

3. Whisk liquid ingredients into dry ingredients; fold in egg whites:

    1¼ - 1½ cups buttermilk (as desired for consistency)
    4 egg yolks
    3 tablespoons olive oil *(p. 14)*
    1 teaspoon vanilla extract
    beaten egg whites

Per Serving with all ingredients   Exchanges: 1 Meat, 0.25 Milk, 3 Bread, 2 Fat; 394 Calories, 14 g protein (14%), 17 g fat (38%), 48 g carbohydrate (48%; 4 g sugars), 4 g dietary fiber, 163 mg cholesterol, 472 mg sodium, $.55

Blender Orange Waffles

4 - 6 Servings

We love the flavor of these waffles! See pp. 202-204, 206 as needed. For benefits of advance mixing see pp. 50-51.

1. Place in blender; blend at high speed 5 minutes until smooth:

    1¾ cups buttermilk *(p. 11; or non-dairy alternative, p. 29)*
    6 oz. can frozen orange juice concentrate (thawed)
    1 egg *(or alternative, p. 269)*
    2 tablespoons olive *(p. 14)*
    1 cup kamut or whole wheat pastry grain *(see grains, p. 13)*
    ½ cup whole dry corn

2. Just before baking, mix in thoroughly, but briefly, using blender and/or rubber spatula, as needed:

    ¾ cup rolled oats, uncooked
    2 teaspoons orange peel, fresh or dried
    ½ - 1 teaspoon salt, to taste
    ½ teaspoon baking soda   "sift" these through a small strainer
    2 teaspoons baking powder *(p. 11)*   with a spoon to break up any lumps.

3. Bake in seasoned or sprayed hot waffle iron or griddle.

Per Serving of 4   Exchanges: 0.25 Meat, 0.5 Milk, 4.25 Bread, 1.25 Fat, 2.25 Fruit; 508 Calories, 16 g protein (12%), 11.5 g fat (20%), 90 g carbohydrate (68%; 27 g sugars), 9.5 g dietary fiber, 57 mg cholesterol, 230 mg sodium, $.65

Blender Oat Pancakes

18 - 4" Pancakes

This makes great waffles, too! We usually omit the sweetening. For benefits of advance mixing see pp. 50-51.

1. Place in blender; blend at high speed 2 minutes until smooth:
   - **1 ¾ cups buttermilk** *(p. 11; or non-dairy alternative, p. 29)*
   - **3 eggs (or yolks if doing step #3)**
   - **2 tablespoons olive oil** *(extra virgin preferred, p. 14)*
   - **1 teaspoon vanilla extract**
   - **2 cups rolled oats, uncooked**

2. mix in thoroughly, but briefly, using blender and/or rubber spatula, as needed:
   - **2 tablespoons *Sucanat*** *(p.15),* **or crystalline fructose, optional**
   - **½ teaspoon salt**
   - **½ teaspoon baking soda**
   - **2 teaspoons baking powder** *(p.11)*

   "sift" these through a small strainer with a spoon to break up any lumps.

3. Optional for lighter cakes--Pour batter into mixing bowl; fold in:
   - **3 stiffly beaten egg whites** *(p. 204)*

4. Bake on moderately hot griddle or in hot waffle iron for waffles.

Per 1 Pancake using 1 egg in recipe
  Exchanges: 0.25 Meat, 0.5 Bread, 0.25 Fat; 71 Calories, 3 g protein (18%), 3 g fat (40%), 7.5 g carbohydrate (42%; 1 g sugars), 1 g dietary fiber, 37 mg cholesterol, 93 mg sodium, $.10

Cottage Pancakes

8 - 5" Pancakes

Light and high in protein. Serve with fresh fruit topping.

1. Separate **4 eggs**; beat egg whites until stiff, but not dry.

2. Blend together in mixing bowl:
   - **4 egg yolks, beaten until light**
   - **1 cup nonfat or lowfat cottage cheese, plain kefir** *(p.28),* **or well drained tofu** *(p.15)*
   - **½ cup flour (spelt, barley, kamut, brown rice, whole wheat pastry, whole wheat, or soy flour)***(see grains, p. 13)*
   - **1 tablespoon olive oil or melted butter**
   - **½ teaspoon vanilla**
   - **¼ teaspoon salt**

3. Fold into batter:
   - **4 stiffly beaten egg whites**

4. Bake pancakes on non-stick or lightly sprayed griddle over moderate heat on both sides.

Per 1 Pancake   Exchanges: 0.75 Meat, 0.25 Milk, 0.5 Bread, 0.25 Fat; 100 Calories, 7.5 g protein (31%), 4.5 g fat (42%), 7 g carbohydrate (28%; 0.5 g sugars), 1 g dietary fiber, 108 mg cholesterol, 100 mg sodium, $.25

208

Carol's Finnish Pancakes   4 - 6 Servings

Moist and custard-like, not your usual pancakes! Bakes into 2 layers with a moist chewy bottom layer and custard-like top layer. Cut into squares and top with fresh fruit, berries, a fruit or berry sauce, or Alice's Fruit Soup (p. 178). Use flour or grain in this recipe. For benefits of advance mixing see pp. 50-51.

AMOUNT: 9" x 13" Baking Pan
Bake: 400°F (205°C) - 20 to 35 minutes

1. Melt butter in 9" x 13" pan in oven while preheating:
   3 tablespoons butter (1½ tbsps. for reduced fat) *(unsalted preferred)*

2. Place in blender; blend at high speed--3 - 5 minutes with grain, or 30 seconds with flour:
   2 cups lowfat or nonfat milk (1½ cups with spelt)
   4 eggs
   ¼ cup honey (increase to ½ cup, if desired, for more sweet)
   1 teaspoon vanilla
   ¼ teaspoon salt
   1 cup flour--whole wheat pastry, spelt, barley, or kamut
   or ⅔ cup whole wheat or whole wheat pastry grain
   or ½ cup + 1 tablespoon spelt or barley grain
   or ¾ cup kamut grain *(see grains, p. 13)*

3. Pour batter into pan over evenly distributed melted butter.

4. Bake at 400° for 20-35 minutes or until knife comes clean out of center.

Per 2¼" x 3" Piece (12 per pan, cut 3 x 4)   Exchanges: 0.5 Meat, 0.25 Milk, 0.5 Bread, 0.5 Fat, 0.5 Fruit; 130 Calories, 4 g protein (14%), 5.5 g fat (38%), 16 g carbohydrate (48%; 8 g sugars), 1 g dietary fiber, 82 mg cholesterol, 48 mg sodium, $.15

CAROB VARIATION

Add in step #2.

⅓ cup carob powder, sifted

Cool slightly; spread over top:
carob chips
chopped nuts
sliced bananas, optional
shredded coconut, optional

Sifting Tip: If you don't have a sifter, stir carob through a strainer.

Per 2¼" x 3" Piece (12 per pan, cut 3 x 4, with ½ c. carob chips, ½ c. walnuts, 2 bananas)
   Exchanges: 0.5 Meat, 0.25 Milk, 1 Bread, 1.5 Fat, 1 Fruit; 236 Calories, 7 g protein (11%), 11 g fat (41%), 29 g carbohydrate (48%; 16 g sugars), 2.5 g dietary fiber, 83 mg cholesterol, 60 mg sodium, $.35

French Toast

A simple standard recipe for French toast with added spark of vanilla. To evenly distribute the cinnamon, sprinkle it over the unbaked side of the toast as the other side bakes. If you add it to the egg, it will just float to the top and heavily coat the first slice or two.

6 - 8 Slices

1. Whisk together with a fork in a shallow bowl shaped to allow easy dipping of the bread:
   - **2 eggs**
   - **½ cup nonfat (skim) or lowfat milk**
   - **1 teaspoon vanilla**
   - **dash salt**

2. Dip bread slices, one at a time, into egg mixture, turning once to coat both sides:
   - **6 - 8 slices whole grain bread** (day old or slightly stale bread makes the best French toast)

3. Toast slices on hot non-stick griddle or griddle sprayed with non-stick spray. Before turning slices to bake second side, dust unbaked sides evenly with:
   - **cinnamon**

Per Slice of 8
   Exchanges: 0.25 Meat, 1.25 Bread; 115 Calories, 6 g protein (21%), 2.5 g fat (22%), 17 g carbohydrate (58%; 2 g sugars), 2 g dietary fiber, 54 mg cholesterol, 212 mg sodium, $.15

French Toast Topper

Kids will especially love this simple gourmet-like topping, yet with much less syrup. The usual butter will not be missed!

1 Serving

To serve, spread evenly over top of each slice French toast:
   - **2 tablespoons unsweetened applesauce**
   - **5 slices banana (about ⅓ banana)**
   - **1 teaspoon warm pure maple syrup** (drizzled over bananas)

Per Serving
   Exchanges: 1.5 Fruit; 64 Calories, 16 g carbohydrate (95%), 1 g dietary fiber, 0 mg cholesterol, 1 mg sodium, $.15

Low Cholesterol French Toast

For French toast lovers who want to avoid the egg yolk (something I don't do--see p.130).

2 Slices

1. Blend together in blender:
   1 egg white
   ¼ cup nonfat (skim) milk
   ½ teaspoon vanilla
   dash salt, optional

2. Pour into wide shallow dish and coat on both sides of:
   2 slices whole grain bread

3. Toast slices on hot non-stick griddle or griddle sprayed with non-stick spray. Before turning slices to bake on second side, dust unbaked sides evenly with:
   cinnamon

Per Slice
   Exchanges: 0.25 Meat, 1.25 Bread; 109 Calories, 7 g protein (25%), 1 g fat (9%), 18 g carbohydrate (66%; 2.5 g sugars), 2 g dietary fiber, 1 mg cholesterol, 253 mg sodium, $.25

Maple Butter French Toast

A yummy eggless French Toast. Controls use of butter and syrup. Delicious served with unsweetened apple-sauce.

2 Slices

1. Whisk together thoroughly and pour onto a dinner plate:
   1 tablespoon melted unsalted butter *(p. 11)*
   2 tablespoons pure maple syrup

2. Coat both sides of:
   2 slices whole grain bread

3. Toast slices on hot non-stick griddle or griddle sprayed with non-stick spray. Before turning slices to bake on second side, dust unbaked sides evenly with:
   cinnamon

Per Slice   Exchanges: 1.25 Bread, 1.25 Fat, 1.25 Fruit; 193 Calories, 4 g protein (8%), 6.5 g fat (30%), 29 g carbohydrate (61%; 14 g sugars), 2 g dietary fiber, 15 mg cholesterol, 182 mg sodium, $.20

Tofu French Toast

*Remember grandmother's milk toast? This recipe is similarly soft and moist. It needs no syrup, but is tasty with a little butter and/or applesauce. A 10 oz. package of Mori Nu Tofu (p. 15) contains 1¼ **cups tofu**--just right for a family recipe of 10 slices French Toast (the recipe below multiplied 5 times).*

2 Slices

1. Vigorously blend together until as smooth as possible with a wire whisk in a small bowl:
   - **¼ cup soft tofu** *(p. 15)*
   - **2 tablespoons water**
   - **1 teaspoon** *Sucanat* *(p. 15)*, **crystalline fructose** *(p. 12)*, **honey, or brown sugar**
   - **¼ teaspoon cinnamon**
   - **⅛ teaspoon nutmeg**
   - **⅛ teaspoon vanilla**
   - **dash salt, optional**

2. Pour mixture on a plate. Coat one side:
   - **2 slices whole grain bread**

   You may need to do a little spooning of the mixture onto the bread to coat sufficiently.

3. Place slices, coated side down, on moderately hot griddle well sprayed with non-stick spray, or on a lightly sprayed non-stick fry pan or griddle.

4. While first side bakes, spoon tofu mixture on unbaked sides of bread to spread evenly.

5. Turn when lightly browned to brown second side.

Per Slice   Exchanges: 0.25 Meat, 1.5 Bread, 0.25 Fat, 0.25 Fruit; 116 Calories, 6.5 g protein (21%), 2 g fat (17%), 18.5 g carbohydrate (62%; 2.5 g sugars), 2 g dietary fiber, 0 mg cholesterol, 219 mg sodium, $.25

Two Fruits Topping

2 Cups

Combine:
- **1 large banana (1 cup), sliced**
- **1 cup fresh pineapple chunks**

Per ½ Cup   Exchanges: 1.25 Fruit; 54 Calories, 13.5 g carbohydrate (91%; 12 g sugars), 1.5 g dietary fiber, 0 mg cholesterol, 1 mg sodium, $.20

Maple Syrup

Some people can't tell the difference between this recipe and real maple syrup. If you can't find real maple syrup, use this recipe in preference to commercial pancake syrup. Cost is about the same as real maple syrup.

Makes ⅝ Cup

Whisk together in saucepan:
> **⅓ cup boiling water**
> **1 cup honey** (mild flavor)
> **½ teaspoon mapline or maple flavor extract**

Per 2 Tablespoons:
   Exchanges: 5 Fruit; 205 Calories, 55 g carbohydrate (100%; 55 g sugars), 0 mg cholesterol, 3 mg sodium, $.25

VARIATION

Crystalline fructose or *Sucanat* *(pp. 12, 15)* may be substituted for honey, but will cost about twice as much per serving. When using these sugars, add a dash of salt to improve flavor; simmer for 3 minutes over moderate heat.

Honey Butter Syrup

Tasty syrup for waffles, pancakes, French toast.

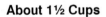

About 1½ Cups

In saucepan thoroughly blend together
with wire whisk over low heat:
> **½ cup (1 stick) unsalted butter, melted** *(p. 11)*
> **1 cup honey** (mild flavor)

Per 2 Tablespoons:
   Exchanges: 1.5 Fat, 2.25 Fruit; 152 Calories, 7.5 g fat (42%), 23 g carbohydrate (58%; 23 g sugars), 20 mg cholesterol, 1 mg sodium, $.15

VARIATIONS

1. Blend in:
> **½ cup finely chopped nuts**
>> (walnuts, pecans, or almonds)
2. Use in place of half the honey:
> **½ cup maple syrup**

Honey Orange Syrup

A tasty topping for waffles, pancakes, or French toast.

About 1¾ Cups

Blend together thoroughly with wire whisk in
a saucepan over low heat:
>   **½ cup (1 stick) unsalted butter, melted** *(p. 11)*
>   **6 oz. can frozen orange juice concentrate, unsweetened**
>   **⅔ cup honey**

Per 2 Tablespoons   Exchanges: 1.25 Fat, 1.75 Fruit; 132 Calories, 6 g fat (42%),
19.5 g carbohydrate (58%; 19 g sugars), 17 mg cholesterol, 1 mg sodium, $.15

Orange Molasses Syrup

For molasses lovers!

Scant 1 Cup

1. Thoroughly blend in saucepan with wire whisk:
>   **½ cup orange juice**
>   **1½ teaspoons arrowroot powder** *(p. 11)* **or cornstarch**

2. Stir in:
>   **½ cup molasses** *(blackstrap preferred, p. 14)*
>   **2 tablespoons *Sucanat*** *(p. 15)* **or crystalline fructose** *(p. 12)*
>   **1 tablespoon unsalted butter** *(p. 11)*

3. Bring to very low boil and cook over medium heat until
   thickened, about 1 minute *(see Ingredient Tip on arrowroot, p. 220).*

Per 2 Tablespoons
*   Exchanges: 0.25 Fat, 1.5 Fruit; 74 Calories, 1.5 g fat (17%),*
15 g carbohydrate (82%; 15 g sugars), 4 mg cholesterol, 26 mg sodium, $.15

Whipped Cream

For an occasional treat over waffles with fruit.

2 Cups

Beat whipping cream on high speed in electric mixer until
foamy. Add sweetener and continue to whip until thickened:
>   **½ pint (1 cup) whipping cream**
>   **2 tablespoons honey or crystalline fructose** *(p. 12)*

Per ¼ Cup   Exchanges: 2 Fat, 0.5 Fruit; 116 Calories, 10 g fat (78%), 6 g carbohydrate
(22%; 6 g sugars), 40 mg cholesterol, $.15

Whipped Fluff Topping

3 Cups

A simple gourmet fruit topping for waffles, pancakes, or fresh fruit. A little lighter and less rich than whipped cream.

Blend together:

1 cup (½ pint) whipping cream, whipped (2 cups whipped)
1 cup sour cream *(fat-free or light preferred, p. 14)*
¼ cup honey or crystalline fructose *(p. 12)*
1 teaspoon vanilla

Per ¼ Cup with fat-free sour cream
   Exchanges: 0.25 Milk, 1.25 Fat, 0.5 Fruit; 100 Calories, 1 g protein (5%), 7 g fat (59%) 9 g carbohydrate (36%; 8.5 g sugars), 27 mg cholesterol, 2 mg sodium, $.20

Almond Sauce

2 Cups

Serve with fresh sliced strawberries or peaches over waffles or pancakes.

Blend together with a wire whisk:

1 cup nonfat or lowfat plain yogurt
1 cup sour cream *(fat-free or light preferred, p. 14)*
½ cup sliced or chopped almonds (toasted, if desired)
⅓ cup honey or maple syrup, to taste
1 teaspoon vanilla, optional

About ¼ Cup with fat-free sour cream; vanilla included
   Exchanges: 0.25 Meat, 0.25 Milk, 0.5 Fat, 1.25 Fruit; 113 Calories, 6 g protein (19%), 3 g fat (23%), 17 g carbohydrate (58%; 16 g sugars), 1 g dietary fiber, 1 mg cholesterol, 20 mg sodium, $.30

Honey Cream Topping

About 1¼ Cups

Serve over waffles, pancakes, and French toast, or unfrosted cake.

Blend together thoroughly in order given with a wire whisk or in electric mixer:

½ cup (1 stick) soft butter
¼ cup honey
½ cup sour cream *(fat-free or light preferred, p. 14)*
1 teaspoon vanilla

Per ¼ Cup with fat-free sour cream
   Exchanges: 4 Fat, 1.25 Fruit; 234 Calories, 19 g fat (73%), 15 g carbohydrate (26%; 15 g sugars), 56 mg cholesterol, 98 mg sodium, $.25

Fresh Fruit Topping

4-6 Servings

Combine:

½ cup fresh pineapple chunks
2 fresh peaches or nectarines, chopped
1 sliced banana
2 tablespoons toasted coconut *(p. 117)*
2 tablespoons chopped pecans, walnuts, or sliced almonds
1 teaspoon crystalline fructose, optional *(p. 12)*

Per Serving of 4   Exchanges: 0.75 Fat, 1 Fruit; 78 Calories, 4 g fat (41%), 11.5 g carbohydrate (56%; 9.5 g sugars), 2 g dietary fiber, 0 mg cholesterol, 1 mg sodium, $.20

Dried Apple Topping

About 3 Cups

A favorite off-season waffle and pancake topping. Delicious with yogurt. Dried apples are the least expensive dried fruit to keep on hand.

1. Soak several hours or overnight:
   2 cups water
   1 cup dried apples, unsulfured *(p. 12)*

2. Drain the apples, saving the juice. Measure the juice and add enough water to make **1 cup liquid**. Pour into saucepan and whisk in:
   ¼ cup honey
   2 tablespoons arrowroot powder *(p. 11)* **or cornstarch**
   ½ teaspoon cinnamon

3. Bring to a low boil over medium heat, stirring constantly with wire whisk. Continue to cook until thickened and clear, about 1 minute. Remove from heat.

4. Snip apples in pieces with kitchen shears, or chop small with a chef's knife. Fold into cooked sauce.

5. To serve, rewarm or keep warm, as needed over low heat.

> **Ingredient Tip:** Arrowroot powder is more unstable than cornstarch. It requires lower heat and is best not boiled vigorously. It generally does not hold or reheat well, although this recipe remains thick upon refrigerating and reheating leftover topping. This may be partly due to the thickening effect of the pectin in the apples. Although arrowroot has twice the thickening power of cornstarch, I prefer to use the same amount of either in recipes.

About ¼ Cup   Exchanges: 1 Fruit; 43 Calories, 12 g carbohydrate (97%; 10 g sugars), 1 g dietary fiber, 0 mg cholesterol, 1 mg sodium, $.10

216

Fresh Apple Topping

A favorite waffle and pancake topping when fresh apples are in abundance. I like tart apples such as Gravenstein, Greening, Newton Pippin, or Granny Smith.

4 - 6 Servings (2½ - 3 Cups)

1. Combine in saucepan, bring to boil, lower heat and simmer until apples are just tender:
   4 apples, cored, peeled or unpeeled; coarsely chopped
   just enough water to prevent sticking while cooking

2. Remove from heat, drain, and stir in, to taste:
   ¼ cup honey or crystalline fructose *(p. 12)*
   ½ teaspoon cinnamon

Per Serving of 4
*   Exchanges: 4 Fruit; 161 Calories, 43 g carbohydrate (99%; 38 g sugars),*
5 g dietary fiber, 0 mg cholesterol, 2 mg sodium, $.40

Berry Topping

During blackberry picking season, this topping makes a delectable treat! Most of the berries are not completely cooked, yet the sauce helps to spread the berry flavor further. To buy fresh berries, purchase 12 oz.

About 2 Cups

1. Blend with wire whisk in saucepan:
   about ½ cup crushed berries (blackberries, blueberries, strawberries, raspberries, etc, fresh or frozen)
   about ½ cup water
   2 tablespoons arrowroot powder *(p. 11)* **or cornstarch**
   1-2 tablespoons honey or crystalline fructose *(p. 12)***, to taste**

2. Cook and stir over moderate heat at very low boil until thickened and clear, about 1 minute (see *Ingredient Tip* on arrowroot, p. 220).

3. Stir in and heat through; do not cook so that berries break down into mush:
   1½ cups berries (cut or quarter strawberries)

About ¼ Cup (with frozen blackberries)
*   Exchanges: 0.75 Fruit; 38 Calories, 9 g carbohydrate (97%; 4.5 g sugars),*
1 g dietary fiber, 0 mg cholesterol, $.30

Pineapple Topping

2½ Cups

An easy waffle and pancake topping alternative when fresh fruit is hard to come by. Great alternative to highly concentrated sweet maple syrup. Also tasty over unfrosted cake.

1. Blend together in saucepan with wire whisk:
   20 oz. can crushed pineapple, unsweetened; undrained
   1½ tablespoons arrowroot powder *(p. 11)* **or cornstarch**
   1 tablespoon honey or crystalline fructose *(p. 12)*, **to taste**

2. Bring to very low boil over medium heat, stirring constantly. Cook and stir about 1 minute until thickened.

Per ¼ Cup
   Exchanges: 0.75 Fruit; 39 Calories, 10 g carbohydrate (100%; 7.5 g sugars),
0.5 g dietary fiber, 0 mg cholesterol, 5 mg sodium, $.10

Pine-Applesauce Topping

2 Cups

Very easy and tasty! Use canned applesauce. I add the drained pineapple juice to our breakfast orange juice.

Stir together to blend:
   1½ cups applesauce, canned unsweetened
   8 oz. can crushed unsweetened pineapple, drained
   ¼ teaspoon cinnamon, to taste

Per ½ Cup
   Exchanges: 1.75 Fruit; 75 Calories, 19.5 g carbohydrate (98%; 15 g sugars),
1 g dietary fiber, 0 mg cholesterol, 6 mg sodium, $.30

Nutty Banana Topping

3 - 4 Servings

Kids will especially enjoy on pancakes or French toast.

1. Blend thoroughly with wire whisk:
   ½ cup peanut butter, slightly warmed
   1 - 2 tablespoons honey, slightly warmed, to taste

2. To serve, spread mixture over pancakes and top with:
   sliced banana
   raisins, optional

Per 1 tbsp. sweetened peanut butter with ⅓ banana, 1½ tsps. raisins
   Exchanges: 0.25 Meat, 0.25 Bread, 1.5 Fat, 1.25 Fruit; 143 Calories, 4 g protein (11%),
7.5 g fat (44%), 17 g carbohydrate (45%; 14 g sugars), 2 g dietary fiber, 0 mg cholesterol,
50 mg sodium, $.15

For Special Occasions

When you have eaten and are satisfied, praise the LORD your God for the good land he has given you. Deuteronomy 8:10

FOR SPECIAL OCCASIONS

SUBJECTS

RECIPES

Beverages

Coffee Cakes

Crepes

Eggs/Sausage

Pizza

Scones

Sweet Yeast Breads

For Special Occasions

The Granola Breakfast Buffet
~
Winsome Waffles
~
An Elegant Egg Menu
~
Company Crepes & Tea
~
Festive Fruit & Hot Bread

Nutrition Goals Menu[1]

Fresh Fruit Tray or Plate Garnish
1-1½ Servings Virginia's Egg Scramble (p. 228)
1-2 Breakfast Sausage (p. 230)
2-3 pc's Blender Blueberry Coffee Cake (p. 236)
1 - 1½ Tbsps. Butter
1 Cup Herb Tea or Decaffeinated Coffee

[1]*Small: $1.55   51% Fat   761 Calories*
[1]*Large: $2,20   52% Fat 1,138 Calories*

[1]This menu is included in the "Average of 7 Breakfasts" Column on the *Nutrition Goals Chart*, pp. 16-17. Small servings represent menu for adult female; large servings represent menu for adult male. I chose this high fat, high cholesterol meal to illustrate that you can enjoy one occasionally without sacrificing the daily nutrition goals. Fresh fruit tray or plate garnish includes thin wedge cantaloupe, thin wedge honeydew melon, 3 strawberries.

Celebrating with Yummies!

As Jesus and his disciples were on their way, he came to a village where a woman named Martha opened her home to him. She had a sister called Mary, who sat at the Lord's feet listening to what he said. But Martha was distracted by all the preparations that had to be made. She came to him and asked, "Lord don't you care that my sister has left me to do the work by myself? Tell her to help me!"

"Martha, Martha," The Lord answered, "you are worried and upset about many things, but only one thing is needed. Mary has chosen what is better, and it will not be taken away from her."
Luke 10:38-42

Having what I consider a *Martha* temperament, and having spent a good portion of my life cooking for large numbers of people in camp and retreat kitchens, I have treasured the lessons from *Luke 10:38-42* concerning hospitality.

The following suggestions will minimize the anxiety and last minute stress of serving guests:

~Serve a menu that is simple to complete at the last minute or just prior to the meal.

~Prepare all the food in advance that you can by at least one day.

~Grocery shop on a different day than your day of major food preparation--two days or more in advance.

~Complete all but the absolutely last minute necessities the night before (see *Breakfast Time Savers*, p. 10).

~Sit down to eat with your guests and enjoy the mutual friendship and fellowship. Arrange table service so you won't need to hop up and down during the meal.

How will you decide the menu? Many women think that they are somehow obligated to revert to typical American fare to satisfy company. I have not done so in 24 years. I have consistently served guests my own nutritious recipes and menus. They have not only enjoyed them, but appreciated them as well. Most people value being served healthier food when it is attractive, tasty, filling, and refreshingly different.

My confidence in serving company meals that are especially appealing comes from years of experience observing people's reactions to conference and camp menus. The following are my favorite special occasion breakfast menus--easy to prepare and well received.

1. The Granola Breakfast Buffet (below)
2. Winsome Waffles *(p. 224)*
3. An Elegant Egg Menu *(p. 225)*
4. Company Crepes & Tea *(p. 226)*
5. Festive Fruit & Hot Bread *(p. 227)*

Granola Breakfast Buffet

This meal is incredibly simple to serve. Practically everything can be done ahead of time except heating the bread.

Granola - 1 or more kinds
2 or 3 Cold Cereals from the Box
Bowl of Fresh Fruit & Raisins
Fruit Flavored Yogurts
Milk
Home Baked Hot Bread
(butter, jam, peanut butter as suits)
Hot Carob (optional)

You can buy your favorite granola or make a favorite recipe or one of the recipes on pp. 116-118 several days ahead. Choose more nutritious, but widely accepted cold cereals (pp. 90-91). For fresh fruit I usually put whole bananas and oranges in an attractive serving bowl. Fresh strawberries are also welcome, and are elegant mixed with fresh or frozen blueberries.

For the hot bread, a coffee cake is a treat that can be baked a ahead and easily reheated. Sweet rolls are also delicious (pp. 233-248).

Here is how I served this breakfast on our daughter Sharon's wedding day for 14 family house guests--buffet style: The night before I set out on trays all the table service items (bowls, plates, glasses, flatware, napkins, etc.--everything needed, including the serving containers for refrigerated items). I put the granolas and raisins in serving bowls and covered them with a towel. Next I set out whole wheat English muffins, butter, jam, and peanut butter, the toaster, and put the bananas in the fruit bowl. At other times I would have made a coffee cake in more relaxed moments on the day before, cut it into serving pieces, arranged them on an oven-proof serving plate and covered it with foil. However, on this particular occasion I was at the church preparing food for the wedding reception instead.

Granola Breakfast Buffet Table

1-plates	7-yogurt	12-tray with butter,
2-cereal bowls	8-milk	jam, peanut butter
3-boxed cereals	9-flatware/napins[1]	13-tray with hot water,
4-granola(s)	10-English muffins	coffee, tea, cream,
5-fruit bowl	(or other hot bread)	sweetener, cups[2]
6-raisins	11-toaster	14-centerpiece (optional)

[1]Or make place settings on dining table   [2]Or set on a side table

Next, I filled the tea pot with water for coffee and tea, and set out jars of instant coffee (regular and decaffeinated) and tea bags. Before retiring I put the table cloth on the buffet table. The next morning all I had left to do was to heat the water, heat the coffee cake, fill the serving containers with refrigerated items--milk, yogurt, oranges or other fruit, and transfer everything from the trays to the buffet table. If suitable, this last step can be done just as well the evening before.

After that, we all helped ourselves and sat down to enjoy the meal together. This is a perfect meal to serve to overnight guests who are going to appear for breakfast at different times after they kept late visiting hours or did something special the night before. This was certainly the case for our family wedding guests!

The Granola Breakfast Buffet with a few boxed cold cereals added is especially appealing for children.

Winsome Waffles

Our #1 company meal, even for dinner! *Blender Waffles*, p. 204, with your favorite grain or grain combination, are a certain winner. I serve fresh fruit topping of sliced bananas, pineapple, with strawberries and/or blueberries when in-season. If fresh fruit is scarce, I serve *Dried Apple Topping*, p. 216, or *Alice's Fruit Soup*, p. 178.

For yogurt I usually serve vanilla yogurt. A berry flavored yogurt is also tasty. Plain yogurt can also be sweetened with either maple syrup or honey. For whipped cream I use the recipe on p. 214 or *Whipped Fluff Topping*, p. 215.

224

Winsome Waffles
Maple Syrup   Butter
Fruit Topping or Toppings
Fruit Yogurt; Whipped Cream
Frozen Orange Juice
Breakfast Sausage (optional)

When serving *Breakfast Sausage*, I mix and shape the sausage patties the night before and refrigerate them. When serving several guests, I cook them in the oven (p. 230).

This meal is so easy to prepare that we often include our guests in the preparation. I set the table and get out all the ingredients. Sometimes, if appropriate, I ask them to bring the fresh fruit and yogurt. When all arrive, we plug in the waffle iron, demonstrate how we make blender waffles, cut up the fruit and set on remaining items together. The guests have fun and learn something new. And they love the waffles! The waffle breakfast is so popular that Emilie Barnes has often served it for her annual Christmas Tea.

An Elegant Egg Menu

A company egg breakfast is delicious but a little more work. You can prepare a do-ahead egg dish such as *Virginia's Egg Scramble*, p. 228. Omelets are yummy, but require a little skill since they make up well only in a small number of servings at a time, requiring last minute preparation. Of course, easy-to-make scrambled eggs such as *Gourmet* or *Holiday Scramble*, pp. 141, 229, are also a special treat. Mix the eggs up the night before and store in refrigerator to reduce last minute preparation. Bake the bread in advance. It can be rewarmed

An Elegant Egg Dish
Breakfast Sausage (optional)
Fruit Juice &/or Fresh Fruit Tray
or Fruit Garnish on Plates
Coffee Cake, Muffins, or Sweet Rolls
Hot Carob or Cocoa (optional)

just before serving. Shape the sausage patties in advance, leaving the cooking only to be done at the last minute.

Company Crepes & Hot Tea

These thin pancakes rolled up with a filling are an unknown art in most American homes, yet are elegant and surprisingly easy to prepare. You can be quite certain that such a breakfast will be something new and different to delight your guests or to serve as a special holiday treat for your family. Crepes are one of the easiest breads to make successfully with almost any whole grain flour.

Cottage Filled Fruit Crepes, p. 250, are colorful and delicious. The crepes and filling can be prepared and refrigerated the night before. The fresh fruit topping can be quickly prepared just before serving. The crepes are filling; all you need to complete this menu is something hot to drink.

**CottageFilled Fruit Crepes
Hot Tea, Coffee, or
Hot Carob, or Cocoa** *(p. 229)*

If you wish to serve a main dish style crepe for brunch or dinner, with a little more to the menu, serve *Chicken Curry Crepes*, p. 251, or *Cheesy Spinach Crepes*, p. 252. These recipes include menu suggestions.

The end of all things is near. . . Above all love each other deeply, because love covers over a multitude of sins. Offer hospitality to one another without grumbling . . . . If anyone serves, he should do it with the strength God provides, so that in all things God may be praised through Jesus Christ. To him be the glory and the power for ever and ever. Amen.
1 Peter 4:7-9, 11

Festive Fruit & Hot Bread

This is a terrific menu on a warm summer morning and one of our favorites. *Cantaloupe Boats* make a beautiful presentation. People

Festive Cantaloupe Boats *(p. 177)*
Home Baked Hot Bread
Butter
Hot Tea & Decaffeinated Coffee

will enjoy eating just because it is a delight to the eyes. Cut the cantaloupe the night before and bake the bread in advance. Use seasonal summer fruits. Another tasty version of this meal is to serve a large bowl of mixed cut fresh fruit such as peaches or nectarines, strawberries, blueberries or other berries, bananas, pineapple, and kiwi. Serve fruit-flavored or vanilla yogurt, whipped cream, or *Whipped Fluff Topping* (p. 215) with it. If desired, you can add small bowls of coconut, granola, and/or chopped nuts to sprinkle over the top of the fruit. If children are present for this meal, just include 2 or 3 choices of boxed cold cereal and milk and they'll be happy.

With all special breakfasts coffee and tea are givens so include items needed for them in your preparations.

The nature of most company yummies is that they are higher in fat, sugar, and calories. I don't let this concern me at all, unless celebrations start coming too often. This often occurs during the Christmas season with Christmas parties and desserts. Why not celebrate the season with friends with a delicious breakfast, instead? It will still likely be higher calorie, fat, and sugar than the daily fare, but generally more balanced and wholesome than the goodie or dessert oriented party.

Even Jesus had guests for a very special breakfast that he prepared himself. They must have been delighted indeed! And you will note (see *John 21*) that he asked them to bring some of the food. This was not mere entertainment, it was hospitality with a purpose.

Do not forget to entertain strangers, for by so doing some
people have entertained angels without knowing it.
Hebrews 13:2 with Genesis 18:1-8

227

Virginia's Egg Scramble

8 - 10 Servings

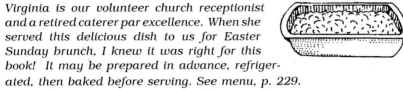

Virginia is our volunteer church receptionist and a retired caterer par excellence. When she served this delicious dish to us for Easter Sunday brunch, I knew it was right for this book! It may be prepared in advance, refrigerated, then baked before serving. See menu, p. 229.

AMOUNT: 9" x 12" glass or pyrex pan

Bake: 325°F (165°C) - 45 to 60 minutes

1. Prepare *Cheese Sauce.* Blend butter and flour; stir in remaining ingredients; cook and stir until thickened over medium heat:
   2 tablespoons melted unsalted butter
   2 tablespoons flour *(unbleached or whole wheat pastry preferred, p. 15)*
   1½ cups lowfat milk
   ½ teaspoon salt
   ⅛ teaspoon pepper
   1½ teaspoons worcesterchire sauce

2. Stir in cheese to melt:
   1 cup firmly packed grated cheddar cheese

3. Prepare *Toasted Bread Crumb Mixture.* Mix together:
   1 cup toasted whole grain bread crumbs
   1½ tablespoons melted unsalted butter

4. Grease or spray baking pan *(p. 271).*

5. Prepare *Scrambled Eggs.* Combine eggs, onion, and mushrooms; scramble in butter until lightly done *(p. 140):*
   12 extra large eggs, beaten
   ¼ cup chopped green onion
   and/or 2 oz. can diced jalapeño or green chiles
   1 cup fresh mushrooms, diced
   3 tablespoons melted unsalted butter

6. Cover bottom of pan with cooked egg mixture. Spread *Cheese Sauce* over top; top with *Toasted Bread Crumb Mixture.* Garnish with **paprika** and **minced parsley.**

7. Refrigerate until ready to bake. Bake at 325° for 45-60 minutes.

Per Serving of 10 (includes green chiles)
Exchanges: 2.5 Meat, 0.25 Milk, 0.25 Bread, 1.5 Fat, 0.25 Vegetable; 260 Calories,
13 g protein (21%), 19.5 g fat (68%), 7 g carbohydrate (11%; 2 g sugars), 1 g dietary fiber,
334 mg cholesterol, 316 mg sodium, $.50

Holiday Scramble

2 - 3 Servings

Make the usual scrambled eggs special with this simple recipe.

1. Wisk together with a fork:
   4 large eggs, beaten until light
   ½ teaspoon salt
   ½ teaspoon thyme leaves
   ¼ teaspoon dry mustard
   ¼ cup sour cream *(fat-free or light preferred, p. 14)*
   ¼ cup Parmesan cheese
   ¼ cup chopped green pepper
   1 tablespoon chopped onion, optional
   2 tablespoons pimiento, chopped

2. Scramble in *(p. 140)*:
   1 tablespoon unsalted melted butter

Per 1 Egg (¼ Recipe)   Exchanges: 1.75 Meat, 0.5 Fat, 0.25 Vegetable; 141 Calories, 9 g protein (27%), 10 g fat (64%), 3.5 g carbohydrate (9%; 2 g sugars), 226 mg cholesterol, 427 mg sodium, $.40

Hot Carob or Cocoa

Note difference in approximate cost and calories of carob and cocoa!

2 Servings

1. Whisk water, carob or cocoa together; bring to a boil; stir and boil 2 minutes;
   ½ cup water (¼ cup with cocoa)
   2 tablespoons cocoa or carob powder *(p. 12)*

2. Reduce heat and stir in remaining ingredients:
   2 cups nonfat (skim) milk
   1 tablespoon honey or crystalline fructose with carob
      (p. 12) **or ¼ cup honey or crystalline fructose with cocoa**
   ¼ teaspoon vanilla (⅛ teaspoon with cocoa)
   dash nutmeg, optional
   dash salt, optional

3. Heat just until hot, but do not boil.

Per Serving Hot Carob (½ Recipe; optional ingredients not included)
*   Exchanges: 1 Milk, 0.75 Fruit; 137 Calories, 9 g protein (24%), 27 g carbohydrate (72%; 22 g sugars), 1 g dietary fiber, 5 mg cholesterol, 134 mg sodium, $.35*

Per Serving Hot Cocoa (½ Recipe; optional ingredients not included)
*   Exchanges: 1 Milk, 0.25 Bread, 3.25 Fruit; 238 Calories, 10 g protein (16%), 50 g carbohydrate (82%; 47 g sugars), 1 g dietary fiber, 5 mg cholesterol, 132 mg sodium, $.45*

Breakfast Sausage

A tasty and nutritions alternative to bacon and pork sausage. See nutrient comparison below. The higher the fat content of the turkey the juicier sausages will be. 85% fat free to 99% fat free[1] ground turkey is available. We find 99% fat free perfectly acceptable for our tastes.

AMOUNT: 6 Servings - 2 Each

1. Mix together thoroughly; shape into 12 small patties:
    1 lb. ground turkey *(p. 13)*
    ½ teaspoon nutmeg
    ½ teaspoon sage
    ½ teaspoon thyme
    ⅛ teaspoon cayenne pepper
    1teaspoon salt (½ tsp. with *Sue's Seasoning*)
    1 teaspoon *Sue's "Kitchen Magic"* Seasoning *(p. 15)*, **optional**

2. Fry in ungreased skillet or bake at 350° for 20-30 minutes until cooked through. Do not overcook.

2 patties (12 per lb.) using 7% fat ground turkey (Sue's Seasoning not included)
Exchanges: 1.75 Meat; 108 Calories, 15 g protein (55%), 5.5 g fat (44%),
47 mg cholesterol, 393 mg sodium, $.40

NUTRIENT COMPARISON

2.66 oz. cooked	Calories	Protein	Fat	Cholesterol	Sodium
Turkey Breakfast Sausage Recipe (7% fat)[1]	108	15 gm	5.5 gm (44%)[1]	47 mg	393 mg
Pork Sausage (Italian)	182	11 gm	14 gm (71%)[1]	44 mg	520 mg
Bacon, cured (broiled or fried crisp)	329	15 gm	39 gm (80%)[1]	47 mg	1072 mg

[1]Brand labels list % of fat by weight which is much lower than fat % of calories (listed in the comparison chart above). For example, 7% fat refers to fat percent by weight, not by caloric value. Fat by weight appears lower in fat than the food item really is in terms of calories. Since % of fat in calories is what is in most people's minds when reading labels, the label usually misleads. The new nutrient data labeling law that now requires a standardized nutrient label may help some, but can also be confusing (see *The 15 Minute Meal Planner*, pp. 292-302). Data for this comparison is taken from *Turkey Store* brand label for ground turkey, *Food Values* by Pennington & Church, 14th edition, 1985 for bacon and pork sausage.

Fruit Pizza

6 - 8 Servings per 13" Round Pizza

For a unique brunch or dessert! Pizza crust can also be made with a portion of Spelt or Kamut Bread dough, pp. 122-123.

1. Prepare *Pizza Crust (**Main Dishes**, p. 237).* Cool completely.
2. For each 13" round pizza crust, blend together thoroughly and spread evenly over the top, not quite to the edge:
   12 oz. light cream cheese
   ¼ cup honey or ½ cup crystalline fructose
3. Top cream cheese layer with attractive arrangement of assorted fruits, working from the center outward; chill before serving:
   banana slices (about ½ banana)   **kiwi slices (1 kiwi)**
   blueberries (about ⅓ - ½ box)   **peach slices (about 2)**
   mandarin oranges (1 can)
   strawberries, cut in half (about 1--12 oz. box)

Exchanges: 0.25 Meat, 2.5 Fat, 2.5 Bread, 3 Fruit; 419 Calories, 10 g protein (9%), 14.5 g fat (30%), 65 g carbohydrate (60%), 8 g dietary fiber, 33 mg cholesterol, 440 mg sodium, $.85

Chicken Ranch Pizza

2 - 3 Servings per 13" Pizza

Unique for brunch or supper! To serve take care! Topping slides off the crust easily! Wrap very loosely in foil to reheat, so topping won't stick. See Fruit Pizza above for pizza crust alternative.

Bake: 350°F (175°C) - 10 to 15 minutes

1. Prepare *Pizza Crust (**Main Dishes**, p. 237).* Cool completely.
2. Spread evenly over top of each 13" crust (or equivalent size):
   1 cup light *Ranch Dressing*
   1 cup mozzarella cheese
3. First saute chicken and garlic and spread over cheese layer; then saute veggies and spread over chicken. Use more butter and oil, as needed; top all with final layer of cheese:
   1 - 2 tablespoons each melted butter and olive oil
   1 - 1½ lbs. boneless, chicken breast, cut in thin strips
   2 - 3 cloves garlic
   ½ - 1 green and/or red bell pepper, chopped
   2 - 4 chopped green onions, as desired
   1 cup fresh mushroom slices
   1 cup mozzarella cheese
4. Bake until crust is done and all is hot through and cheese melts. about 10 - 15 minutes.

Per ⅙ pizza serving (using 1 tbsp. each butter and oil, and 1½ lbs. chicken)
Exchanges: 2.5 Meat, 1 Fat, 3 Bread, 0.5 Vegetable, 0.75 Fruit; 460 Calories; 20 g protein (18%), 17 g fat (32%), 58 g carbohdydrate (50%; 12 g sugars), 8.5 g dietary fiber, 26 mg cholesterol, 905 mg sodium, $.90

Cinnamon Scones

12 Scones

Light and flaky, especially with barley flour.

Bake: 400°F (205°C) - 12 to 15 minutes

1. Blend together thoroughly in mixing bowl:
   1¾ cups whole wheat pastry flour *(see grains, p. 13)*
   ¼ cup barley flour (or additional ¼ cup pastry flour)
   6 tablespoons *Sucanat* *(p. 15)* **or ¼ cup crystalline fructose** *(p. 12)*

2. Cut in with 2 table knives or pastry blender until coarse meal is formed:
   ¼ cup cold unsalted butter

3. Make a well in center, add and stir in just to mix:
   ½ cup + 2 tablespoons buttermilk *(p. 11)*

4. Cover bowl; let stand at room temperature overnight *(pp. 50-51).*

5. Make a **topping** with a blend of:
   1 tablespoon crystalline fructose
   ¼ teaspoon cinnamon

6. Mix into dough thoroughly, but briefly, with a mixing spoon:
   ½ teaspoon baking powder *(p. 11)*
   ½ teaspoon baking soda
   ½ teaspoon salt
   ½ teaspoon cinnamon

   "sift" these through a small strainer with a spoon to break up any lumps.

7. Knead dough 8 strokes on floured surface. Divide in half and pat each piece into about ½ inch thick circle. Cut each circle into 6 wedges with a floured knife. Let stand 10 minutes.

8. Preheat oven to 400°.

9. Place wedges on ungreased cookie sheet and top each with **fructose-cinnamon topping** (step #5).
   Bake at 400° for 12-15 minutes.

Per Scone   Exchanges: 1 Bread, 0.75 Fat, 0.5 Fruit; 139 Calories, 2.5 g protein (7%), 4 g fat (27%), 22 g carbohydrate (65%; 6 g sugars), 2 g dietary fiber, 11 mg cholesterol, 137 mg sodium, $.10

Company Jam Scones

14 Scones

A delicious continental breakfast with a cup of tea. Substitute fresh cut strawberries for the jam or spread if you wish.

1. Bake a double recipe of **Scones (Lunches & Snacks**, *p. 39).*

2. ~~Make recipe of *Whipped Cream*, p. 218.~~

3. To Serve: Cut **scone** open; spread half with **2 teaspoons all-fruit jam or spread** *(p. 13).* Top with other half and dollop with **whipped cream**.

Almond Coffee Cake

Our most often served blender coffee cake. See pp. 82-83 for additional blending in the blender tips or for standard mixing with flour. To mix by hand with flour use **2 cups pastry, kamut or barley flour** *or* **2⅓ cups spelt flour.**

AMOUNT: 11.5" x 8" (preferred) or 9" x 13" Baking Pan
Bake: 325°F (165°C) - 30 to 40 minutes

1. Place in blender; blend on highest speed 3 minutes until smooth:
   1 cup buttermilk *(p. 11; or non-dairy alternative, p. 29)*
   ¼ cup olive oil, optional (for more cake-like texture)
   ¾ cup honey (warm slightly if not easily pourable)
   grain choice (not flour) of
      1⅓ cups whole wheat pastry grain
      or 1½ cups spelt, kamut or brown rice
      or 1¼ cups barley grain

2. Meanwhile, for **topping** blend together in order given with a fork:
   2 tablespoons butter *(unsalted preferred)*
   2 tablespoons *Sucanat* **or crystalline fructose** *(pp. 12, 15)*
   ½ cup uncooked rolled oats
   ½ cup chopped or sliced almonds
   (with kamut only) 1 teaspoon cinnamon

3. Cover blender; let stand at room temperature overnight *(pp. 50-51).*

4. Grease or spray baking pan *(p. 271).*

5. Preheat oven to 325°.

6. Just before baking, add and reblend on highest speed for 1 minute:
   2 eggs *(or alternative, p. 269)*

7. Mix into blender batter thoroughly, but briefly, using blender and/or rubber spatula, as needed:
   ½ teaspoon salt   "sift" these through a small strainer
   1 teaspoon baking soda   with a spoon to break up any lumps.
   1 teaspoon baking powder *(p. 11)*
   2 teaspoons cinnamon (omit with kamut)
   ¼ teaspoon ginger

8. Pour batter into baking pan. Distribute **topping** evenly over top with fingers, pressing it slightly into batter with a fork.

9. Bake at 325° for 30-40 minutes or until knife or toothpick comes clean out of center of cake. Serve cake hot.

Per Piece (15 per pan - cut 3 x 5) without optional oil
  Exchanges: 0.25 Meat, 1 Bread, 0.75 Fat, 1.25 Fruit; 182 Calories, 4 g protein (9%), 5 g fat (24%), 31 g carbohydrate (68%; 16 g sugars), 2 g dietary fiber, 33 mg cholesterol, 139 mg sodium, $.25

Apple Coffee Cake

I use tart green apples for this blender coffee cake. See pp. 82-83 for additional blending in blender tips, our recommended procedure to improve nutritional benefits (as in Almond Coffee Cake, p. 233) or for standard mixing with **2 cups flour.**

AMOUNT: 11.5" x 8" (preferred) or 9" x 13" Baking Pan
Bake: 325°F (165°C) - 30 to 40 minutes

1. Preheat oven. Grease or spray baking pan *(p. 271)*.

2. Cook apples with water over medium heat until tender; drain, and coat evenly with cinnamon; set aside:
    2 cups apples, peeled thin slices cut in half
    ¼ cup water
    1 teaspoon cinnamon

3. Place in blender; blend on high speed 4-5 minutes until smooth:
    1 cup buttermilk *(p. 11; or non-dairy alternative, p. 29)*
    2 eggs *(or alternative, p. 269)*
    ¾ cup honey (warm slightly if not easily pourable)
       or ⅔ cup honey for less sweet cake
    choice of whole grain (not flour): 1⅓ cups whole wheat pastry
       grain or 1½ cups kamut or spelt or 1¼ cups barley grain

4. Meanwhile, for **topping** blend together in order given with a fork; set aside:
    2 tablespoons butter *(unsalted preferred)*
    2 tablespoons *Sucanat* **or crystalline fructose** *(pp. 12, 15)*
    ½ cup uncooked rolled oats or ¼ cup flour
    1½ teaspoons cinnamon
    ½ cup chopped walnuts

5. Mix into blender batter thoroughly, but briefly, using blender and/or rubber spatula, as needed:
    ½ teaspoon salt   "sift" these through a small
    1 teaspoon baking soda   strainer with a spoon to
    1 teaspoon baking powder *(p. 11)*   break up any lumps.

5. Pour batter into baking pan. Spread **apple slices** evenly over the top and press into batter slightly with a fork. Add **topping**.

6. Bake at 325° for 30-40 minutes or until knife or toothpick comes clean out of center of cake. Serve cake hot.

Per Piece (15 per pan - cut 3 x 5) without nuts
   Exchanges: 0.25 Meat, 1 Bread, 0.75 Fat, 1.5 Fruit; 194 Calories, 4 g protein (8%),
5.5 g fat (25%), 33 g carbohydrate (67%; 18 g sugars), 3 g dietary fiber, 33 mg cholesterol, 139 mg sodium, $.25

Apricot Pecan Coffee Cake

Coffee cake in the blender! See pp. 82-83 for additional blending in blender tips, our recommended procedure to improve nutritional benefits (as in Almond Coffee Cake, p. 233) or for standard mixing with **2 cups flour.**

AMOUNT: 11.5" x 8" (preferred) or 9" x 13" Baking Pan
Bake: 325°F (165°C) - 30 to 40 minutes

1. Preheat oven. Grease or spray baking pan *(p. 271).*

2. Cover **1 cup dried apricots halves** with hot water and let stand to soften for 1-2 hours. Drain and chop into small pieces.

3. Place in blender; blend on high speed 4-5 minutes until smooth:
    1 cup buttermilk *(p. 11; or non-dairy alternative, p. 29)*
    2 eggs *(or alternative, p. 269)*
    ¾ cup honey (warm slightly if not easily pourable)
    or ⅔ cup honey for less sweet cake
    1 teaspoon vanilla
    choice of whole grain (not flour): 1⅓ cups whole wheat pastry grain or 1½ cups kamut or spelt or 1¼ cups barley grain

4. Meanwhile, for **topping** blend together in order given with a fork; set aside:
    2 tablespoons butter *(unsalted preferred)*
    ¼ cup *Sucanat* or crystalline fructose *(pp. 12, 15)*
    ½ cup uncooked rolled oats
    ½ cup chopped pecans (¾ cup for more sumptuous cake)
    1 teaspoon cinnamon

5. Mix into blender batter thoroughly, but briefly, using blender and/or rubber spatula, as needed:
    ½ teaspoon salt   "sift" these through a small
    1 teaspoon baking soda   strainer with a spoon to
    1 teaspoon baking powder *(p. 11)* break up any lumps.

6. Pour batter into baking pan. Spread **apricot pieces** evenly over the top and press into batter slightly with a fork. Add **topping**.

7. Bake at 325° for 30-40 minutes or until knife or toothpick comes clean out of center of cake. Serve cake hot.

Per Piece (15 per pan - cut 3 x 5)
Exchanges: 0.25 Meat, 1 Bread, 0.75 Fat, 2 Fruit; 214 Calories, 4 g protein (7%), 5.5 g fat (23%), 37 g carbohydrate (69%; 21 g sugars), 3 g dietary fiber, 33 mg cholesterol, 143 mg sodium, $.35

Blueberry Coffee Cake

*Coffee cake in the blender! See pp. 82-83 for additional blending in blender tips, our recommended procedure to improve nutritional benefits (as in Almond Coffee Cake, p. 233) or for standard mixing with **2 cups flour.***

AMOUNT: 8" or 9" Square Baking Pan
Bake: 325°F (165°C) - 30 to 40 minutes

1. Preheat oven. Grease or spray baking pan *(p. 271)*.

2. Place in blender; blend on high speed 4-5 minutes until smooth:
   ½ cup buttermilk *(p. 11; or non-dairy alternative, p. 29)*
   2 eggs *(or alternative, p. 269)*
   ⅓ cup honey
   choice of whole grain (not flour): 1 cup whole wheat pastry grain or 1⅛ cups kamut or spelt or 1 cup barley grain

3. Meanwhile, for **topping** blend together in order given with a fork; set aside:
   2 tablespoons butter *(unsalted preferred)*
   ⅓ cup *Sucanat* or crystalline fructose *(pp. 12, 15)*
   ½ cup uncooked rolled oats
   ½ chopped walnuts

4. Mix into blender batter thoroughly, but briefly, using blender and/or rubber spatula, as needed:
   ½ teaspoon salt   "sift" these through a small
   ½ teaspoon baking soda   strainer with a spoon to
   2½ teaspoons baking powder *(p. 11)* break up any lumps.
   1 teaspoon cinnamon

5. Pour batter into baking pan. Spread **1 cup fresh or frozen blueberries** evenly over the top and press into batter slightly with a fork. Add **topping**.

6. Bake at 325° for 30-40 minutes or until knife or toothpick comes clean out of center of cake. Serve cake hot.

Per Piece (15 per pan - cut 3 x 5)
   Exchanges: 0.25 Meat, 0.75 Bread, 0.75 Fat, 1 Fruit; 155 Calories, 3.5 g protein (9%), 5 g fat (31%), 23 g carbohydrate (60%; 11 g sugars), 2 g dietary fiber, 33 mg cholesterol, 118 mg sodium, $.25

> **Adding Fruit Tip:** If fruit is folded into coffee cake it usually sinks to the bottom. Spreading it over top of the batter in baking pan just before the topping helps to prevent this. It still sinks further into the batter during cooking.

Cowboy Coffee Cake

*Originally a camp favorite, we turned this into a
family blender recipe. See pp. 82-83 for additional
blending in blender tips, our recommended procedure to
improve nutritional benefits (as in Almond Coffee Cake, p. 233) or for
standard mixing with* **2 cups flour.**

AMOUNT: 11.5" x 8" (preferred) or 9" x 13" Baking Pan
Bake: 325°F (165°C) - 30 to 40 minutes

1. Preheat oven. Grease or spray baking pan *(p. 271)*.

2. Place in blender; blend on high speed 4-5 minutes until smooth:
   1 cup buttermilk *(p. 11; or non-dairy alternative, p. 29)*
   2 eggs *(or alternative, p. 269)*
   ¾ cup honey (warm slightly if not easily pourable)
      or ⅔ cup honey for less sweet cake
   choice of whole grain (not flour): 1⅓ cups whole wheat pastry
      grain or 1½ cups kamut or spelt or 1¼ cups barley grain

3. Meanwhile, mix together and use half cup only in topping (#4):
   ¾ cup chopped walnuts
   ¾ cup date dices or chopped dates
   ¾ teaspoon cinnamon

4. For **topping** blend together in order given with a fork; set aside:
   2 tablespoons butter *(unsalted preferred)*
   2 tablespoons Sucanat or crystalline fructose *(pp. 12, 15)*
   ½ cup uncooked rolled oats
   ½ cup cup date-nut mixture

5. Mix into blender batter thoroughly, but briefly, using blender
   and/or rubber spatula, as needed:

½ teaspoon salt	"sift" these through a small
1 teaspoon baking soda	strainer with a spoon to
1 teaspoon baking powder *(p. 11)*	break up any lumps.
1 teaspoon cinnamon	
1 teaspoon nutmeg	

6. Fold remaining date-nute mixture into batter.

7. Pour batter into baking pan. Distribute **topping** evenly over top
   with fingers, pressing it slightly into batter with a fork.

8. Bake at 325° for 30-40 minutes or until knife or toothpick comes
   clean out of center of cake. Serve cake hot.

Per Piece (15 per pan - cut 3 x 5)
   *Exchanges: 0.25 Meat, 1 Bread, 1 Fat, 1.75 Fruit; 220 Calories, 4.5 g protein (8%),
   6.5 g fat (27%), 36 g carbohydrate (65%; 20 g sugars), 3 g dietary fiber, 33 mg cholesterol,
   138 mg sodium, $.25*

Orange Coffee Cake

A blender coffee cake. See pp. 82-83 for additional blending in blender tips, our recommended procedure to improve nutritional benefits (as in Almond Coffee Cake, p. 233) or for standard mixing with **3 cups flour.**

AMOUNT: 11.5" x 8" (preferred) or 9" x 13" Baking Pan
Bake: 325°F (165°C) - 30 to 40 minutes

1. Preheat oven. Grease or spray baking pan *(p. 271)*.

2. Grate **1 tablespoon grated orange peel**; set aside.
   Squeeze oranges (about 2) to make **1 cup fresh orange juice**

3. Place in blender; blend on high speed 4-5 minutes until smooth:
   ½ cup buttermilk *(p. 11; or non-dairy alternative, p. 29)*
   1 cup fresh orange juice
   2 eggs *(or alternative, p. 269)*
   ¾ cup honey (warm slightly if not easily pourable)
      or ⅔ cup honey for less sweet cake
   choice of whole grain (not flour): 2 cups whole wheat pastry grain or 2¼ cups kamut or spelt or 1⅔ cups barley grain

4. Meanwhile, for **topping** blend together in order given with a fork; set aside:
   2 tablespoons butter *(unsalted preferred)*
   2 tablespoons *Sucanat* **or crystalline fructose** *(pp. 12, 15)*
   half of the grated orange peel (1½ teaspoons)
   ½ teaspoon cinnamon
   ½ cup uncooked rolled oats

5. Mix into blender batter thoroughly, but briefly, using blender and/or rubber spatula, as needed:
   ¾ teaspoon salt   "sift" these through a small
   ½ teaspoon baking soda   strainer with a spoon to
   2 teaspoons baking powder *(p. 11)* break up any lumps.
   remaining orange peel

6. Pour batter into baking pan. Distribute **topping** evenly over top with fingers, pressing it slightly into batter with a fork.

7. Bake at 325° for 30-40 minutes or until knife or toothpick comes clean out of center of cake. Serve cake hot.

Per Piece (15 per pan - cut 3 x 5) without nuts
   Exchanges: 0.25 Meat, 1.25 Bread, 0.25 Fat, 1.5 Fruit; 192 Calories, 4 g protein (8%), 3 g fat (13%), 36 g carbohydrate (79%; 17 g sugars), 3 g dietary fiber, 33 mg cholesterol, 147 mg sodium, $.25

238

Pineapple Coffee Cake

Coffee cake in the blender. See pp. 82-83 for additional blending in blender tips, our recommended procedure to improve nutritional benefits (as in Almond Coffee Cake, p. 233) or for standard mixing with **2 cups flour.**

AMOUNT: 11.5" x 8" (preferred) or 9" x 13" Baking Pan
Bake: 325°F (165°C) - 30 to 40 minutes

1. Preheat oven. Grease or spray baking pan *(p. 271)*.

2. Place in blender; blend on high speed 4-5 minutes until smooth:
   juice drained from 8 oz. can crushed pineapple
   buttermilk to make 1 cup total with the juice
   (p. 11; or non-dairy alternative, p. 29)
   2 eggs *(or alternative, p. 269)*
   ¾ cup honey (warm slightly if not easily pourable)
   or ⅔ cup honey for less sweet cake
   choice of whole grain (not flour): 1⅓ cups whole wheat pastry grain or 1½ cups kamut or spelt or 1¼ cups barley grain

3. Meanwhile, for **topping** blend together in order given with a fork; set aside:
   2 tablespoons butter *(unsalted preferred)*
   2 tablespoons *Sucanat* or crystalline fructose *(pp. 12, 15)*
   ½ cup uncooked rolled oats
   8 oz. can drained crushed pineapple

4. Mix into blender batter thoroughly, but briefly, using blender and/or rubber spatula, as needed:
   ½ teaspoon salt   "sift" these through a small
   1 teaspoon baking soda   strainer with a spoon to
   1 teaspoon baking powder *(p. 11)*   break up any lumps.

5. Pour batter into baking pan. Distribute **topping** evenly over top with fingers, pressing it slightly into batter with a fork.

6. Bake at 325° for 30-40 minutes or until knife or toothpick comes clean out of center of cake. Serve cake hot.

Per Piece (15 per pan - cut 3 x 5)

Exchanges: 0.25 Meat, 1 Bread, 0.25 Fat, 1.5 Fruit; 164 Calories, 3 g protein (8%), 2.5 g fat (14%), 32 g carbohydrate (78%; 17 g sugars), 2 g dietary fiber, 33 mg cholesterol, 140 mg sodium, $.20

Zucchini Coffee Cake

Coffee cake in the blender. See pp. 82-83 for additional blending in blender tips, our recommended procedure to improve nutritional benefits (as in Almond Coffee Cake, p. 233) or for standard mixing with **2 cups flour.**

AMOUNT: 11.5" x 8" (preferred) or 9" x 13" Baking Pan
Bake: 325°F (165°C) - 30 to 40 minutes

1. Preheat oven. Grease or spray baking pan *(p. 271)*.

2. Grate zucchini; set aside:
   1 generous cup shredded zucchini, unpeeled

3. Place in blender; blend on high speed 4-5 minutes until smooth:
   1 cup buttermilk *(p. 11; or non-dairy alternative, p. 29)*
   2 eggs *(or alternative, p. 269)*
   ¾ cup honey (warm slightly if not easily pourable)
      or ⅔ cup honey for less sweet cake
   **choice of whole grain (not flour): 1⅓ cups whole wheat pastry
      grain or 1½ cups kamut or spelt or 1¼ cups barley grain**

4. Meanwhile, for **topping** blend together in order given with a fork; set aside:
   2 tablespoons butter *(unsalted preferred)*
   ½ cup uncooked rolled oats
   ½ chopped walnuts (or fold into batter with zucchini in step #6)

5. Mix into blender batter thoroughly, but briefly, using blender and/or rubber spatula, as needed:
   ½ teaspoon salt
   1 teaspoon baking soda
   1 teaspoon baking powder *(p. 11)*
   1½ teaspoons cinnamon

   "sift" these through a small strainer with a spoon to break up any lumps.

6. Stir **grated zucchini** into batter with a fork.

7. Pour batter into baking pan. Distribute **topping** evenly over top with fingers, pressing it slightly into batter with a fork.

8. Bake at 325° for 30-40 minutes or until knife or toothpick comes clean out of center of cake. Serve cake hot.

Per Piece (15 per pan - cut 3 x 5) with nuts
   Exchanges: 0.25 Meat, 1 Bread, 0.75 Fat, 1.25 Fruit; 181 Calories, 4 g protein (10%), 5.5 g fat (25%), 30 g carbohydrate (66%; 15 g sugars), 2.5 g dietary fiber, 33 mg cholesterol, 137 mg sodium, $.20

Peach Bran Coffee Cake

*See pp. 82-83 for additional blending in blender tips, our recommended procedure to improve nutritional benefits (as in Almond Coffee Cake, p. 233) or for standard mixing with **1 cup flour.***

AMOUNT: 8" or 9" Square Baking Pan
Bake: 325°F (165°C) - 35 to 40 minutes

1. Preheat oven and grease or spray baking pan *(p. 271)*.

2. For topping blend together in order given with a fork:
   2 tablespoons melted butter
   3 tablespoons *Sucanat* *(p. 15)*, **crystalline fructose** *(p. 12)*,
      or brown sugar
   ¾ teaspoons cinnamon
   ½ cup uncooked rolled oats

3. Drain **16 oz. can unsweetened peach slices**, reserving juice. Dice each peach slice into 4 pieces and set aside. Heat juice.

4. To blender add **⅓ cup of the reserved hot peach juice**. In large mixing bowl mix together thoroughly; set aside:
   1 cup wheat bran *(p. 11)*
   remaining peach juice

5. Add to juice in blender; blend on high speed 3-4 minutes until smooth:
   2 eggs *(or alternative, p. 269)*
   ½ cup honey (slightly warmed - 15 seconds in microwave)
   ⅔ cup whole wheat pastry grain (not flour) *(see grains, p. 13)*

6. Mix in thoroughly, but briefly, using blender and/or rubber spatula, as needed:

½ teaspoon salt	"sift" these through a small
1 teaspoon cinnamon	strainer with a spoon to
2½ teaspoons baking powder *(p. 11)*	break up any lumps.

7. Pour batter into **bran mixture**; blend thoroughly, but briefly.

8. Spread batter evenly in baking pan. Spread **peaches** over the top, pressing slightly into batter with fork. Add **topping**.

9. Bake 325° for 35-40 minutes or until knife or toothpick comes clean out of center.

Per Piece (16 per pan - cut 4 x 4)
   Exchanges: 0.25 Meat, 0.5 Bread, 0.25 Fat, 1.25 Fruit; 121 Calories, 2.5 g protein (8%), 2.5 g fat (17%), 23.5 g carbohydrate (76%; 13 g sugars), 2.5 g dietary fiber, 31 mg cholesterol, 83 mg sodium, $.20

Sweet Roll Dough

*Use this recipe for breakfast sweet rolls--Date Pecan Ring, Swedish Tea Ring, Cinnamon or Prune Rolls (pp.243-245). I also make these recipes with Delicious Whole Wheat Dough (**Soups & Muffins**, p. 96, or **Yeast Breads**, pp. 20, 21 or Spelt or Kamut Bread dough (pp. 122-123).*

1. In glass measuring cup blend yeast and honey into the water with wire whisk and let stand 5-10 minutes until it bubbles up:
   ¼ cup lukewarm water
   ½ teaspoon honey or other sugar (assists yeast growth)
   2 teaspoons (1 package) active dry yeast

2. Blend in mixing bowl, cover with a damp cloth and let stand overnight or several hours in a place away from excessive heat and drafts:
   1¼ cups cool water
   2 cups whole wheat , spelt, or kamut flour *(see grains, p. 13)*
   yeast mixture (step #1)

3. Blend in and beat vigorously for 200 strokes or on medium speed in electric mixer for 5 minutes:
   ¼ cup honey or other sweetener
   ⅛ teaspoon vitamin C crystals (or 500 mg. crushed)
   2 tablespoons olive oil or melted butter
   1 egg
   1¼ teaspoons salt
   1 cup whole wheat, kamut or spelt flour

4. Add enough remaining flour to begin kneading easily; gradually use additional flour as needed during kneading process to prevent sticking to hands or work surface; knead 10-15 minutes (or 300-400 strokes) until dough is resiliant and resistent to kneading motion:
   about 1¾ - 2 cups whole wheat or Kamut flour
   or about 2¾ - 3 cups spelt flour

5. Place in bowl greased with melted butter, turning dough over to grease the top; cover with damp cloth and let rise in warm place until double, about 1 - 1½ hours (see rising tip below).

6. Press down gently, turn over in bowl, cover and let rise until double, about 30 - 40 minutes (see rising tip below).

7. Press down gently, knead lightly a few times on working surface, cover with a damp cloth and let rest 10 - 15 minutes.

8. Shape and complete dough for desired recipe, pp. 243-245.

Rising Tip: The time for rising is merely a rule of thumb. Use the finger poke test: Poke into dough about ½ inch with finger. If hole does not fill up, the dough is sufficiently risen.

Date Pecan Ring

1 Ring - 15 Rolls

Makes a beautiful gift or special holiday breakfast treat.

1. Prepare **Sweet Roll Dough,** p. 244 (or use one of the other recipes listed at the top of *Sweet Roll Dough* recipe).

2. Roll dough out as for **Cinnamon Rolls** (step #2, p. 244). Spread evenly, not quite to edges with:
   ⅓ cup honey
   ½ cup chopped dates
   ½ cup chopped pecans

3. Shape and cut on cookie sheets as for **Swedish Tea Ring** below, or cut into individual rolls as for **Cinnamon Rolls** (steps #4, 5, p. 244). Overlap cut rolls in a ring on cookie sheet or pizza pan, leaving plenty of room to rise (*see* illustration below).

4. Let rise until almost double, about 20-25 minutes; bake as for **Cinnamon Rolls** (steps #6, 7 p. 244).

Per Roll of 15 with whole wheat flour
Exchanges: 1.75 Bread, 1 Fat, 1.5 Fruit; 234 Calories, 6 g protein (10%), 6 g fat (21%), 43 g carbohydrate (69%; 14 g sugars), 6 g dietary fiber, 14 mg cholesterol, 183 mg sodium, $.25

unbaked

baked

Swedish Tea Ring

1 Ring - 15 Rolls

1. Make **Cinnamon Rolls** or **Prune Rolls** (pp. 244-45) following steps #1-4 of cinnamon roll recipe until dough is rolled with filling inside. Even up thickness of the roll with your hands.

2. Place the seamed edge of the roll on a lightly greased cookie sheet, shaping it into a round or oval ring. Securely pinch ends together to close the ring.

3. With scissors, make cuts two-thirds the way through ring on outside edges at 1" intervals. Twist each cut section so that the cut side of each roll overlaps the next (similar to *Date Pecan Ring* illustration above).

4. Brush with **beaten egg** for a glossy surface, if desired.

5. Let rise and bake as for **Cinnamon Rolls** (steps #6, 7, p. 244).

Cinnamon Rolls

A Family favorite!

AMOUNT: 15 Rolls (9" x 13" Pan)
Bake: 325°F (165°C) - 25 to 30 minutes

1. Prepare **Sweet Roll Dough,** p. 244 (or use one of the other recipes listed at the top of *Sweet Roll Dough* recipe).

2. Roll dough out with rolling pin to 9" x 15" rectangle about ½ inch thick.

> **Tip:** If the dough has been kneaded in an electric bread kneader, use water on hands and working surface (pastry sheet or smooth counter surface) to prevent sticking. Do not overdo the amount of water! If dough is kneaded by hand you will need a floured surface for dough and lightly floured hands.

3. Evenly spread over surface of dough, not quite to the edges:
   ⅓ cup honey or other sweetener *(p. 15)*
   cinnamon, generously -- about 1 teaspoon
   ½ cup raisins, soaked and drained, optional
   ½ cup chopped walnuts, optional
   1 apple, grated, peeled or unpeeled, optional

4. *Illustrated,* p. 245: Roll dough up firmly from the long side, sealing the edge by lifting it up and over the top of the roll, pinching the edge to the roll. Turn the seam downward. Even up the roll with hands.

5. *llustrated*, p. 245: Slide a piece of thread or dental floss under the roll, cross it over the top and "slice" it through the dough. Cut each roll 1" thick.

6. *Illustrated,* p. 245: Lay rolls, cut side down, in greased pan *(p. 271)*. Allow room between them for rising. Let rise until almost double, 20 - 25 minutes.

7. Bake at 325° about 25 - 30 minutes or until golden on bottom.

Per Roll of 15 with whole wheat flour, and honey and cinnamon only
    Exchanges: 1.75 Bread, 0.25 Fat, 1 Fruit; 190 Calories, 5.5 g protein (11%), 3 g fat (14%), 38 g carbohydrate (76%; 11 g sugars), 5 g dietary fiber, 14 mg cholesterol, 183 mg sodium, $.15

Per Roll of 15 with whole wheat flour; includes optional ingredients
    Exchanges: 0.25 Meat, 1.75 Bread, 0.75 Fat, 1.5 Fruit; 239 Calories, 6 g protein (10%), 5.5 g fat (20%), 44 g carbohydrate (70%; 16 g sugars), 6 g dietary fiber, 14 mg cholesterol, 184 mg sodium, $.25

Prune Rolls

Sue's favorite sweet rolls.

AMOUNT: 15 Rolls (9" x 13" Pan)
Bake: 325°F (165°C) - 25 to 30 minutes

1. Combine together in bowl and let stand 2 hours or more:
   ½ cup pitted dried prunes
   boiling water to cover well

2. Prepare **Sweet Roll Dough,** p. 244 (or use one of the other recipes listed at the top of *Sweet Roll Dough* recipe).

3. Drain prunes, saving the juice. Place prunes in blender. Puree into a sauce, adding saved juice as needed to blend easily.

4. Follow illustrations below and recipe for **Cinnamon Rolls** *(steps #2-7, p. 244)* to roll out, shape, rise, and bake the rolls, spreading over dough:
   ⅓ cup honey
   prune sauce mixture
   ½ cup chopped walnuts

Per Roll of 15 with 4¾ cups whole wheat flour
   Exchanges: 0.25 Meat, 1.75 Bread, 0.75 Fat, 1.5 Fruit; 233 Calories, 6.5 g protein (10%), 5.5 g fat (21%), 42.5 g carbohydrate (69%; 14 g sugars), 6 g dietary fiber, 14 mg cholesterol, 183 mg sodium, $.25

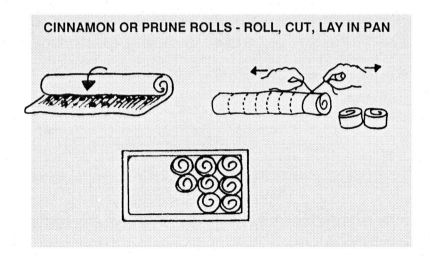

CINNAMON OR PRUNE ROLLS - ROLL, CUT, LAY IN PAN

Orange Snails

Delicately orange flavored sweet rolls for breakfast. Fun to make!

AMOUNT: 18 Rolls
Bake: 350°F (175°C) - 15 minutes

1. Grate peel, and squeeze juice of **1 orange** to make:
   about 2-3 teaspoons orange peel
   1 tablespoon orange juice (place in separate container; in step #6 you will add 1 tablespoon beaten egg to this juice to use as a glaze over top of the rolls)
   ½ cup orange juice + water or more juice (as needed for ½ cup)

2. In measuring cup, blend yeast and sweetener into water; let stand about 5-10 minutes until it bubbles up:
   ¼ cup warm water (100° - 110°)
   bit of honey or pinch of sugar (assists yeast growth)
   2 teaspoons (1 package) active dry yeast

3. Scald milk, cool in mixing bowl; blend in remaining ingredients; cover with damp cloth and let stand at room temperature overnight several hours away from drafts and excessive heat:
   ½ cup nonfat milk, scalded (scum forms on top, not boiling)
   ½ cup orange juice (from step #1)
   yeast mixture
   2½ cups whole wheat or spelt flour *(see grains, p. 13)*

4. Blend in and beat vigorously for 200 strokes or 5 minutes on medium speed in electric mixer:
   ¼ cup melted unsalted butter
   ¾ cup *Sucanant* *(p. 15)* **or crystalline fructose** *(p. 12)*
   1 teaspoon salt
   grated orange peel

5. Cover bowl with a towel and let batter rise until spongy in texture in a warm place, about 30-45 minutes.

6. Before you stir eggs into the batter, add **1 tablespoon beaten egg** to 1 tablespoon reserved orange juice (step #1). Stir remaining eggs into batter; stir in enough flour to make a dough easy to turn out onto a smooth surface. Work in remaining flour as needed to prevent sticking to hands or work surface while you knead; knead about 10 minutes (or 300-400 strokes) until dough is resiliant and resistent:
   3 beaten eggs
   3 - 3¼ cups whole wheat flour or 4¼ - 4½ cups spelt flour
   Continued, p. 247.

7. Place dough in bowl greased with melted butter; cover with damp cloth; set in warm place to rise until double, about 1½ hours.

8. Press dough down gently in center; fold sides into center, pressing down; knead 5 times and let rest while greasing 2 cookie sheets.

9. Divide dough into 18 equal pieces. Shape each piece into a 12"-14" rope with hands (lightly greased with oil, if needed).

10. Coil each rope, pinching end securely underneath. Lay on greased cookie sheets, leaving space to rise between each.

 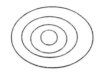

11. Cover rolls with a towel and set in warm place to rise until double, about 45 minutes.

12. Brush tops of rolls with **reserved 2 tablespoons juice-egg mixture**. Dust with *Sucanat* **or crystalline fructose**.

13. Bake at 350° for 15 minutes or until lightly browned.

14. Remove from baking sheets immediately and cool on wire rack.

15. Serve warm. To reheat, place in baking pan, cover with foil, and heat at 350° until just nicely warmed, about 10 minutes.

Per Roll of 18 with 5½ cups whole wheat flour
Exchanges: 0.25 Meat, 1.75 Bread, 0.5 Fat, 0.75 Fruit; 191 Calories, 6 g protein (13%), 4 g fat (19%), 33 g carbohydrate (68%; 7 g sugars), 4.5 g dietary fiber, 43 mg cholesterol, 152 mg sodium, $.20

Per Roll of 18 with 6¾ cups spelt flour
Exchanges: 0.25 Meat, 2.25 Bread, 0.5 Fat, 0.75 Fruit; 219 Calories, 7 g protein (12%), 4 g fat (16%), 43 g carbohydrate (72%; 7 g sugars), 7.5 g dietary fiber, 43 mg cholesterol, 151 mg sodium, $.30

Baked Donuts

We like these baked better than deep fried.
Easy to make! For recommended procedure to
improve nutritional benefits, see pp. 50-51.

AMOUNT: 14 Large Donuts
Bake: 425°F (220°C) - 8 to 10 minutes

1. For *cinnamon sugar* blend together with a fork; set aside:
   3 tablespoons *Sucanat* *(p. 15)* **or crystalline fructose** *(p. 12)*
   1 teaspoon cinnamon

2. In large mixing bowl, beat the eggs; blend in remaining ingredients in order given:
   2 eggs
   1 cup *Sucanat* or crystalline fructose
   ¼ cup olive oil *(p. 14)*
   1 cup buttermilk *(p. 11)*

3. In separate bowl blend dry ingredients:
   4½ cups whole wheat pastry flour *(see grains, p. 13)*
     or 5½ cups spelt flour
   4 teaspoons baking powder *(p. 11)*   "sift" these through a small
   1 teaspoon baking soda   strainer with a spoon to break
   ½ teaspoon salt   up any lumps.
   ½ teaspoon nutmeg
   1 teaspoon cinnamon

4. Blend dry ingredients into liquid ingredients. Chill dough to make easier to roll out.

5. Roll dough out on lightly floured surface to about ½" thickness. Cut donuts with 3" donut cutter dipped in flour.

6. Place on cookie sheet. Brush lightly with **melted butter**; sprinkle with **cinnamon-sugar**. Also set the donut holes on cookie sheet to bake.

7. Bake at 425° for 8-10 minutes. Or, to deep fry, bring canola oil to 375°; fry in oil 2-3 minutes each side; drain on paper towel.

Per Baked Donut of 14 with whole wheat pastry flour   Exchanges: 0.25 Meat, 2 Bread,
0.75 Fat, 1.25 Fruit; 253 Calories, 5 g protein (9%), 5 g fat (20%), 43 g carbohydrate
(72%; 13 g sugars), 4 g dietary fiber, 31 mg cholesterol, 183 mg sodium, $.25

Per Baked Donut of 14 with spelt flour   Exchanges: 0.25 Meat, 2.25 Bread, 0.75 Fat,
1.25 Fruit; 267 Calories, 8 g protein (11%), 6 g fat (18%), 51 g carbohydrate (71%; 13 g sugars),
8 g dietary fiber, 31 mg cholesterol, 183 mg sodium, $.40

Blender Breakfast Crepes

These very thin pancakes, suitable for rolling up with a filling, make an elegant breakfast, topped with fresh fruit or a sauce, and are surprisingly easy to make. Practically any whole grain or whole grain flour works well. We use our seasoned omelet pan for crepes (see p. 145). Leftover crepes freeze well; wrap snuggly in saran wrap, then foil.

AMOUNT: 8 - 6" Crepes

1. Place in blender and blend 30 seconds if using flour, or 3 minutes if using grain:
   ¾ cup nonfat (skim) milk
   1½ teaspoons olive oil
   ⅛ teaspoon salt
   1½ teaspoons honey (for crepes served with fruit only)
   ¼ teaspoon cinnamon (for crepes served with fruit only)
   ½ cup flour or ⅓ cup whole grain (raw, uncooked)
      kamut, whole wheat pastry, spelt, or other grain *(see pp. 12, 13)*

2. Cover blender and let batter stand overnight at room temperature (see pp. 50-51).

3. Preheat seasoned crepe pan over moderately high heat until drops of water sizzle gentle in pan.

4. Add to batter and reblend on highest speed for 1 minute:
   1 egg

5. Lightly spray pan with non-stick spray, wiping out any excess gently with a paper towel.

6. Pour **3 tablespoons batter** (fill a ¼ cup measuring cup 3/4 full) into hot pan, quickly tilting pan to swirl the batter evenly to edges of pan.

   > **Tip:** Since the flour sinks quickly to the bottom, the batter must be stirred before making each crepe. Briefly reblend in blender or pour the batter into another container so you can stir it up easily by hand before making the next crepe.

7. Bake until browned at edges, about **1-2 minutes**; loosen along edge with table knife or shish kabob stick; lift gently with fingers, loosening from pan carefully as you turn over to bake on second side.

8. Respray pan only as needed to prevent crepes from sticking.

9. Stack crepes on plate until ready to fill. See recipes, pp. 250-52 to complete the crepes.

Per Crepe (all ingredients with whole wheat pastry flour)
   Exchanges: 0.25 Meat, 0.5 Bread, 0.25 Fat; 58 Calories, 2 g protein (16%), 2 g fat (27%), 8 g carbohydrate (57%; 2 g sugars), 1 g dietary fiber, 27 mg cholesterol, 71 mg sodium, $.10

Quinoa Crepes

These are light and soft and great for persons who are gluten intolerant or allergic to many common grains. While other grains can easily be used for Blender Crepes, p. 249, quinoa requires a little special preparation first to remove the bitter taste (see p. 75.).

1. Before making **Blender Breakfast Crepes**, p. 249, rinse and soak the quinoa grain overnight following the procedure as given in *Creamy Quinoa*, p 106. Use:
   ¼ cup + 2 teaspoons quinoa

2. Drain well; rinse 30 seconds before using in the recipe.

Per Crepe   Exchanges: 0.25 Meat, 0.25 Bread, 0.25 Fat; 53 Calories, 2.5 g protein (18%), 2 g fat (33%) 6.5 g carbohydrate (49%; 2 g sugars), 1 g dietary fiber, 27 mg cholesterol, 72 mg sodium, $.10

Cottage Filled Fruit Crepes

A beautiful simple breakfast for a special morning. Serve with favorite herb tea or Hot Carob or Cocoa. See menu, p. 230.

AMOUNT: 8 - 6" Crepes (3 to 4 Servings)

1. Make **Blender Breakfast Crepes**, p. 249.

2. While crepes are cooking, make filling--
   Blend together in mixing bowl:
   1½ cups fat free or low fat cottage cheese
   4 teaspoons maple syrup *(p. 13)*
   rounded ¼ teaspoon finely grated lemon peel
   ⅛ teaspoon vanilla

3. Make fruit topping--Cut fruits up in small chunks, halves, or slices (except small berries):
   about 3 cups mixed fresh fruit
     (as nectarine or peach,
     blueberries, strawberries, grapes,
     kiwi, bananas, pineapple)

4. Place on side of each crepe, roll up, place seam side down:
   3 tablespoons cheese filling

5. To serve place 2 or 3 crepes side-by-side on attractive serving plates. Center **fruit topping** over the rolled crepes.

Per Serving of 2 Crepes with ¾ cup fresh fruit)
Exchanges: 0.25 Meat, 0.75 Milk, 0.75 Bread, 0.5 Fat, 2.25 Fruit, 249 Calories,
17 g protein (26%), 4 g fat (14%), 39 g carbohydrate (60%; 23 g sugars),
4.5 g dietary fiber, 58 mg cholesterol, 146 mg sodium, $.80

Chicken Curry Crepes

*Great for dinner, brunch, or leisurely breakfast. May
be prepared, covered, and refrigerated the night before baking. In any
case I at least cook the chicken and onion well in advance of making the
crepes.*

AMOUNT: 8 - 6" Crepes (3 - 4 Servings)

1. Cook chicken--Chop in small cubes, cover with water in sauce
   pan and boil 10-15 minutes, or until cooked through:
   1 lb. boneless, skinless chicken breast

2. Steam onion until cooked:
   ¼ cup chopped onion

3. Make ***Blender Breakfast Crepes***, p. 249, omitting
   honey and cinnamon.

4. For sauce whisk together in mixing bowl:
   ¼ cup plain nonfat yogurt *(p. 15)*
   ¼ cup sour cream *(fat-free preferred, p. 14)*
   1 teaspoon curry powder
   1 tablespoon honey
   1 tablespoon lemon juice
   ⅜ teaspoon salt

5. Fold into sauce:
   chopped cooked chicken
   cooked chopped onion
   1 avocado, peeled and diced

6. Place about ¼ **cup filling** on side of each crepe, roll up and
   place seam side down on oven proof serving plate. Cover
   loosely with foil; heat through in 350° oven about 15 minutes.

7. Serve as desired with **extra sour cream, salsa, or cottage cheese.**

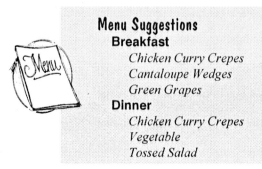

Menu Suggestions
Breakfast
Chicken Curry Crepes
Cantaloupe Wedges
Green Grapes
Dinner
Chicken Curry Crepes
Vegetable
Tossed Salad

Per Crepe of 8 (does not include extras for topping)
   *Exchanges: 1 Meat, 0.25 Milk, 0.5 Bread, 0.75 Fat, 0.25 Fruit; 157 Calories, 14 g protein (40%),
6 g fat (20%), 12 g carbohydrate (40%; 5 g sugars), 1.5 g dietary fiber, 55 mg cholesterol, 200 mg
sodium, $.70*

Cheesy Spinach Crepes

Texture is wonderfully light, like a souffle. Great for dinner, brunch, or leisurely breakfast. May be prepared, covered, and refrigerated the night before baking.

AMOUNT: 15 - 6" Crepes (5 - 7 Servings)

Bake: 350°F (175°C) - 20 minutes, uncovered

1. Make double recipe of **Blender Breakfast Crepes**, p. 249, omitting honey and cinnamon.

2. Prepare (steam, drain well, press out water, chop):
   1 large bunch fresh spinach

3. Blend in mixing bowl in order given:
   4 large eggs
   1½ cups nonfat or lowfat cottage cheese
   ¼ cup + 2 tablespoons grated cheddar cheese
   chopped steamed spinach
   salt and pepper, to taste

4. Place **about 3 tablespoons filling** on the side of each crepe and roll up; place seam side down in lightly greased or sprayed 9" x 13" bake pan *(p. 271)*.

5. Combine and spread over the top:
   3 tablespoons melted unsalted butter
   ¼ cup + 2 tablespoons Parmesan or Romano cheese

6. Bake uncovered at 350° for 20 minutes or until hot through and egg is lightly cooked.

Menu Suggestions

Breakfast
Cheesy Spinach Crepes
Fresh Pineapple Wedges
Parsley Garnish

Dinner
Cheesy Spinach Crepes
Corn on the Cob and/or
Steamed Carrot Rounds
Tossed Salad with Tomato Wedges

Per Crepe (of 15; salt, salsa not included)
   Exchanges: 0.75 Meat, 0.25 Milk, 0.5 Bread, 0.5 Fat, 0.25 Vegetable; 134 Calories, 9 g protein (27%), 7 g fat (46%), 9 g carbohydrate (26%; 2 g sugars), 1.5 mg dietary fiber, 96 mg cholesterol, 161 mg sodium, $.30

Health Bonuses

I pray that you may enjoy good health and that all may go well with you, even as your soul is getting along well.
3 John 2

HEALTH BONUSES

SUBJECTS

RECIPES

Baking Powder, Homemade

Fresh Juices

Other

Sourdough

Other

A Potpourri

I will give you. . . riches stored in secret places. . . Isaiah 45:3

This section was especially challenging and fun to work on, but I will admit I have had a hard time defining what unifies the items that I selected to put in it. At first, I thought of folk remedies, but not every item is a folk remedy. Then I thought of food supplements. But sourdough and fresh juices, for example, are certainly not food supplements. Besides, most people think of food supplements as what comes out of a vitamin bottle. "Super-foods" next suggested itself, but while that fits flaxseed, it doen't serve for *Butter Spread.* Then I tried out "health bonuses." While I can't say that quite fits, either, it is seems to be the most inclusive.

Maybe you could say this section is a hodge-podge of nutritional bonus information that didn't fit anywhere else that I couldn't pass up. It focuses on foods that have a lot to offer, but that are not often thought of as ingredients to be used in the diet on a regular basis.

If, after doing what you can with your diet, you still have a chronic common problem, some of the health bonuses in this section may provide help. Such problems include:

~skin problems	~muscular weakness
~allergies	~lack of energy/vitality (fatigue)
~constipation	~gall stones or kidney stones
~depression	~recurring infections or illness
~digestive discomfort	~high blood cholesterol and/or
~nervous conditions	triglycerides

Items introduced in this section are just that - an introduction. I did not intend to be thorough or exhaustive, but to raise your awareness of what is available and to encourage you to do your own further research. You can incorporate health bonuses into your daily regimen for the sake of prevention, even if you don't have any of the above listed recurring problems.

The key to the effectiveness of these health bonuses is regular use in a recommended amount. Sporadic use won't accomplish much and would be a poor use of your food dollar. None of what I suggest in this section is a prescription for anything, but general guidelines to give you a starting reference point. Individual needs vary widely, so what benefits you may gain from taking advantage of one or more health bonuses will depend on how you adjust your use of them to accomplish the results you want.

Breakfast lends itself well to many of these health bonuses, for example: *Potassium Tonic* upon arising, lecithin and/or brewer's yeast added to a breakfast shake, or fresh juice to start the day.

Juice It!

About ten years ago I got braces on my teeth, for the second time. My ability to chew fresh fruits and vegetables dissappeared in one dental visit! Along with this ability went the enjoyment. Who wants lettuce leaf and carrot bits wrapped around one's metal bands?

This was a tolerable sacrifice until my energy level began to drop. I decided it was time to recover some of the sacrificed nutrients. I bought a vegetable juicer and a book or two on juicing, and I became very excited about juicing!

Freshly prepared juices will add vital nutrient support to any diet. Here are the facts: According to the *Food Pyramid* presented to the American public by the USDA and replacing the *Basic 4 Food Groups*, we should be eating 3-5 servings of vegetables and 2-4 servings of fruits every day. The average American doesn't begin to meet this recommendation! On the average we eat only 1 serving of fruit and 1.8 servings of vegetables daily.[1] Increasing our intake of fresh raw foods is our greatest dietary need. This is true for most of us even if we are eating a better than typical a American diet.

Nutritionally, what do fresh raw foods have to offer? They provide the broad range of vitamins and minerals, plus vital water content. In addition they provide amino acids (easily digestible proteins) plus nutritional properties we are still barely aware of. Green vegetables provide cleansing and building chlorophyll. Yet, most important of all and most overlooked are *enzymes* that only raw foods supply. An enzyme is an activity or energy factor that is carried by a protein molecule. An enzyme is a *catalyst* in all biological processes. That is, it causes changes to occur in the body without itself being changed. For example, enzymes break down and digest food so that it can be absorbed into the blood stream. Other enzymes then build the digested food into muscle, bones, nerves, blood, glands and virtually every part of the body. Enzymes are essential to every process in the body. For example, besides food digestion and assimilation, they are essential to the storing of sugar, elimination, removal of toxins, reproduction, and a strong immune system.

There are over 1,000 different known enzymes in our body. Each enzyme does a specific task, like only one key that fits into one lock. The names of most enzymes end in *-ase,* as in lactase, the lactose

---

[1]As reported in *American Journal of Public Health* 80:1443, 1990 based on a 4 year study of 11,000 persons who took part in the National Health and Examination Survey from 1976-80.

(milk sugar) digesting enzyme. We are born with a large enzyme reserve, but we lose enzymes daily through digestion and elimination. The more high-stress a diet we consume, the faster this enzyme reserve will be depleted. It is important to support this reserve.

Cooked food supplies no enzymes because all enzymes are killed at 129°F. Thus cooked foods require more of the body's enzyme activity for digestion, assimilation, and elimination, than do raw foods. It was once thought (and by many still is) that raw food enzymes were irrelevant to health because they were inactivated by the acid in the stomach and also, because the body had its own supply. Research has shown, however, that not all of these raw food enzymes are inactivated, but that they remain active in the upper part of the stomach where acid does not affect them. And even those that are inactivated, are reactivated in the small intestine. Furthermore, they assist both in partial digestion of the raw food itself and are absorbed into the blood stream where they assist in other metabolic processes. It is in this way that the enzymes of raw foods are vital to the preservation of the body's enzyme reserve.

Enzymes are essential to energy, strength, and longevity. For most of us, a much higher proportion of the diet in raw fresh foods will assist in preserving our enzyme reserve. Raw fresh foods not only include fresh fruits and vegetables, but also sprouted whole grains and legumes, nuts and seeds, and certified raw dairy products. The role of raw food enzymes in the human body has not yet been widely researched, accepted or recognized. An excellent booklet to read is *Food Enzymes* by Humbart Santillo BS, MH. Phoenix, Arizona: Hohm Press, 1991, $4.95, available at health food stores.

Fruit and vegetable juicing is an ideal way to get not only a high intake of enzymes, but also a powerful supply of nutrients and cleansing liquid. The fiber is separated from the juice allowing you to take in more at one time and to digest and assimilate it speedily.

A key question asked is, *What about the fiber*? Don't we need the fiber? The answer is no, not in this way. To make 1 cup of carrot juice, for example, requires one pound of carrots. Practically, no one eats a pound of carrots to get the fiber. I am not recommending that fresh salads or fruits be replaced with juices, although in some situations they will fill a real need. For example, juices are an excellent solution for children who won't eat their fruits and vegetables and for those who either cannot chew or digest high-fiber foods well. They won't be missing any fiber they wouldn't eat anyway, yet will receive many otherwise missed nutritional benefits.

When should you include fresh juices? Anytime! I often have a tall glass of apple-carrot or apple-carrot-celery juice for breakfast, or maybe apple-grape or a citrus combination. Fresh juice can be taken with meals but is best for digestion at least 30 minutes before a meal. It will certainly curb your appetite for a big meal!

Both cleansing to the system and energizing, juices make an excellent choice for a fast of a few days. One to three days on juices alone can be very beneficial, yet not deplete you of energy. It is an easy and enjoyable way to benefit from a fast from solid foods.

I am often asked what I think of taking food supplements. Many people experience dramatic results from taking them. I am not one of these people, but have taken a variety of supplements for years as a matter of "insurance," based upon what I know about my own nutrient needs. There are many complex interactions to consider in how nutrients are utilized in our bodies. We can't possibly know and understand them all. Yet when we consume them in foods of high nutritional value, all the components, known and unknown, work together *synergistically* (p. 55). This is why fresh juices excel. They are a tasty and inexpensive way, compared to food supplements, to obtain power-packed nutrition.

What kind of juicer should you buy? There are a wide selection of juicers on the market. The *Juiceman* juicer is fast becoming a household word. The "Juiceman" himself is Jay Kordich, author of *The Juiceman's Power of Juicing* (a "must" book, and my favorite on juicing). I personally have a *Phoenix* juicer ($160-$180--a very modest price for a good juicer). Like the *Juiceman*, it is a continuous juicer, meaning that the pulp is extracted from the juice into a separate container from the basket and the juice. In some juicers the pulp accumulates in the basket. This limits how much juice you can make before cleaning out the basket. I prefer a continuous juicer with a sturdy motor and one with juice and pulp containers that do not vibrate out of position while juicing.

Fresh juice should be consumed immediately after it is prepared as the nutritional value and delicious taste are very perishable. Do you want to take it to work with you? Jay Kordich will tell you exactly how to carefully preserve it using a thermos in *The Juiceman's Power of Juicing.*

How much of your busy day will it take to prepare a glass of fresh juice? About 5 minutes to prepare the fresh food and juice it, and about 3-4 minutes to clean up everything you used, including the juicer. I call that a quick meal-in-a-glass! When you clean up, plan to feed the fiber to the compost pile. Yes, the fiber can be used in baking. Some juice books give recipes for the fiber. But you'll use precious little in a recipe compared to the amount collected in your juicer. You won't want to be baking all the time just to use up the fiber, so give it to the compost. Your garden will love it!

Is it necessary to buy organic produce for juicing? Several authors suggest that you should. Yet, Dr. Norman Walker, the grandfather of juicing in his 1936 classic, *Fresh Vegetable & Fruit Juices* (1986 reprint of the 1978 revised edtion) states that toxic pesticide residues collect in the fiber, not in the juice. Thus it is not essential to have organic produce, but do get the freshest you can obtain. Keep in mind that storage time, storage conditions, and the quality of soil that fresh foods are grown in will all affect the nutrient value.

What fresh fruits and vegetables are best for juicing? High vitamin A and C foods are the most important. Here is a simple list of common fruits and vegetables that will make a surprising variety of juice combinations.

Vegetables	Fruits
carrots	apples
celery	grapes (in season)
cucumber	pineapple
parsley	melons (in season)
beets (occasionally)	oranges
cabbage	grapefruit
spinach	lemons
	kiwi

HOW TO PREPARE FRESH FOODS FOR JUICING

1. Scrub well with vegetable brush. Rinse leafy greens well.

2. Cut firm vegetables into 1"-2" pieces.

3. Cut apples in half. Lay flat side on cutting board and score into 1-2" chunks.

4. Peel citrus fruits and cut into wedges with knife. Kiwis and very small pieces of lemon do not need to be peeled.

5. Follow juicer instructions for feeding vegetables and fruits into juicer.

Sue's Carrot-Apple Juice

About 2 Cups

Use any kind of apple you wish.
This is my favorite combination.

Prepare produce for juicing (p. 259) and
process in vegetable juicer:

> **1 lb. carrots (about 6 medium)**
> **(or 1 cup juice)**
> **1 small red delicious apple**
> **1 small Granny Smith apple**

Per Recipe   Exchanges: 2.5 Fruit, 7.25 Vegetable; 324 Calories, 6.5 g protein (7%),
1.5 g fat (4%), 80 g carbohydrate (89%; 29 g sugars), 150 mg sodium, $.65

> For persons concerned about food combining,
> apples go with both fruits and vegetables.

Carrot-Apple-Celery Juice

About 2 Cups

Use any kind of apple you wish; One green apple and
half red apple is my favorite combination.

Prepare produce for juicing (p. 259)
and process in vegetable juicer:

> **2 or 3 large carrots**
> **2 large ribs celery**
> **½ red apple**
> **1 green apple**

Per Recipe   Exchanges: 2 Fruit, 4.5 Vegetable; 218 Calories, 4.5 g protein (7%),
1 g fat (5%), 54 g carbohydrate (88%; 30 g sugars), 191 mg sodium, $.55

> I enjoy "sipping" my juice with a straw.

Sue's Apple-Grape Juice

About 1¼ Cups

My favorite apple combination with grapes.

Prepare produce for juicing (p. 259)
and process in vegetable juicer:

> **1 red apple**
> **1 green apple**
> **about 1 cup red grapes**

Per Recipe   Exchanges: 4 Fruit; 246 Calories, 1.5 g protein (2%), 1.5 g fat (4%),
64 g carbohydrate (94%; 18 g sugars), 5 mg sodium, $.55

Kiwi-Apple Juice

Packs in almost 300 mg. vitamin C!

Prepare produce for juicing (p. 259) and process in vegetable juicer:
4 kiwi fruit, unpeeled
1 apple

Per Recipe   Exchanges: 4.25 Fruit; 256 Calories, 3.5 g protein (5%), 2 g fat (6%), 63 g carbohydrate (89%; 40 g sugars), 16 mg sodium, $1.30

Cantaloupe Cooler

About 1⅓ Cups

A high C, high A Combination! Don't expect an orange-colored juice. It will be pea-green when juiced with peeling, yet will be tasty.

Wedge the cantaloupe, rind and all, cut into chunks, and process in vegetable juicer:
1 lb. cantaloupe

Per Recipe   Exchanges: 1.25 Fruit; 70 Calories, 1.5 g protein (8%), 0.5 Fat (3%), 17 g carbohydrate (89%; 18 g sugars), 28 mg sodium, $.45

Watermelon Nectar

About 1 Cup

In contrast to cantaloupe juice, I don't care for the taste when unpeeled. I peel this and process in the blender. It's mostly water anyway.

Puree in the blender at high speed until liquified:
½ lb. peeled watermelon chunks (about 10 oz. before removing the peel)
1 teaspoon crystalline fructose *(p. 12)* or other sweetener, optional
2 ice cubes

Per Recipe   Exchanges: 0.25 Fruit; 86 Calories, 1.5 g protein (6%), 1.5 g fat (13%), 20 g carbohydrate (81%; 19 g sugars), 2 g dietary fiber, 4 mg sodium, $.25

Citrus Combo

About 1 Cup

Squeeze juice of:
½ grapefruit (⅓ to 3/8 cup)
1 orange (⅜ to ½ cup)
½ lemon (2-2½ tablespoons)

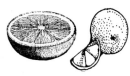

Per Recipe   Exchanges: 1.75 Fruit; 107 Calories, 2 g protein (7%), 0.5 g fat (3%), 27 g carbohydrate (90%; 21 g sugars), 0 mg sodium, $.55

Olive Oil

Observe the commands of the LORD your God, walking in his ways and revering him. For the LORD your God is bringing you into a good land...with wheat and barley, vines and fig trees, pomegranates, olive oil and honey. Deuteronomy 8:6-9

Olive oil has a rich Biblical tradition. Historically it has been most widely used in the Mediterranean countries. Average oil consumption in this region is 40%, but with far lower incidence of heart disease and less cancer than in the U.S.A. Part of olive oil's secret is its *monunsaturated fat* that lowers blood cholesterol but does not correspondingly lower the good HDL blood cholesterol component. It is also a probablility that a high fat diet (around 40%) with olive oil may lower blood cholesterol more effectively than a low fat diet.

The latest research indicates other benefits of olive oil, as well: it may regulate blood sugar levels, lower blood pressure, assist in prevention of breast cancer and act as an *antioxidant*. This latter property is extremely valuable. An antioxidant inhibits the oxidation of fats that causes free radicals in the body. Free radicals contribute to build up of plaque on artery walls, cancer, aging, and possibly numerous other diseases. The most important antioxidant of olive oil is its *oleic acid*. Oleic acid is monounsaturated fat.

Extra Virgin Olive Oil[1] is my peferred choice (light olive oil is the occasional exception used in *Butter Spread*, p. 264). It is produced by the first crushing of olives between steel rollers or stone, preserving the quality of the fatty acids and its natural preservatives. Protected from light, it will keep fresh and its antioxidant properties will stay intact for many years. Its strong flavor is not conveyed in most baking. I also use olive oil in oil salad dressings. Olive oil has a wonderful ability to coat leafy greens and spread its unique flavor without using very much. I use olive oil or a combination of olive oil and butter when fat is desired for cooking or stir-frying over direct heat (see **Main Dishes**, p. 27). As a general practice I have transitioned almost entirely to olive oil in cooking and baking, salad dressings and in *Butter Spread*.

Because olive oil is so highly monounsaturated (77%), it will keep longer than all the other oils at room temperature. It is the only oil that will turn semi-solid if refrigerated, making it difficult to pour. I

[1]Purchase at health food stores, Trader Joe Markets, many supermarkets. See also SunOrganic Farm mail order offers organic extra virgin olive oil (see p. 79 for address).

store olive oil in the cupboard. For long term storage during very hot and humid weather you may wish to refrigerate it. Remove it from the refrigerator for awhile before using it to warm it up to a a pourable state.

Canola Oil

Canola was developed through traditional breeding methods from *rapeseed* (related to the mustard family, with yellow flowers,grown in Europe and India) until the desired characteristics were achieved. The primary concern in the use of oil from rapeseed has focused on its traditionally high erucic acid content considered a risk to health. *Canola*, the Canadian source of the oil, contains less than 5% erucic acid. Nevertheless, canola oil has recently come under attack via the Internet[1] (see my response at *www.suegregg.com* under Questions & Answers).

Admittedly canola oil has an excellent balance of quality fats: a high percentage (62%) of monounsaturated fat, very low amount of saturated fat (6%) and good amounts of both omega-6 (linoleic 22%) and omega-3 (linolenic 10%) essential fatty acids. For this reason and because of its mild flavor I used it for some time in *Butter Spread* (p. 264) and in some baking (see **Main Dishes**, pp. 26-27) because of its mild flavor. However, over the last two years I have found myself using olive oil exclusively in place of canola oil. I believe the reason is that canola oil is still somewhat of an "unknown quantity" with the verdict still out on its safety and its health benefits. I also believe that research cited against the overuse of polyunsaturated oils (including canola oil) is worthy of careful attention (see articles available at *www.westonprice.org*). This same research exonerates saturated fats (particularly butter) from being the heart disease-cancer culprits.

The most unrefined canola oil available is *Spectrum Naturals Spectravac-Processed Fresh Unrefined Guaranteed Organic Canola Oil*. It is available at health food stores under refrigeration. Produced in 8.5 oz. dark bottles, it is expensive, about $4.50 per cup. It is also very strong flavored . Most will not want to handle this price or strong flavor. I recommend *Spectrum Naturals 100% Expeller Pressed Canola Oil*, available in quart jars at health food stores. It is milder in flavor and lower in price. However, at this time, I suggest caution in the use of much canola oil. Olive oil and butter are both very safe and well-documented nutritonal alternatives.

[1]Udo Erasmus in *Fats that Heal, Fats that Kill* (Alive Books, 1993) is cited in this attack giving what I consider a false impression of his view of canola oil. I highly recommend this book for understanding the entire subject of fats.

Saturated Fat & Essential Fatty Acids

Almost all margarines are made from polyunsaturated fats that have been hydrogenated or partially hydrogenated which makes them solid at room temperature. *Hydrogenation* and *partial hydrogenation* alter the chemical structure of the oil's essential fatty acids. Hydrogenation renders them unavailable to the body, while partial hydrogenation turns a high proportion into harmful *trans-fatty acids*.

Butter, on the other hand, is naturally solid at room temperature, and as a short-chain fatty acid it is one of the most easily digested fats, has antimicrobial properties that protect the body from viruses, yeasts and pathogenic bacteria in the digestive system, and boosts the health of the immune system. It's vitamin A content, which promotes health of the heart, is the best source in America and most easily absorbed.[1] The high percentage of *saturated fat* in butter, however, is what frightens people into the persistent use of margarines, in addition to the higher cost. *Butter Spread* is my challenge to margarine. Equal portions of butter and olive oil lessens the amount of saturated fat while including a high amount of monounsaturated fat and a small usable portion of essential fatty acid (linoleic). *Butter Spread* provides:

~24% less saturated fat.
~21% increase in monounsaturated fat.
~a small increase in linoleic acid (an essential fatty acid).
~50% reduction in sodium content.
~50% reduction in cholesterol content.
~an acceptable flavor of always spreadable consistency
   direct from the refrigerator.

[1]*Sally W. Fallon, MA and Mary G. Enig, Phd, The Ploy of Soy, "Why Butter is Better," p. 11, Price-Pottenger Nutrition Foundation, Inc., 1995*

Butter Spread

My alternative to hydrogenated margarines, although I don't use it exclusive of butter. Keep refrigerated until ready to use. It will return to liquid at room temperature in a very short time.

Gradually whisk oil into butter until completely smooth and no lumps remain:

½ cup (1 stick) butter, very soft
½ cup light or extra virgin olive oil *(according to taste preference*

Per 1 Tbsp. (includes lecithin): Exchanges: 2.5 Fat; 111 Calories, 13 g fat (100%), 15 mg cholesterol, 48 mg sodium, $.10

Butter Spread Comparison Chart

Sat = Saturated fat
Mono = Monounsaturated fat
Poly = Polyunsaturated fat
   Linoleic Acid - Essential Fatty Acid
   Linolenic Acid - Essential Fatty Acid

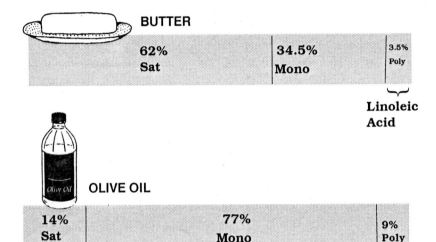

BUTTER

| 62%
Sat | 34.5%
Mono | 3.5%
Poly |

Linoleic
Acid

OLIVE OIL

| 14%
Sat | 77%
Mono | 9%
Poly |

8% Linoleic Acid
1% Linolenic Acid

Butter Spread } ½ cup butter
                   ½ cup olive oil

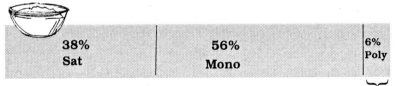

| 38%
Sat | 56%
Mono | 6%
Poly |

Sodium reduced by half
Cholesterol reduced by half

Linoleic
Acid

Flaxseed

*. . .none herbe is so needful to so many dyurrse uses
to mankynde as the flexe. Bartholomew, medieval
herbalist, A Modern Herbal, Vol. I*

A Little History

Flaxseed has a long history. It is mentioned in the Bible several
times. It was one of the crops, along with the barley crop, destroyed
during the plague of hail at the time of the Exodus (*Exodus 9:31*).
Linen cloth is made from the fibers of the flax plant. Rahab had stalks
of flax drying on her roof in Jericho when she hid the Israelite spies
(*Joshua 2:6*). The curtains of the tabernacle were made of linen
(*Exodus 26:1*), as well as Aaron's priestly garments (*Lev. 6:4*), and the
strips of cloth in which Jesus' body was wrapped (*John 2:5*). Historically, linen has been used widely from the making of sails and fishnets
to ropes and candle wicks. Flaxseed has also been used medicinally
as an herb and for its oil. Therapeutic uses are found in writings that
date back to 650 B.C. The scientific name of flaxseed is *Linum
usitatissimum,* meaning "the most useful."

What is It?

Flax seeds are small brown seeds that are shiny, oval, and flat. The
plant grows gracefully about 1-2 feet high and sometimes 3 feet, and
has turquoise blue flowers. Flax seeds come from the pods of the
plant. Flaxseed oil has been used for hundreds of years as an edible
oil in European households.

In contrast to the processing of most oils, flaxseed oil is pressed
from the seeds with little or no heat. A more familiar use of the oil in
America is the inedible linseed oil used in art and painting. But
hundreds of research studies have been done revealing the value of the
edible oil to human health. Flaxseed is the highest known source of
linolenic acid (LNA), the omega-3 essential fatty acid that is commonly
lacking in the diet of most Americans. Omega-3 as a food supplement
source from fish oils has been highly publicized in recent years as
valuable in controlling cholesterol. Yet flaxseed is a much richer
source of Omega-3.

What are Benefits of Flaxseed?

Flax seeds contain soluble fiber which assists in regulating cholesterol levels (see chart, p. 52). They also contain another fiber, lignin,
an anti-cancer agent. The mucilage of flax seeds is beneficial both in
controlling blood cholesterol and as a laxative to encourage regularity. Externally, flax seeds have been used as a poultice for bruises,
boils, and other skin problems.

The oil of the flaxseed is rich in vitamins A, B-1, B-2, D, and E, lecithin (p. 270) and phosphatides that assist in fat digestion, and most of the major and trace minerals. One tablespoon oil provides 5,500 I.U. of beta carotene (provitamin A), and 7,300-8,500 mg. omega-3 fatty acids.

Flaxseed oil has incredible benefits and the list is long. If you have any chronic condition, flaxseed oil would be worth checking into for possible assistance (see reading resources, p. 268). For a few examples, flaxseed oil has been found helpful in arthritis, in asthma relief, in preventing colon and breast cancer, in improving moods, in PMS, in producing healthier skin, in diminishing allergic responses, in increasing vitality and energy and in lowering high blood pressure.

Where Is it Found?

Flaxseed is grown principally in India, Holland, Russia, Argentina, the United States, Canada, and also in England and Ireland. Both the seeds and the edible oil are available at health food stores. While the seeds have been available in America for many years, the oil has been made available only within the last few years. Excellent brands of flaxseed oil include *Omega Nutrition, Arrowhead Mills, Spectrum Naturals, Bio San C-Leinosän* and *Barlean.* Bottles are small (about 8 oz.), and must be stored in the refrigerator case.

How Do You Use It?
I use both oil and seeds. The oil is best assimilated when thoroughly mixed with cottage cheese. The sulfur-rich amino acids in the cheese assist in the assimilation of omega-3 fatty acids into the bloodstream. Flax seeds are less costly than the oil. For example 3 1/3 tablespoons seeds at $.15 provide the same amount of fat as 1 tbsp. oil at $.45.

To use flaxseed or oil start with a small amount--1 tablespoon seed or 1 teaspoon oil. Increase gradually to 1 tablespoon oil or 2 tablespoons seed ground to ¼ cup (whole flaxseeds should be ground, p. 120). Both the seed and the oil are very pleasant in taste.

Several ways flaxseed can be used easily include:
~Flaxseed oil and/or ground flax seeds added to cottage cheese
   (see recipe, p. 268)
~Ground flax seeds sprinkled over hot cereal *(see Sue's Breakfast, p. 111)*
~Ground flax seeds in *Roman Meal* cereal *(p. 107)*
~Ground or oil in shakes *(p. 184, Sue's Apple Bran Shake, p. 185)*
~Ground sprinkled over fruit or yogurt
~Ground flax in waffles/pancakes *(p. 204)*
~Ground flax or oil in vegetable juice drinks
~1½ tsps. oil in 6 oz. orange juice (as drink or salad dressing)

How Should Flaxseed be Stored?

Keep whole flax seeds at room temperature 2-3 months or up to 1 year in refrigerator or freezer. Grind flax seeds that can be used up in a week, storing them in refrigerator or freezer.

Flaxseed oil is highly perishable. It may be frozen in the bottle to extend the shelf life and is pourable from the bottle even from the freezer. Flaxseed oil will stay fresh in the refrigerator up to 3 months from the pressing date. It is helpful if both the pressing date and "use by" dates are listed on the bottle. Once it is opened it is best used within 3-6 weeks (longer if kept in freezer).

For Further Reading

Fats that Heal, Fats that Kill by Udo Erasmus, Alive Books, 1993

Flaxseed Oil and The Power of Omega-3 by Ingeborg M. Johnston, C.D, and James R. Johnston, Ph.D., A Good Health Guide Book

How to Fight Cancer & Win by William L. Fischer, pp. 109-150

Sue's Super Cottage "Dessert"

Eat this just as it is or top with fresh fruit. It has the real "health-food" look, but I find it very tasty, especially with fresh lemon peel added. I eat it often for breakfast.

Whisk together thoroughly:
- **½ cup fat free cottage cheese**
- **3 tablespoons nonfat plain yogurt**
- **2 teaspoons flaxseed oil** *(p. 12)*
- **1 teaspoon maple syrup, optional**
- **few gratings lemon peel, optional**
- **2 or 3 drops vanilla extract, optional**
- **2 tablespoons ground flax seeds** (from 1 tablespoon whole seeds)
- **1 tablespoon lecithin granules, optional** *(p. 13)*
- **1-2 teaspoons brewer's yeast, optional** *(p. 265)*

Per Serving (all ingredients)
Exchanges: 0.25 Meat, 1 Milk, 0.25 Bread, 3.5 Fat, 0.5 Fruit; 221 Calories, 31 g protein (47%), 9.5 g fat (32%), 14 g carbohydrate (21%; 10 g sugars), 3 g dietary fiber, 5 mg cholesterol, 56 mg sodium, $.85

VARIATION   *A tasty tossed salad topping, or a salad in itself.*

Optional: Blend cheese, yogurt, and oil in blender. Omit other ingredients and add, as desired, finely chopped:
> **carrot, cucumber, radish, green onion, parsley, chives, green pepper, celery, tomato**

Tasty additional seasonings include, as desired:
> **dill weed, celery seed, garlic powder, soy sauce, basil, tarragon, lemon juice, apple cider vinegar**

Egg Alternatives

Flaxseed Binder

The mucilagenous property of flax seeds make them a good alternative for eggs. They do not add lightness, but give the essential "binding" effect of eggs in baking. This will keep well for 2 weeks in the refrigerator. Amount is equivalent to 5 or 6 eggs.

1. Bring to a boil, stirring with a wire whisk:
   ¾ cup cold water
   ¼ cup ground flaxseed (2 Tbsp. whole seed, ground, *p. 120*)

2. Boil 3 minutes while stirring.

3. Cool and refrigerate in tightly covered container.

4. Use per egg: **⅛ cup (2 tablespoons) flaxseed binder.** Thoroughly whisk into first liquid ingredient in the recipe before adding the next ingredient.

> **Measuring Tip:** Flaxseed Binder is hard to measure exactly because it will stick to itself like glue. Pull it up with a fork into a ⅛ cup measure or scoop out a heaping tablespoon (equivalent to ⅛ cup). An exact measure is not important.

About ⅛ Cup (⅕ Recipe)   *Exchanges: 0.25 Fat; 19 Calories, 1 g fat (58%), 2 g carbohydrate (29%; 0 g sugars), 1 g dietary fiber, 0 mg cholesterol, $.02*

Arrowroot Binder

Per 1 egg, whisk together until smooth, bring slowly to boil over moderate heat, stirring constantly until clear:
   ⅓ cup cold water
   1 teaspoon arrowroot powder *(p. 11)*

Others

Quail Eggs Use **2 quail eggs per 1 large egg**. Available in some health foods stores (i.e. Gooch's Market in Glendale, CA.) or mail order from: Big Country Game Bird Farm, Abilene, TX (915) 677-0866.

Duck Eggs Use **1 duck egg for 2 chicken eggs.** Inquire through local health food stores. Available from Woodland Farms, La Puente, CA (818) 336-1624.

Tofu **¼ cup tofu per 1 egg** works in some recipes, but can make a difference in texture. Use soft tofu or blend thoroughly in blender with other liquid ingredients.

Ener-G Egg Replacer Use **1½ teaspoons per egg**. Contains potato starch, tapioca base; available at health food stores.

Lecithin

What is It?

Lecithin (LESS-a-thin) is a waxy complex fatty substance made up of phospholipids and essential fatty acids, and containing phosphorus, choline, and inositol (two of the B-vitamins). It is best know as a fat *emulsifier*. That is, it disperses fats and most notably cholesterol, in the blood, so that it does not collect on the walls of the arteries. It is available as a bottled liquid, in granules or capsules, and is available at health food stores.

Where is It Found?

The human body manufactures lecithin in the liver as long as the necessary nutrients are supplied by the diet. Lecithin acquired its name from the Greek word for egg yolks, the highest source of lecithin. It is also present in soybeans, unrefined oils such as safflower, soybean, and sunflower, legumes, nuts, and wheat germ. Much of it is made unusable through heat processing or cooking. Liquid lecithin and granules are produced primarily from soybeans.

What Does It Do?

Lecithin has a combination of positive effects upon fats, from their breakdown and absorption, to their proper balance and utilization in the body. There have been studies done, though not on a broad scale, to indicate lecithin's cholesterol lowering effect. In addition, lecithin is known to contribute to healthy brain function, to prevent formation of gallstones and kidney stones, to assist the nervous system, and to help clear up skin problems. Synergistically (p. 55) lecithin improves the utilization of vitamin A. Externally, it has been used as a folk remedy for hemorrhoids, diaper rash, skin rashes, and psoriasis.

An Experiment: To visualize *emulsifying action*, add 2 tablespoons oil to ¼ cup water in a glass or glass measuring cup. Notice that the oil remains on top, separated from the water. Thoroughly whisk in 1 tablespoon liquid lecithin or lecithin granules. Let stand several hours or overnight. If you notice that the fat and lecithin are blended, yet as a separate "glob" in the water, warm the mixture a little and stir again. After several hours you will notice that the water and oil are no longer separated. The oil molecules have been dispersed throughout the water by the lecithin.

How Should Lecithin be Stored?

Lecithin may be stored indefinitely at room temperature. Do not refrigerate; it will be impossible to pour.

How Do You Use It?

Easy ways to include lecithin in the diet include:
~liquid lecithin or granules in hot cereal
~lecithin granules in breakfast shakes (see p. 184)
~lecithin granules in *Sue's Super Cottage "Dessert"*, p. 268

Use 1 or 2 tablespoons liquid or granular lecithin daily, or several times a week. To receive benefit use it on a regular basis. There is no known toxic level for lecithin. One tablespoon granules contains 12 grams fat. One tablespoon liquid lecithin contains 15 grams fat.

GREASING BAKING PANS

Using the non-stick spray is a fast and easy way to grease pans. Read the ingredients label on non-stick spray can. You'll notice three listed ingredients: oil, lecithin, and propellant. Oil alone used for greasing will not prevent sticking of baked goods to the pan. Lecithin used alone is effective, but very sticky to work with and very expensive. But a blend of liquid lecithin and oil works well. When using non-stick spray, I recommend an olive oil spray, such as *Pam* and *Bertolli*, two brands found in many supermarkets and health food stores.

If you want to cut cost and avoid the propellant of non-stick spray, you can grease the pans by blending your own supply of liquid lecithin with olive oil. The oil and lecithin can be premixed and kept at room temperature for ready use, or blended at the time you grease the pan. To premix, combine 1 part lecithin with 2 parts olive oil and store at room temperature.

To grease pans without mixing oil and lecithin in advance, pour a small amount of liquid lecithin into the bake pan. For muffins I pour it into one muffin cup. Next, pour about twice as much oil over the lecithin. Evenly distribute the oil and lecithin over the baking pan surface with wax paper. With a little experience you'll know about how much is needed to cover the surface of the pan you are using.

Wheat Bran

Wheat bran consists of 6 outer layers of the wheat kernel (see chart, p. 53). It is a rich source of *insoluble fiber* and most effective for relieving constipation (see chart, p.52). Coarser bran is more effective than finer bran. The bran also contains iron, calcium, phosphorus, potassium, sodium, niacin, and good traces of several B-vitamins.

An Experiment: Stir some freshly ground wheat flour through a strainer. The coarse particles left in the strainer are the bran.

To use wheat bran as a high-fiber supplement, increase use gradually. Up to 3 tablespoons daily is an average suggested amount. To improve wheat bran's nutritional benefits, soak the bran in water overnight (see pp. 50-51): thoroughly blend about 2 tbsps. boiling water with a fork into 3 tbsps. bran (a proportion of 2 parts water to 3 parts bran). If you get diarrhea, it is a sign of too much bran. If you have diverticulosis, diverticulitis, or Crohn's disease, consult your doctor before using bran. Diverticulosis affects about 30-40% of Americans over 50. A high fiber diet can prevent this condition.

Wheat bran is available in both supermarkets and health food stores, but generally more economical from health food stores. It is called *Miller's* unprocessed wheat bran. In comparison, cold boxed cereals such as *Bran Buds, Raisin Bran,* or *100% Bran* contain sugar and sodium. Plain bran works just as well in recipes, and at much lower cost. Unprocessed bran costs about $.07 per cup as compared to about $.48 per cup of 100% bran cereal.

Wheat bran will keep at room temperature about 1 month, and in the refrigerator or freezer 2-3 months.

Ways to use wheat bran:
~*Blender Bran Muffins*, p. 192
~*Peach Bran Coffee Cake*, p. 341
~Add to shakes, p. 184
~Add to hot cereals, p. 115
~Add to *Simple Granola*, p. 117
~*Banana Date Bran Muffins*, **Soups & Muffins,** p. 65
~*Carrot Bran Muffins*, **Soups & Muffins,** p. 63
~*Date Bran Muffins*, **Soups & Muffins,** p. 55
~*Minute Bran Muffins*, **Soups & Muffins,** p. 61

Wheat Germ

Wheat germ is a valuable source of Vitamin E and B-vitamins, a good source of calcium, and iron, and contains a variety of minerals. It also contains *octacosonol*, an ingredient now thought to be responsible for improved stamina and strength. Undoubtedly it works synergistically (p. 55) with vitamin E and the other nutrients in wheat.

Wheat germ is the valuable heart of the wheat kernel, the embryo with the life in it (see chart, p.53), and the most nutrient-rich portion. Without the germ the wheat kernel will neither sprout nor grow.

One-fourth cup of wheat germ contains 8.5 grams protein, as much as a glass of milk. It is also high in phosphorus in proportion to its calcium. The calcium of 8 oz. of milk or yogurt will balance the phosphorus of ¼ cup wheat germ.

Wheat germ extracted from the whole grain turns rancid very quickly, in about 10 days. Many health food stores carry wheat germ packaged in plastic bags and store them on the shelf at room temperature. I do not recommend purchasing these. Not only are rancid foods unhealthy, but they taste bitter. I recommend wheat germ that is toasted, vacuum packed, and guaranteed fresh. For some brands available at supermarkets and health food stores see p. 15. While there is some nutrient loss in toasted wheat germ, toasting destroys the enzymes that hasten rancidity, and greatly improves the flavor. Toasted wheat germ will keep under refrigeration up to 6 months after opening. I prefer to keep it in the freezer after it is opened.

Ways to use wheat germ:
~Add to shakes, p. 184
~Add to hot cereals, p. 115
~Add to *Simple Granola*, p. 117
~Add to *Yummy Oatmeal*, p. 118
~Purchase *Oat Bran Cereal with Toasted Wheat Germ*, p. 91
~Sprinkle over Mixed Fresh Fruit
~Stir into yogurt
~Add to muffins (¼ cup in place of ¼ cup flour in 2 cup recipe)
~Use in *Wheat Germ Muffins*, p. 197
~Add to waffles/pancakes (same proportion as for muffins)
~Add to yeast breads (1 cup wheat germ to 6 cups flour)
~Use it to replace oatmeal or oat bran in meat loaf
~Use in *Turkey Burgers* (**Main Dishes**, p. 184) in place of oat bran
~Use in *Sweet 'n Sour Meat Balls* (**Main Dishes**, p. 201)
~Use in *Mexicali Burgers* (**Main Dishes**, p. 286)
~Use in place of bread crumbs to coat chicken, fish, top casseroles

Brewer's Yeast

What is It?

Yeast is a *fungus* that grows off of other plants. Brewer's yeast is not the same as baker's yeast used to raise breads. It is a pasteurized non-active, non-leavening yeast used as a food supplement. Most brewer's yeast is grown on hops and is a by-product of the beer brewing industry. *Lewis Laboratories* brand (see below) is grown on sugar beets. Nutritonal yeast, food yeast, primary yeast, and torula yeast, also non-leavening yeast food supplements, are grown on blackstrap molasses or wood pulp.

Where is It Found?

All types of yeast food supplements may be found at health food stores. Take my word for it, they can and usually do taste "yuck!" I guarantee that the best tasting is *Lewis Laboratories Brewer's Yeast.* The label states: "This is the only brewer's yeast that actually tastes good! Absolutely NO after-taste. Totally digestible, it will change your idea of what Brewer's Yeast really is." Try this one before any other brand. If you can't find it, inquire of the health food store manager or write to Lewis Laboratories International, Ltd., 49 Richmondville Avenue, Westport, CT 06880. A 16 oz. can costs about $8.30--about $.14 per level tablespoon.

What Does it Do?

Brewer's yeast is the richest, and an inexpensive source of B-complex vitamins, including B-12 (It does not contain B-17). One of the best protein sources, containing 4-4.5 grams protein per table-spoon, brewer's yeast has 18 of the amino acids, plus 14 minerals, and nucleic acids (RNA). Here are some benefits claimed for it:

~May prevent constipation
~Assists immunity against degenerative diseases
~Slows skin aging (dry and wrinkled skin)
~May clear up acne and eczema
~May increase breast milk supply
~Build strong nails
~Assist in control of migraines
~Aids sugar metabolism
~Reduces nervousness, fatigue
~Improves physical and mental efficiency
~Excellent supplement during pregnancy
~Important during radiation/chemotherapy treatments

Often, when we see a list of nutrients a food contains, we don't think of the benefits. Then we see the list of the benefits and we can't believe how a food could contribute to all those. That's because we don't translate a list of nutrients into benefits. We have generally been taught a very short list of nutritional benefits. For example, vitamin C helps prevent colds, or the B-vitamins help to calm nerves, or calcium helps build bones and teeth. The fact is each individual nutrient accomplishes a host of benefits. And all the nutrients working together accomplish more than they do alone (synergism). So you can imagine why there are many benefit claims, for example, for brewer's yeast.

Richest Source of B-Vitamins!

What Are the B-Vitamins?

Most of us can name about 4 of the B-vitamins. Yet there are at least 13: B-1 (thiamine), B-2 (riboblavin), B-3 (niacin), B-6 (pyridoxine), B-12, B-17 (amygdalin), biotin, folic acid, choline, inositol, pantothenic acid, para-aminobenzoic acid (PABA). B-13 (orotic acid) is also a B-vitamin, but not yet recognized as one of the B-vitamins in this country. Singly or taken together, the B-vitamins make an incredible contribution to health.

How Do You Use It?

The taste of brewer's yeast takes some getting used to, but it is worth it for the nutritional whallop it packs. Trust me that *Lewis Laboratories* brand is good tasting. But you will still want to start with, and perhaps continue to use, a modest amount at a time. An interesting phenomenon occurs in labeling on some of these products. The serving size is often listed as "heaping" tablespoons. If you actually measure 2 heaping tablespoons (rather an inexact amount), the serving size of *Lewis Laboratories Brewer's Yeast*, will be about ¼ cup. Unless you are a health maveric, ¼ cup of any brewer's yeast at one time would probably sink your taste buds! In addition, like beans or worse than beans, it can cause flatulence. Start with 1 teaspoon with a goal of 1 tablespoon maximum at a time. If you use it to assist in a particular problem such as migraine headaches, or increasing breast milk supply, you may need to use considerably more on a daily basis (as 2-4 tablespoons), dividing it up into palatable, non-flatulence producing portions. Persons with candida or osteoporosis are cautioned not to use brewer's yeast.

Ways to use brewer's yeast:
~Add to *Sue's Cottage "Dessert"*, p. 268
~Add to shakes (p. 184), *Sue's Apple Bran Shake*, p. 185
~Sprinkle over yogurt, hot cereal, salads
~Add to meat loaf, casseroles
~Stir into fruit/vegetable juices

How Should Brewer's Yeast be Stored?

Store it at room temperature; I haven't been able to find out how long, so store it in the refrigerator or freezer after 6 months.

Apple Cider Vinegar

Dear Friend, I pray that you may enjoy good health and that all may go well with you even as your soul is getting along well. 3 John 2

Called the champion *folk remedy* by Dr. D. C. Jarvis in his book *Folk Medicine,* and "The Master Mineral" and "The Youth Mineral" by Dr. Paul Bragg, apple cider vinegar excels in potassium. Dr. Bernard Jensen calls potassium "The Great Alkalizer."

Potassium has gained such a reputation for many reasons. Here are a few major contributions of potassium to health:
~Balances pH (acid-alkaline balance of the blood)
~Increases muscular and nerve strength and vitality
~Reduces fatigue and increases vigor
~Fights viruses and bacteria
~Improves brain function
~Promotes healthy hair and skin tone
~Softener of the artery walls
~Increases efficiency of all body processes and elimination
~Pain reducer

When the *pH balance* of the body becomes too acid, the body becomes susceptible to a wide variety of disease conditions and break-down. The typical American diet supplies an over-abundance of acid-producing foods. Apple cider vinegar helps balance pH. In addition to potassium, apple cider vinegar contains the full range of major and trace minerals, and *malic acid*, which assists in removing toxins from the body.

Many health conscious persons today are taking expensive potassium-rich supplements. Yet, at a fraction of the cost, apple cider vinegar provides a rich potassium tonic. One quart of the highest quality apple cider vinegar will provide a daily potassium tonic for over 3 months for just about $.03 per 2 teaspoons a day. At a health food store you can buy apple cider vinegar made from the whole apple. I recommend raw, unfiltered organic apple cider vinegar that contains the "mother." The mother is the cloudy mixture of beneficial enzymes and bacteria that is usually removed by heat or filtering. Why not get the full benefit? Most health food stores have at least one brand of apple cider vinegar with the mother in it. *Spectrum Naturals* is one brand. If the mother is present, the vinegar will be cloudy in appearance.

276

There are many more ways you can use apple cider vinegar to promote health, both externally and internally. Two excellent resources include *Apple Cider Vinegar Health System* by Paul & Patricia Bragg, available at health food stores or through Health Science, Box 7, Santa Barbara, CA 93102, and *The Vinegar Book* by Emily Thacker, Tresco Publisher, 718-12th Street N.W., Canton, OH 44703. You may also enjoy reading *Folk Medicine* by Dr. D.C. Jarvis.

> **Folk Remedy** Something utilized by a wide variety of people and found to be beneficial for particular problems through experience, but not clinically studied or established by medical or scientific research.

Potassium Tonic

Drink first thing in the morning before breakfast. Honey is also high in potassium. Brush teeth after drinking.

Mix together:
  1 glass warm or cool water
  2 teapoons apple cider vinegar
  1-2 teaspoons honey, to taste

Per Serving -- Exchanges: 0.5 Fruit; 23 Calories, 6 g carbohydrate (100%; 6 g sugars), $.10

Health Tip Use raw-unfiltered organic apple cider vinegar with "mother" in it (p. 276) in your salad dressings and on your salads with olive oil.

Lemon Tea

Another health drink to start the day, lemon juice is cleansing to the system. Drink 30 minutes before the meal.

Mix together:
  1 cup warm water
  juice of ½ fresh lemon
  1 teaspoon honey

Per Serving   Exchanges: 0.75 Fruit; 29 Calories, 8 g carbohydrate (96%; 8.5 g sugars), $.25

Leavening

*The kingdom of heaven is like unto leaven, which a woman
took, and hid in three measures of meal, till the whole was
leavened.   Matthew 13:33 (King James)*

Ingredients that make baked goods rise are called *leavening
agents*. The word leaven comes from the Latin word, *levare*--to raise.
Leavenings release gasses into the batter or dough, increasing the size
and porous structure of the baked product. These gasses are
primarily carbon dioxide, but also may be air or steam. Air may be
added by folding in beaten egg whites, or by *creaming* (vigorously
beating, the sugar and fat together). Steam raises a product when
water is exposed to a high temperature, for example when baking
popovers. Both air and steam are physical ways to leaven.

Carbon dioxide gas is produced chemically by adding an alkaline
ingredient to an acid medium. *Acid and alkaline* react in moisture
to produce carbon dioxide. This is accomplished in two ways:

1) **Baking soda**, bicarbonate of soda, is added as the alkaline
ingredient to an acid liquid used in the recipe--fruit juice, buttermilk,
yogurt, or sour milk. The chemical reaction is immediate.

> **Experiment:** Stir ¼ teaspoon baking soda into 2 tablespoons
> room temperature water. Note what happens. Repeat this in
> 2 tablespoons orange juice or vinegar in another glass. Note
> that the fizz that forms is more dramatic in the vinegar.

2) **Baking powder** is made up of an acid and alkaline ingredient
combined with a filler to keep them separate and non-reactive during
storage.

Most baking powders used today contain a *phosphate* acid agent.
This allows for only part of the acid-alkaline reaction to take place
when added to the dough or batter, while the remaining action occurs
during baking. These are called *double acting* baking powders. They
may contain two phosphate ingredients--calcium acid phosphate and
sodium aluminum phosphate. This allows for even less release of
carbon dioxide before baking, and more during baking. In *single
acting* baking powders (formerly more common) tartaric acid, from
cream of tartar produced from grapes, is used instead of a phosphate.

> Baking soda and baking powder are
> often used in combination in recipes.

Carbon dioxide gas is also produced when *yeast* comes into contact with moisture in a warm environment. Yeast may be purchased commercially as active dry yeast, or *wild yeasts* may be collected from the air in a *sourdough* starter (p. 282).

> **Experiment:** Fill a glass measuring cup with ½ lukewarm water (warm but not hot to wrist). Pour in 1 package (or 2 teaspoons) active dry yeast and ¼ teaspoon sugar or honey. Let stand 5-10 minutes. Watch mixture bubble up. This is called *proofing* the yeast.

There are several problems with leavenings. Those who have candida cannot use yeast, and baked products with yeast require more time to prepare than many are willing to take. This makes the use of baking soda and baking powder attractive, yet they too pose several problems.

Baking soda, and baking powder that contains sodium bicarbonate can alter the pH balance of the batter so that some of the B-vitamins are destroyed if too much is used. This loss can be reduced by limiting the total leavening to 1 teaspoon per cup of flour. Baking soda gives a particularly light texture with buttermilk or soured milk. Usually 1 teaspoon baking soda is recommended per cup of milk. I reduce this to ½ teaspoon soda or less per cup in most recipes and add a baking powder that contains potassium bicarbonate instead of sodium bicarbonate. *Low sodium* (or aluminum free, grainless) baking powder contains potassium bicarbonate in place of sodium bicarbonate for the alkaline agent.

In most double acting baking powders, another problem is the presence of aluminum in the second alkaline agent used--sodium aluminum phosphate. Aluminum has been implicated in health problems and is probably best avoided. *Rumford* and low sodium baking powders do not contain aluminum.

Most baking powders use cornstarch for the filler, including *Rumford*. If you are allergic to corn, get low sodium baking powders, such as *Featherweight* brand which uses potato starch. If you are allergic to both of these try a homemade baking powder (p. 280).

Baking soda will keep at room temperature for 1½ years, and baking powder for 6 months. To test whether either is still active, whisk 1 teaspoon into ⅓ cup boiling hot water. Vigorous fizz and bubbles indicates active ingredients. Usually baking powder containers and baking soda boxes are labeled with expiration dates.

COMMERCIALLY AVAILABLE BAKING POWDERS

Rumford double acting
alkaline ingredient: sodium bicarbonate
acid ingredient: calcium acid phosphate
filler: cornstarch

some supermarkets
and
health food stores

Low Sodium (or aluminum free, grainless) double acting
alkaline ingredient: potassium bicarbonate
acid ingredient: calcium phosphate
filler: potato starch

health food stores

Calumet; Clabber Girl double acting   supermarkets

    alkaline ingredient: bicarbonate of soda (baking soda)
    acid ingredients: calcium acid phosphate
                    sodium aluminum phosphate (_Calumet_)
                    sodium aluminum sulfate (_Clabber Girl_)
    filler: cornstarch

HOMEMADE BAKING POWDERS

Do not delay baking when using these. They are all _single acting._

Corn-Free, Aluminum-Free Baking Powder

For 1 teaspoon baking powder, combine:
½ teaspoon cream of tartar (supermarket spice shelf)
¼ teaspoon baking soda
¼ teaspoon arrowroot powder _(p. 11)_

Low Sodium Baking Powder   (no corn or aluminum)

Blend thoroughly, sifting several times; store in tightly closed container. Use same amount as called for in recipe.
½ cup arrowroot powder _(p. 11)_
    (cornstarch or potato starch can be used)
½ cup cream of tartar
¼ cup potassium bicarbonate (purchase at at a pharmacy)

Non-Filler Allergy-Free Leavening

Blend thoroughly with the dry ingredients per 1 cup flour:
½ teaspoon baking soda
⅛ teaspoon vitamin C crystals[1] (be sure contains no corn)

[1] 1 tablespoon lemon juice or apple cider vinegar may be added to the liquids in place of vitamin C crystals.

Sensational Sourdough

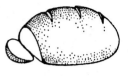

I agree with Mel London, author of *The Bread Winners' Cookbook*, that "the taste [of sourdough] is like no other taste in the bread world." Unfortunately commercially available sourdough breads made from whole grain flours are rare.

During the American westward expansion, as prospectors regularly carried and baked with these doughs, they achieved the popular title of *sourdough*. Sourdough dates back to Old Testament times, however. The ancient Hebrews used sourdough extensively.

Sourdough is a *lactic-acid* ferment made by allowing a mixture of flour and water to collect *wild yeasts* from the surrounding air. It is then used to make breads, biscuits, and pancakes. Baking with sourdough produces nutritionally superior breads because the lactic-acid ferment is beneficial for eliminating toxic wastes from cells. And because sourdough breads are partially "predigested" by the lactic-acid fermentation process before baking, they are more easily digested by the body. This may help some persons who are wheat sensitive and helps to maximize nutritional benefits (see pp. 50-51). Sourdough breads keep longer and the flavor is improved with age when frozen.

Sourdough starter is easy to make, and you can make new starter anytime you want to with little loss and little ado. Acquiring some famous starter that has been in the family or among friends for generations or that came out of San Francisco isn't a necessity.

The science of sourdough is not hard to understand. First a blend of warm water and flour collects some wild yeast from the air as it sits at room temperature for a few days. Some commercial yeast is usually added to give it a head start, but it can be made without it for an even truer sourdough flavor. Refrigeration then preserves it. To use it, warming it again to room temperature to activate the yeast. It will remain dormant if left cold. A portion of it is saved and fed with a little more flour and water in equal portions in order to keep the volume of your supply constant, and to keep it from getting too sour.

If you neglect your starter and don't use it often enough, it is neither a mortal nor a moral failure and there are easy remedies for it (p. 282). Experiment with it and let the kids try. It will be a wonderful practical science lesson for them.

Sourdough Starter

There are a number of varied ways to make sourdough starter along with many confusing instructions. I have found this recipe to be the simplest, and easy to follow. Expect varying results as flavor of sourdough bread depends on degree of sourness of the starter and type of wild yeast collected in it from the air, sometimes being just right and other times leaving something to be desired. Don't give up too soon!

1. Blend equal amounts of flour and water in a quart-size non-metal bowl or crock with a wooden spoon (sourdough reacts with metal) and let stand 5-10 minutes till bubbly:
   - **½ - 1 cup lukewarm water or potato water** (95° - 105°)
   - **1 - 2 teaspoons active dry yeast**
   - **½ - 1 teaspoon honey, optional**
   - **½ - 1 cup whole wheat pastry flour or rye flour** (these work best, but any whole grain flour can be used)

2. Blend in additional equal amounts of flour and water:
   - **½ - 1 cup lukewarm water or potato water** (95° - 105°)
   - **½ - 1 cup whole wheat pastry flour or rye flour**

3. Cover loosely with cheesecloth or light towel; set in a corner for 3-7 days, until distincly sour in odor. Normally a dark liquid forms on top. Stir down once daily and before storing.

4. Store in covered non-metal container in refrigerator.

5. **To Use Refrigerated Starter:** Remove starter from refrigerator 12 hours before using in recipe; stir down any dark liquid. Measure out portion to use in recipe, always saving an unused portion.

6. Replenish the unused portion of starter with equal parts of:
   warm water and flour--usually ½ - 1 cup each
   Cover and refrigerate. After you have replenished the starter give it at least 24 hours before using it again.

Special Tip: If dark liquid rises to the top at any time, just stir it back in. It is not a sign of failed or spoiled starter. If mold appears at any time, just remove it. Discard starter only if any pink color is present.

For Best Results: Your starter may be more effectively pungent the second time around. Use it twice weekly, or at minimum once every 2 weeks to prevent its becoming too sour. If you don't use it often enough you can do one of the following:
1. Freeze it in 1 cup portions.
2. Throw half away and replenish the remainder (#6 above). Repeat with unused starter every 10 days.
3. Discard it and make new starter.

To Use Sourdough Starter in Recipes

Sourdough starter can be used in yeast breads, English muffins, pancakes, waffles, biscuits, and muffins using these general guidelines.

1. Use ½-1 cup starter in an average recipe. Reduce liquid and flour in the recipe by same amount that is in the starter.

2. Several hours or the night before make a *sponge* by blending the starter with the main liquid used in the recipe (e.g. the milk), and part, or all of the flour as needed to keep the sponge at a batter consistency. Let stand overnight.

3. In the morning blend in remaining ingredients. Other leavenings may be omitted, reduced, or included, as desired. Blend them (except proofed yeast) with remaining flour before combining with liquid ingredients. If no flour remains to be added, dissolve leavening with 1 tablespoon water and stir into batter.

Sourdough Pancakes

This is the waffle recipe, p. 204, with sourdough starter added according to the guidelines listed above.

AMOUNT: About 18 - 4" Pancakes

1. The night before blend together with a wooden spoon:
    1 cup sourdough starter *(see step #5, p. 282)*
    1 cup buttermilk *(p. 11; or non-dairy alternative, p. 29)*
    1½ cups spelt flour or other flour *(see grains, p. 13)*

2. Just before baking, blend in:
    1 egg *(or alternative, p. 269)*
    2 tablespoons oil *(extra virgin olive oil preferred, p. 14)*
    1 teaspoon salt
    (optional) **½ teaspoon baking soda dissolved in 1 tablespoon water**

3. Bake on hot griddle sprayed with olive oil non-stick spray.

Per Pancake (of 18)
    Exchanges: 0.75 Bread, 0.25 Fat; 72 Calories, 2.5 g protein (13%), 2 g fat (25%)
    12 g carbohydrate (62%; 1 g sugars), 2 g dietary fiber, 12 mg cholesterol, 144 mg sodium, $.10

Sourdough English Muffins

Truly a family favorite. Unless I hide these in the freezer, they are gone in less than 2 days! These are "baked" in a fry pan on stove top.

AMOUNT: 2 Dozen Muffins
Bake: 5 minutes each side

1. The night before: Bring water to a boil, remove from heat and thoroughly blend in the milk:
   3 cups water
   1 cup nonfat dry milk powder *(p. 14)*

2. Cool milk to lukewarm. Make *sponge*--Whisk in flour until smooth, then stir in sourdough starter with a non-metal spoon:
   4 cups whole wheat or spelt flour *(see grains, p. 13)*
   ½ cup sourdough starter *(see step #5, p. 282)*

3. Cover sponge with a damp cloth and let stand overnight.

4. Optional for quicker rise: In a glass measuring cup blend yeast and honey into lukewarm water and allow to stand 10 minutes until bubbles up:
   ¼ cup very warm (but not hot) **water**
   2 teaspoons (1 package) **active dry yeast**
   ½ teaspoon honey

5. Blend into sponge with a wooden spoon; dough will be quite stiff:
   2 teaspoons salt
   optional yeast mixture (step #4)
   3-4 cups whole wheat or spelt flour (usually takes less flour without yeast mixture; a little more spelt flour than wheat may be needed)

6. Knead dough about 10 minutes, either by hand or electric dough kneader. Turn dough out on surface lightly dusted with **cornmeal.** Divide into 24 equal pieces with lightly floured hands.

7. Flatten each piece with fingers or rolling pin to ½" thick. Cut with floured rim of glass, about 3½" diameter. Place close together on greased cookie sheet; cover with towel and set in a warm place to rise until double in size, 1-3 hours. Continued p. 285.

Rising Tip: Longer rising time is required when sourdough starter is used without additional yeast. However, if muffins without yeast are allowed to rise in oven at 150° (no higher), they may double in size in 1 hour.

8. Bake on ungreased griddle or fry pan over medium heat about 5 minutes on each side; cool on wire rack.

9. While warm, divide each muffin in half with tines of a fork inserted around the side (a knife will "pack" the dough together diminishing the texture characteristic of English muffins).

> **Tip:** If some muffins are doughy inside, raise the baking temperature a bit. If desired, bake the inner sides of the muffins a little after cutting them open with a fork.

Note: Muffins may be frozen whole, thawed and then forked open for toasting.

Per Muffin Half (with 7 cups whole wheat flour; includes optional yeast and honey)
Exchanges: 1 Bread; 75 Calories, 3 g protein (17%), 15 g carbohydrate (78%; 2 g sugars), 2 g dietary fiber, 1 mg cholesterol, 102 mg sodium, $.10

Sourdough Biscuits

This is the biscuit recipe, p. 125, adapted to sourdough.

AMOUNT: 12 Biscuits
Bake: 425°F (220°C) - 12 to 15 minutes

Several hours ahead or night before
1. Blend together for *sponge* using a non-metal spoon:
>   **½ cup sourdough starter** *(see step #5, p. 282)*
>   **½ cup + 2 tablespoons buttermilk** *(p. 11; non dairy alternative, p. 20)*
>   **or ¾ cup buttermilk** with grains other than spelt
>   **1 cup spelt flour or other whole grain flour** *(see grains, p. 13)*

2. In separate bowl blend together and set aside:
>   **¾ cup spelt flour or other whole grain flour**
>   **½ teaspoon salt**
>   **½ teaspoon baking soda**

3. Just before baking, blend into sponge:
>   **3 tablespoons oil** *(extra virgin olive oil preferred, p. 14)*
>   **separate bowl of flour, salt, and soda**

4. Drop by spoonfuls on greased cookie sheet and bake 12-15 minutes at 425°.

Per Biscuit of 12   Exchanges: 1 Bread, 0.75 Fat; 105 Calories, 3 g protein (11%), 4 g fat (30%), 17 g carbohydrate (59%; 1 g sugars), 3 g dietary fiber, 0 mg cholesterol, 123 mg sodium, $.15

Sourdough Bread

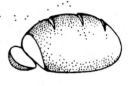

This bread is an adaption of Spelt Bread, p. 122, to sourdough. Any bread recipe including Kamut Bread, p. 123 or Delicious Whole Grain Dough (Soups & Muffins, p. 96) may be similarly used, following guidelines given on p. 283.

AMOUNT: 2 Rounded or 2 Medium Loaves (8½" x 4½" Pans)
Bake: 350°F (175°C) -35 to 45 minutes

1. Remove *Sourdough Starter* from refrigerator and bring to room temperature (step #5, p. 282).

2. For *sponge* blend together in non-metal bowl with non-metal mixing spoon, cover, and let stand overnight or several hours:
   1½ cups warm (not hot) water
   1 cup sourdough starter
   3½ cups spelt flour *(see grains, p. 13)*

3. Replenish unused portion of starter and return to refrigerator (step #6, p. 282).

4. Optional--In glass measuring cup whisk yeast and honey into warm water and let stand until bubbles up, 5-10 minutes:
   ¼ cup very warm (but not hot) **water**
   2 teaspoons (1 package) **active dry yeast**
   ½ teaspoon honey

5 Blend into sponge mixture in order given and beat vigorously for 200 strokes:
   2 teaspoons salt
   ⅓ cup honey, optional
   ⅓ cup oil *(extra virgin olive or canola oil preferred, pp.11, 14)*
   yeast mixture, optional (step #2)
   a portion of 4½ - 6 remaining cups spelt flour (No more than keeps batter easty to beat vigorously).
   See flour Tip below.

6. Complete recipe as for **Spelt Bread**, p. 122, steps 5 - 9. To shape loaves in bread pans follow *Shaping Loaves*, pp. 122-123, or shape into nicely rounded loaves and place on lightly greased cookie sheet to rise.

> **Flour Tip:** Amount of flour should be added by "feel" and not any exact measurement. If grain other than spelt is used, less flour will probably be needed. The amount also depends on the total liquid used. Thus if the optional yeast in step #2 is omitted, less flour will be required.

> **Rising Tip:** Sourdoughs often require a longer rising time.

Come & Have Breakfast

When they landed, they saw a fire of burning coals
there with fish on it, and some bread. John 21:9

This is one of my favorite stories in the Bible. This must have been a glorious morning for the disciples of Jesus. Here they are, weary from fishing all night without a bite. Then Jesus comes along the Galilean shore--resurrected! He tells them to dip their nets again--this time for a large catch. Can't you just imagine their excitement? They were so excited they even counted every fish--153!

But that's not all. As they dragged the net ashore, a heart-warming campfire breakfast awaited them--fresh caught fish and hearty bread prepared and served by the Lord, himself. What an identification with, and exaltation of one of our most menial tasks!

It wasn't the catch or the meal, though, that captured their hearts, but WHO provided both catch and meal. What a host! What a Provider! What Power! What Love! What a Lord! When Peter realized that it was Jesus, he couldn't wait. He jumped overboard!

Have you "jumped overboard" to meet Jesus yet? Has your life been as *all night catching nothing*? This Man, God's Messiah, has prepared "a catch" and a "heavenly feast" of abundant life for you. He invites you to receive it: *Come and have breakfast!*

"I am the bread that came down from heaven. . . .
I tell you the truth, he who believes has everlasting life. I am the
bread of life. Your forefathers ate the manna in the desert, yet they
died. But here is the bread that comes down from heaven, which
a man may eat and not die. I am the living bread that came down
from heaven. If a man eats this bread he will live forever. This
bread is my flesh, which I give for the life of the world. . . .Whoever
eats my flesh and drinks my blood has eternal life, and I will raise
him up at the last day. . . he who feeds on this bread will live forever.
. . .The words I have spoken to you are spirit and they are life."
John 6:41, 47-51, 54, 63

Have you received this heavenly meal?

John 1:12

Index

296

**SCRIPTURES &
SCRIPTURE REFERENCES**

SueGreggCookbooks

A Comprehensive Wholefoods Cooking System
Over 1450 Pages and 894 Recipes plus Menus

THE BASIC COOKBOOK SET

MAIN DISHES includes over 270 recipes and 138 menus at an average cost of about $1.75. 52 low budget meals average only $1.20. 58 low fat meals average just 20% fat (of calories). Menus include all food groups with vegetarian options. Data for exchanges, calories, carbohydrate, protein, fat, and fiber. Satisfies the "meat and potatoes" appetite. Index, 292 pages.

MEALS IN MINUTES outlines flexible once a month or once a week cook-ahead plans for stocking your freezer with 26 low fat/high fiber recipes. Now you can have quick meals when time and energy are short. Double, triple, multiply recipes for mega-cooking. Shopping and assembly lists. Index, 90 pages.

SOUPS & MUFFINS, the easiest way to get whole grain variety. 36 muffin and bread recipes from 12 grains with alternatives for wheat & dairy allergies. 27 favorite soup recipes nutritionally improved. Soup and muffin combination menus save $$$. Index, 102 pages.

More than **BREAKFASTS** *with Blender Batter Baking & Allergy Alternatives* gives you fresh whole grain blender batter recipes for waffles, pancakes, coffee cakes, muffins, and crepes without a grain mill. Introduces Kamut® and spelt. Cinnamon rolls, smoothies, cereals, egg variations, fruit dishes, toppings and spreads. Wheat, dairy, and egg allergy alternatives. Research resources for children. Index, 312 pages.

DESSERTS *with Lowfat & Allergy Alternatives* provides recipes for wholesome sweets without white flour or hydrogenated fats. Familiar favorites along with Poppy Seed Cake and Sweet n' Spicy Pudding plus alternatives for both chocolate and carob. Whole grain Angel Food Cake at 0% fat! Over 125 recipes. Includes 45 recipes with 30% or less fat. Index, 176 pages.

LUNCHES & SNACKS *with Lessons for Children* includes a guide for young cooks in preparing lunches from set up to clean up. Recipes written "by-the-numbers" avoid confusion. Nutrition quizzes for discussion. Children can master basic kitchen skills, learn nutritional why's, and prepare complete meals by their teens. Index, 168 pages.

MASTER INDEX & MENU PLANNER Includes a recipe index, subject index, and ingredient index to the *SueGreggCookbooks*. Plan a month's menus in 20 minutes to save time, cost, "what's for dinner" frustration, and meet nutritional goals. Keyed to the cookbooks but flexible enough to merge your own favorites. Special sections on feeding babies and children, the food connection in the Biblical redemption story, and updates. 312 pages

For current prices see www.suegregg.com or call 800-998-2783

COOKING with CHILDREN
Cooking Experiences where Children & Parents Learn together

Uses **Lunches & Snacks** as text with step-by-step photo recipe demonstrations on CD that present children with opportunities to be "caught" by their interests. Permits parents to introduce younger children to a variety of cooking experiences with recipes that have special appeal to them. Lessons emphasize hands on learning by doing, practicing kitchen safety, handling kitchen tools, learning measurements, identifying nutritional values, keeping a tidy work area, and experiencing a variety of tastes and textures. If children fix it, they will eat it. By age 13 they may replace mom in the kitchen! Call 1-800-998-2783 for quote with cookbook package combinations. Preview at www.suegregg.com

BAKING with WHOLE GRAINS
A Comprehensive Semester Course for Families with H.S. Students

Master 16 basic whole grain recipes. Introduces blender batter baking, fresh flour quick breads, and whole grain yeast breads. Emphasizes a biblical focus, nutritional value, convenience, taste appeal, cost control, and research. Provides opportunities for creative activities, bonus projects, and serving others. **Course Materials: Breakfasts 3rd ed.**, text, **Student Notebook & Curriculum Guide, CD** with 30 recipe demonstrations, floppy disk with tests & answers. Compter requirements: Microsoft Internet Explorer & Adobe Acrobat Reader (both available free on the internet). Call for quote on package combinations with cookbooks, 2nd & 3rd student and group discounts. Preview at www.suegregg.com

SPECIALTY COOKBOOKS

THE CREATIVE RECIPE ORGANIZER Keep new recipes safe! Recipe revision examples with guide to ingredient changes for nutritional improvement. Taste tips. Measurement tables. Herbs & spice organizer. Food & cooking term glossary. Avoid tear out hazards of three ringbinders. Over 200 pages ready for taping, gluing, post-it-noting, and copying try someday ideas.

YEAST BREADS Includes both machine (e.g. Bosh, DLX) and hand instructions for all-purpose dough, recipes for whole grains, rolls, sweet rolls, bagels, Italian bread sticks, pizza along with sourdough and sprouted breads. Bread baking technique and trouble shooting. Not for autobake machines. 75 p.

HOLIDAY MENUS Celebrate with traditional but wholesome fare. Perfect Turkey and Cheese Ball recipes. Menus for Thanksgiving, Christmas, Easter, Passover, Autumn Harvest, and Company. 78 p.

FOUR FOOD STORAGE PLANS *for Health and Hospitality, A Preparedness Guide for Families.* Biblical and historical basis for storing food and for becoming resourceful in ministering to others. Save money building your own food storage plan as you "Eat what you store, and store what you eat." Long term and short term food reserves compared. Some recipes modified for stove top cooking. Shopping lists for each menu plan for 4 weeks. How to save money. Charts for shelf life of most basic foods. How to prepare dehydrated foods and grow sprouts. Shopping resources for ingredients. Over 55 recipes specially adapted for stove top cooking. 310 pages.